A Cookbook by
The Junior League of
Savannah, Inc.

As the tiny settlement of Savannah—Georgia's first outpost founded in 1733—emerged in the nineteenth century as a world port in the cotton trade, its citizens developed a special style all their own. Those were the days of all-day shooting parties at nearby rice plantations, island picnics with dancing until dusk and mellow afternoons spent tasting Madeira at highly polished mahogany tables. The Earl of Warwick praised Savannah for its hospitality; newspaper writers wrote glowingly of gaslit balls for seven hundred guests where the music was exquisite, the dancing nimble and the champagne flowing. New Year's calls were a tradition and local gourmets fixed their mouths, "turtle fashion" for the Savannah delicacy, terrapin soup.

Today, Savannah is revered for its original city plan, its elegantly restored townhouses situated around tree-shaded squares, and a style of cooking and entertaining that has earned it the epithet, Hostess City of the South.

Here the Junior League of Savannah shares a bit of that style in the form of 464 recipes from the city's best cooks along with enthralling glimpses into Savannah's social and culinary history.

Each recipe has been tested three times and it is certain that the reader will find something tempting for every occasion. Picnickers might choose cold lemon chicken, Savannah red rice and marinated green salad topped off with crème de menthe brownies or cold strawberry soufflé. Salmon mousse and asparagus might fill any luncheon bill, while baked Ogeechee shad, hot curried Georgia peaches and dove pilau are not to be missed. For New Year's Day, there's only one choice: Dugger's Hoppin' John.

Some of the recipes are for up-to-the-minute dishes that might be served at a low-country supper next week. Others are traditional favorites from the days when, as New York socialite Ward McAllister put it, "a Savannah dinner party was an event to live for." Either way the emphasis is on simple but elegant food, well within the ability of the busy person who cares about graceful living and stylish entertaining, but who must accomplish it with less help than in days past.

About the Junior
League of Savannah

The Junior League of Savannah was chartered in 1926 and currently is composed of more than 700 active and sustaining members. Since its beginning, the League has contributed countless volunteer hours and over $537,000 to 33 community organizations. Major projects have included substantial participation in the founding of four Savannah institutions: the Community Children's Theatre, the Savannah Speech and Hearing Center, the Coastal Plains chapter of the Georgia Conservancy and the Voluntary Action Center.

In 1969, Historic Savannah Foundation awarded the Savannah Junior League the prestigious Davenport Trophy in recognition of the League's ongoing financial and volunteer support in the preservation of Savannah's architecturally significant buildings.

Recently the League has conducted Treasure Trunks, an educational program of the Telfair Academy of Arts and Sciences. It organized the Adler Conference on Child Abuse and Neglect and a series of similar professional seminars and has contributed both funding and volunteer hours to the establishment of Savannah's public radio station.

League headquarters are located in the historic district at 330 Drayton Street, Savannah, Georgia 31401. Profits from all fundraising activities are reinvested in projects that serve the community.

Savannah Style

A Cookbook
by
The Junior League of Savannah, Inc.

The purpose of the Junior League is exclusively educational and charitable and is to promote voluntarism: to develop the potential of its members for voluntary participation in community affairs; and to demonstrate the effectiveness of trained volunteers.

Cover design, "An Oyster Roast," from an original oil by Ray Ellis.

Text Illustrations by Jenellen Hibberd Young

Ray Ellis is a noted local and national artist, and artist for *South by Southeast* and *North By Northeast*. We sincerely thank him for sharing his outstanding talents with us.

ISBN 0-9613411-0-6

Additional copies of book ($16.95) may be obtained by addressing:

The Junior League of Savannah, Inc.
P.O. Box 1864
Savannah, Georgia 31402

First Printing — 20,000 copies
Second Printing — 30,000 copies
Third Printing — 15,000 copies
Fourth Printing — 15,000 copies
Fifth Printing — 20,000 copies
Sixth Printing — 25,000 copies
Seventh Printing* — 20,000 copies
Eighth Printing* — 36,000 copies
(*__Southern Living__ ® **Hall of Fame** edition)

Acknowledgements

Our thanks to the active and sustaining members of the Junior League of Savannah, Inc. for so graciously sharing their many treasured recipes and for their enthusiastic support during the long months of testing, re-testing, research and editing that have resulted in the publication of this book. Special appreciation goes to Rosalie Morris for launching the project; Jenellen Young for agreeing to serve as illustrator and general art director; Pat Harper for compiling the findings of ten industrious researchers and writing the accompanying text; Camille Searcy, Sara Gaines, Marion Reid and JoAnn Morrison for spearheading a team of over thirty dedicated testers; Diana Barrow for her organizational assistance with indexing; and Elaine Simmons for the difficult task of typing and editing.

Cisty Davis, *Chairman*
Mimi Rippin, *Assistant Chairman*

Contents

SAVANNAH
STYLE

Introduction

In setting out to publish its first cookbook, the Junior League of Savannah established several guidelines for selecting recipes. First, the recipes had to be uncomplicated—the sort that can be prepared without a kitchen staff complete with *pâtissier* and *sous chef.*

Second, the ingredients had to be fresh—or at least as unprocessed as possible. We wanted to steer clear of recipes in which you add a can of cream soup to a can of green beans and top with a can of French-fried onions.

Third, the preparations had to be simple enough to accomplish without spending all day at it. In short, this book is written for busy, active people who still care about graceful living and stylish entertaining, but who must accomplish it with less help than our forebears.

In sifting through old family favorites and their own working files, League members came up with more than a thousand recipes of which 435 thrice-tested offerings have been included in this book. Some are landmark dishes that have graced Savannah tables since colonial days. Others are typical of what the reader might be served if invited to a Savannah supper party next week. Still others are house specialties at some of the city's leading restaurants.

While focusing on simple, but elegant food, both traditional and trendy, it was tempting to take a look at how people in this historic seaport have entertained and mused themselves and their friends over the years. So this is what we've done.

In between recipes for Shrimp Monterey and Savannah Red Rice, you'll get an inkling of how Savannahians have cooked, shopped, picnicked and partied—especially in the city's nineteenth century heyday when it was a world port in the cotton and naval stores trade.

As many people have pointed out, Savannahians often have thought they lived better than most other people in the rest of Georgia and certainly in the North. In 1831, a local woman whose name has now been lost to history wrote to a friend in Providence, Rhode Island, ''I have really hoped that you would come to Savannah this winter... certainly the hospitality of the inhabitants is not exceeded and hardly equalled anywhere—in other places you will find one or two Lady Bountifuls, but here they are all bountiful.''

Nearly a hundred years later the Earl of Warwick praised Savannah hospitality after he visited the home of Mr. and Mrs. William Washington Gordon. "I have had my full share of kindness from all sorts and conditions of people," wrote the nobleman, ". . . but I have never lived for a week in surroundings more novel, pleasing, and restful. It was an experience that stands out in my memory like a landmark, and I cannot recall it without feelings of renewed gratitude to my gracious hostess and her husband."

One of the most famous nineteenth century Savannahians was Ward McAllister, who grew up in Savannah but lived most of his adult life in New York. There he became an intimate friend of Mrs. William Astor and is credited with cutting the list of New York Society to four hundred people—the number that could fit into Mrs. Astor's ballroom. After that, he reportedly became known as "Mr. Make-a-Lister."

Once McAllister declared that there were gentlemen in the South who "cultivated the belief that they alone lived well, and that there was no such thing as good society in New York and other Northern cities." Maybe he was telling the truth or perhaps he wasn't, but one thing is certain—early accounts of Madeira tastings, balls, shooting parties and summer visits to the salt marshes leave no doubt that Savannahians have always known how to live well.

That's not to say these Georgians have led a charmed existence. The city has suffered Yellow Fever epidemics, major fires, an earthquake and William Tecumseh Sherman. Sons have been lost at war and sand gnats have invaded the finest picnics. But over the years Savannahians have seemed to develop that special quality that lets one rise above the ordinary.

That's why it is hoped that this book will share with the reader not only a taste of Savannah's finest foods, but also a sense of the city's inimitable style.

Savannah Style

SPIRITS

Spirits

Ask any Savannahian to name the city's most famous drink and chances are he'll say Chatham Artillery Punch.

It is said that the concoction possesses a kick greater than the two brass cannons presented the Chatham Artillery by George Washington. It was first devised in the 1850's to honor a rival military organization, the Republican Blues, and since then has laid to rest, at least temporarily, many an unknown soldier and countless known ones.

The original recipe was brewed in ice-filled horse buckets into which were placed sugar, lemon and a quart each of brandy, whiskey and rum. Then the bucket was filled with champagne. Revised recipes call for the addition of green tea, but the popular punch still, though it tastes as mild as syllabub, conquers like a cyclone.

Although not so widely enjoyed now, Madeira wine is another beverage that played a special part in Savannah's social history.

When the colony's trustees met in London in October, 1732, to discuss the founding of Georgia, they dispatched botanist William Houston to the island of Madeira to secure cuttings of the grapevines there for delivery to the New World.

The vines never took hold in Georgia, but the wine did and it came to symbolize gracious living in Savannah throughout the nineteenth century.

The primary reason for the wine's success lay in its improved quality due to the long sea voyage and the warmth of the local climate.

Some Savannahians had a special way with Madeira. Experts even from abroad wrote of how William Neyle Habersham could improve so greatly the stock of wine he kept in the solarium above his ballroom.

According to Ward McAllister, afternoon wine parties were the custom in Savannah from 1800 up until the Civil War. Guests were asked to come and taste Madeira at 5 p.m., after dinner which in those days was served at three in the afternoon. The mahogany table, polished to a sheen that reflected the face, was set with finger bowls each containing four pipe-stemmed glasses, with olives, parched ground nuts and almonds and half a dozen bottles of Madeira. There you sat, tasted and commented on these wines for an hour or more.

The Earl of Warwick was fêted with a Madeira party and was suitably impressed when he visited the William Gordons. As he later described it: "The etiquette was for each man to attend to his neighbor's glass, and only one man shirked his obligations . . . His feeble sense of duty put the onus of fourteen bottles upon eleven men, all of whom had done justice to the wines that preceded the Madeira; but we did our duty, and the decanters were empty when we left the table. It was at once a rare and choice wine; I do not think its like could be bought in England for any money."

Beverages

Chatham Artillery Punch

Serves 200

2 gallons tea (green tea—1
  pound tea to 2 gallons
  water. Soak overnight in
  tin bucket and strain.)
Juice of 3 dozen lemons
5 pounds brown sugar
2 gallons Catawba wine
2 gallons Santa Cruz rum

1 gallon Hennessy (3-Star)
  brandy
1 gallon dry gin
1 gallon rye whiskey
2 quarts cherries
2 quarts pineapple cubes
10 quarts champagne

Mix the tea with lemon juice, preferably in cedar tub, then add brown sugar and liquors. Let this mixture "set" for at least 1 week, or preferably 2 weeks, in *covered* container.

After "setting" period and when ready to serve, pour *over* cake of ice. Never chill in refrigerator or used crushed ice. When this is done, add cherries, pineapple cubes and champagne, pouring in slowly and mixing with circular motion. The punch is now ready to serve.

Champagne Punch

Serves 25

1½ cups sugar
2 cups lemon juice
2 fifths sauterne, chilled

1 fifth champagne, chilled
Lemon slices, fresh strawberries
  and orange slices

Combine sugar and lemon juice, stir until dissolved. Pour over ice in punch bowl. Add sauterne and champagne. Mix well and float fruit slices on top.

Festive Fruit Punch   Serves 24

46 ounces canned orange juice
46 ounces canned pineapple juice
1 pint lemon juice
1 quart sugar (or to taste)
1 tablespoon almond flavoring
1 tablespoon vanilla
1 quart ginger ale
2 to 3 (46 ounce) cans water

Combine all ingredients in punch bowl. Add ice mold, if desired.

Peach Fuzzie   Serves 6

6 ounces pink lemonade, thawed
6 ounces vodka
6 ounces water
2 to 3 peaches, pitted and unpeeled
Crushed ice

Place first 3 ingredients in blender. Add peaches and blend until well mixed. Fill with crushed ice and blend until smooth.

Sylvan Island Freeze   Serves 12

Half of (15 ounce) can Coco Lopez
2 cups pineapple juice
2 cups orange juice
12 ounces rum
1 tablespoon grenadine

Blend small amounts of the above mixture with crushed ice until slushy. Serve in stemmed glasses garnished with orange slices, pineapple chunks or maraschino cherries.

Iced Sherry Cobbler   Serves 4

1½ tablespoons
  confectioner's sugar
1 teaspoon fresh lemon
  juice

¾ cup ice, crushed
¾ cup sherry

Place sugar and lemon juice in a tumbler. Add ice. Pour sherry over all. Pour from tumbler to tumbler to mix. Serve in sherry glasses.

Iced French Brandy   Serves 2

2½ ounces brandy
½ ounce heavy cream
6 scoops French vanilla ice
  cream

2 cherries, for garnish

Place above ingredients, except cherries, in blender and blend until smooth and thick. Pour into goblet and garnish with a cherry. If mixture is too thin, add more ice cream. It is important that French vanilla ice cream be used in this recipe.

Whisper

Coffee ice cream
Brandy

Crème de cacao, optional

Put one scoop of coffee ice cream per serving in blender. Add one jigger brandy and 1 ounce crème de cacao per serving. (Put one jigger of each for pot, too.) Mix in blender for a delicious and easy after-dinner drink. Number of servings depends on number of scoops of ice cream used. Allow one scoop per person. Jamocha ice cream can be used if coffee ice cream is not available.

Plantation Mint Julep   Serves 20

4 cups water   Crushed ice
3 cups sugar   Kentucky bourbon
Leaves from 15 to 20 large
    mint stalks

Boil water in heavy saucepan; add sugar and mint leaves and allow to boil for 10 minutes. Let cool. Put mixture into a jug and refrigerate. Allow to stand for at least 30 days.

To make julep, pour 1½ ounces of sugar mixture and 3 ounces of bourbon over shaved ice. Stir and serve with short straws and a mint sprig garnish.

The Chart House Amaretto Sour   Serves 3

1½ ounces Amaretto   4 ounces sweet and sour mix
1 egg white   Handful of crushed ice
4 teaspoons confectioner's
    sugar

Combine all ingredients in blender and blend until frothy.

A specialty of The Chart House restaurant.

Lemon Cream Frappé   Serves 2

3 ounces lemon juice   3 ounces gin
3 tablespoons confectioner's   3 ounces half-and-half
    sugar

Blend the first 3 ingredients, then add cream. Blend all together with a few ice cubes until frothy. Serve in 4-ounce wine glasses.

Whoopee Eggnog

Serves 20

12 egg yolks
1½ cups sugar
1 pint bourbon
1 pint dark rum
½ to 1 pint rye
1 quart homogenized milk

1 cup sweet sherry
1 quart vanilla ice cream
2 cups heavy cream
⅓ cup confectioner's sugar
6 egg whites
Nutmeg

Beat egg yolks until fluffy and light in color. Add 1 cup sugar. Slowly add, while beating mixture constantly, the bourbon, rum and rye. While still beating, add milk. Reserve 2 tablespoons sherry. Blend remaining sherry with ice cream and beat into egg and liquor mixture. Whip cream until it forms soft peaks. Whip in confectioner's sugar, folding into this the 2 tablespoons sherry. Set aside. Beat whites of 6 eggs until stiff and dry. Add remaining ½ cup of sugar. Sprinkle with nutmeg. Fold whipped cream into egg yolk, liquor and ice cream mixture and top with egg white mixture.

To increase or decrease alcoholic content of this eggnog, the same ratio of alcoholic beverages should be maintained.

Holiday Eggnog

Serves 36

1 dozen eggs, separated
1¾ cups sugar
1 fifth dark rum
1 quart milk

½ teaspoon vanilla
1 quart heavy cream
Nutmeg

Combine egg yolks with sugar, beating until thick. Add rum, milk and vanilla and mix well. Refrigerate overnight. Before serving, beat egg whites until stiff and whip the cream. Fold egg whites and whipped cream into egg mixture. Sprinkle with nutmeg.

Sangria

Serves 12 to 15

1 litre dry red wine
2 ounces Cointreau or
  orange liqueur
2 ounces sweet brandy
4 tablespoons sugar

Champagne or club soda
1 lemon, seeded and sliced
1 orange, seeded and sliced
1 apple, seeded and sliced

Mix the first 4 ingredients in a 2 litre jug or decanter. Add champagne or club soda to fill the remainder of the jug just before serving. Garnish with fruit and serve over cracked ice, or serve well-chilled in wine glasses.

White Sangria

Serves 64 in 6-ounce glasses
48 in 8-ounce glasses

6 oranges, sliced
6 lemons, sliced
2 cups sugar

3 gallons white wine
8 bottles (28 ounces each) club
  soda

Mix together and soak in the refrigerator for 24 hours the oranges, lemons and sugar. Refrigerate wine and soda. When ready to serve, mix all ingredients and serve very cold while the soda is bubbly.

Wassail

Serves 40

1 gallon cider
2 sticks cinnamon
½ cup honey
Whole cloves

1½ cups orange juice
1½ cups lemonade
½ teaspoon nutmeg
2 teaspoons lemon rind

Heat cider, cinnamon sticks, honey and cloves in large saucepan. Bring to boil over medium heat; simmer, covered, 5 minutes. Add remaining ingredients. Simmer a little longer. Lace with rum or brandy, if desired.

Hot Cranberry Drink

Yields 6 to 8 Cups

1 tablespoon whole cloves
3 2-inch cinnamon sticks,
 broken
2 cups cranberry juice
 cocktail

2 cups unsweetened pineapple
 juice
½ teaspoon whole allspice
⅓ cup light brown sugar

Put liquids and brown sugar in bottom of percolator. Put spices in top of percolator. Perk 10 minutes. Serve in punch cups garnished with lemon slices.

Hot Spiced Cider

Serves 16

1 cup orange juice
1 cup sugar
⅓ box (1 ounce) whole stick
 cinnamon

⅓ box (1 ounce) whole allspice
⅓ box (1 ounce) whole cloves
1 gallon apple cider

Combine orange juice and sugar. Put in bottom of a large coffee pot. Place spices in basket; pour apple cider over and perk.

Hot Mulled Cider

Serves 4

½ cup brown sugar
¼ teaspoon salt
2 cups cider
1 teaspoon whole allspice

1 teaspoon whole cloves
3 inches stick cinnamon
Dash nutmeg
Orange slices

Combine brown sugar, salt and cider. Tie spices in small piece of cheese cloth; add to cider. Slowly bring to a boil; cover and simmer 20 minutes. Remove spices. Serve hot with orange slice floaters, cinnamon stick muddlers.

Hot Buttered Rum   Serves 6

¼ cup butter, softened   6 whole cloves
⅓ cup dark brown sugar   Boiling water
¼ teaspoon nutmeg, freshly   Rum
  grated

Mash together butter and sugar. Add nutmeg and mix well. Into pre-heated mugs, place a dollop of mixture and top with a clove. Pour in 1 jigger of boiling water and 1 jigger of rum. Stir well.

Serve in small pottery mugs, if available.

Iced Irish Coffee   Serves 4

½ cup milk   1 teaspoon instant coffee
¼ cup Irish whiskey   Heavy cream, whipped
1 quart coffee ice cream   Stick cinnamon

Put milk and whiskey into blender. Spoon in ice cream and instant coffee. Cover and blend until smooth. Pour into chilled glasses, top with whipped cream and add cinnamon stick as stirrer.

Mexican Coffee   Serves 1

2 tablespoons Kahlua   Heavy cream, whipped
½ cinnamon stick   Semi-sweet or unsweetened
Hot, strong coffee   chocolate, grated

Place Kahlua and cinnamon stick in coffee cup. Add coffee to fill cup. Top with spoonful of whipped cream and sprinkling of grated chocolate.

Spanish Coffee   Serves 6

Half of 1 lemon   3 ounces Kahlua
1 tablespoon sugar   6 cups coffee
3 ounces brandy   1 cup heavy cream, whipped

   Rub half of lemon around the rim of 6 stemmed water goblets
and dip in sugar that has been spread on waxed paper. Set aside.
Heat brandy and pour ½ ounce into each glass. Flame. Pour ½
ounce Kahlua into each glass. Fill with coffee and top with whipped
cream. If a sweeter coffee is preferred, add sugar to glass before
topping with whipped cream.

Iced Mocha Mint Coffee   Serves 4

6 ounces bittersweet   Fresh mint
   chocolate   Sugar
½ teaspoon cinnamon   Cream
4 cups hot, double-strength
   coffee

   Melt bittersweet chocolate over boiling water and stir in cinnamon. Stir the mixture gradually into coffee. Pour coffee into tall
glasses filled with ice and top with fresh mint. Serve with sugar and
cream.

ON THE SALTS

On The Salts

Within ten miles or so from the heart of downtown Savannah lie a number of wonderful residential areas on the banks of the rivers and creeks that wind their way through the low country.

Now Savannahians live year-round in these little settlements like Vernonburg and Beaulieu, but in earlier days these idyllic spots served primarily as summer colonies for city residents trying to escape the devastating heat. It was called summering "on the salts."

Early accounts of life "on the salts" note the state of the breeze from day to day. There was said to be much rivalry between groups as to whether the exposure to the sea breezes was better at White Bluff, Montgomery, Isle of Hope or some other waterside location.

One favorite Savannah story that attests to that competition depicts a luncheon scene on the piazza of the summer home of Josephine and William Neyle Habersham. Mrs. Habersham's mother boasted that the breezes were so much stronger at her home farther down the river that the silver sometimes blew right off the table. "But, Mother Ann," replied her son-in-law, "that happened because your family's silver is so much lighter than the Habersham silver!"

Many of the summer resorts were served by trains, but the Stiles family, which spent its summers on Green Island, was one family that couldn't wholly depend on locomotion to get them to their country place.

Instead they were met at Montgomery by family servants rowing a boat jokingly called "The Ark." The travelers had to get aboard by the high tide to reach the island in an hour or so and it must have made quite a picture—the boat laden with mattresses, furnishings and provisions for the long stay and the ladies reclining amidst it all.

Accounts of life at these summer houses during the 1870's, '80's and '90's describe fishing, crabbing, rowing and berry-picking as some of the favorite pastimes. Swimming, then called "bathing," was done primarily within the confines of a bathhouse, the men in long-sleeved jerseys and knee-length shorts and the ladies covered with clothing from head to toe.

The men went to town each day to conduct their business, while the women oversaw the gardening and housekeeping. Apparently, families entertained casually. Noted one hostess, who often had eight to fourteen people at her table, "We live chiefly from what the waters furnish and vegetables of which we can get a full supply. Housekeeping does not give me much trouble even when the house if full of company, for, as we only profess to be marooning, not much is expected of us."

Marinated Shrimp Monterey

Serves 8 to 10

¼ cup sugar
1 teaspoon paprika
1 teaspoon salt
¼ teaspoon dry mustard
1 cup oil
¼ cup tarragon vinegar
½ cup catsup
Juice of 1 lemon

1 tablespoon Worcestershire sauce
1 tablespoon steak sauce (optional)
3 medium onions, thinly sliced
1½ pounds small shrimp, cooked and peeled

Combine above ingredients except onions and shrimp to make a sauce. Pour over onions and shrimp. Marinate in refrigerator overnight. Serve with crackers, using toothpicks. Can be served hot.

Shrimp Paste

Spreads 50 to 60 Crackers

1 pound shrimp
3 ounces cream cheese, softened
1 tablespoon onion, grated
1 stalk celery, chopped

1 teaspoon cider vinegar
Dash salt
Dash Worcestershire sauce
Mayonnaise, enough to moisten

Cook shrimp, grate onion and chop celery. Place all ingredients except mayonnaise in blender or food processor. Mix well. Add enough mayonnaise to moisten into a spreadable consistency. Refrigerate. Better if made several hours or a day in advance. Keeps well for several days in refrigerator.

Shrimp Butter
Serves 12

½ cup mayonnaise
1 cup butter
8 ounces cream cheese
2 shakes Worcestershire
  sauce
¼ teaspoon salt
¼ teaspoon pepper

1 clove garlic, crushed
2 tablespoons onion, minced
2 hard-cooked eggs, chopped
½ pound shrimp, cooked and
  chopped
Crackers or Melba rounds

Beat together first 8 ingredients. Add eggs and shrimp. Chill. Spread on crackers or Melba rounds and serve.

Caviar Egg Mold
Serves 8 to 10

2 green onions, tops
  included
3 ounces cream cheese
6 eggs, hard-cooked
½ cup mayonnaise
2 teaspoons lemon juice
½ teaspoon salt

1 tablespoon unflavored gelatin
2 tablespoons hot water
½ cup Spanish onions, chopped
1 cup sour cream
3½ ounces canned red or black
  caviar

In food processor or blender, place green onions (cut in fourths) and cream cheese. Blend until onion is chopped. Add eggs, mayonnaise, lemon juice and salt. Blend again until eggs are smooth. Add gelatin which has been dissolved in hot water and allowed to sit 5 minutes (stirred well). Blend 2 seconds. Pour into mixing bowl and stir in Spanish onions. Pour mixture into an oiled 2 cup mold and refrigerate overnight until set. Unmold and spread sour cream over mold. Spoon and spread caviar over top of sour cream. Serve with Melba rounds or wheat crackers.

Savory Shrimp Mold   Serves 6

1 envelope unflavored
 gelatin
½ cup cold water
1 cup boiling water
2 chicken bouillon cubes
¾ to 1 cup mayonnaise
2 teaspoons horseradish
1 teaspoon instant onion,
 minced

2 teaspoons parsley, minced
2 tablespoons lemon juice
Dash Worcestershire sauce
Dash Tabasco
2 pounds shrimp, cooked,
 peeled, and diced or ground
Salt and pepper

Soften gelatin in cold water; add boiling water and bouillon cubes, stirring until gelatin and cubes are dissolved. Chill until slightly thickened. Fold in remaining ingredients. Pour into mold and chill until firm.

Fondue Neufchâtel   Serves 8 to 10

1 clove garlic
1½ cups dry white wine
1 teaspoon lemon juice
2 cups Jarlsberg cheese,
 grated
2 cups Gruyère cheese,
 grated

1 teaspoon flour
1 tablespoon dry mustard
1 tablespoon chives, snipped
Pepper and cayenne, to taste
French bread, for serving

Rub inside of fondue pot with clove of garlic. Heat wine with lemon juice carefully. Mix flour with grated cheeses. Combine the two mixtures and heat until cheeses melt. Pour into fondue pot and add other seasonings.

Best if made day before serving.

Swiss Cheese Fondue

Serves 12

1 pound Swiss cheese,
  grated
1 tablespoon flour
1 clove garlic
1 cup dry white wine

2 tablespoons kirsch
¾ teaspoon salt
½ teaspoon pepper
¼ teaspoon nutmeg
French bread, cubed

Dredge cheese in flour. In a baking dish, rubbed with garlic, bring wine almost to a boil. Add cheese slowly, stirring constantly until melted. Add seasonings. When mixture starts to boil, add kirsch and serve at once with French bread cubes for dunking.

Shrimp Dip Divine

Yields Approximately 2 cups

10 ounces shrimp, cooked
  and peeled
8 ounces cream cheese,
  softened
½ cup mayonnaise

1 medium onion, finely
  chopped
2 teaspoons prepared mustard
Dash Tabasco

Chop shrimp and combine with remaining ingredients.

Eggs Everglade

Serves 10 to 15

1 package unflavored
  gelatin
¼ cup cold water
1 cup chicken broth

3 eggs, hard-cooked
1 teaspoon curry powder
¾ cup mayonnaise

Soften gelatin in water, then dissolve in boiling chicken stock. Put all ingredients in blender and pour into greased mold. Serve on a bed of lettuce for a salad or unmold and garnish with caviar. Serve with crackers.

Chicken Liver Spread
Serves 12

¼ pound chicken livers
2 chicken bouillon cubes
1 bay leaf
1 small onion, chopped
2 stalks celery, chopped

½ teaspoon salt
¼ teaspoon pepper
2 tablespoons sour cream
2 tablespoons mayonnaise

Simmer all ingredients except sour cream and mayonnaise in small saucepan with just enough water to cover. Drain. Chop livers, but not too fine. Moisten with sour cream and mayonnaise. Season to taste. Curry powder may be added, if desired. Chill and serve as appetizer on crackers.

Delectable Spinach Dip
Serves 8

10 ounces frozen spinach, thawed
½ cup fresh parsley, chopped
½ cup green onion (use tops)

½ teaspoon salt
½ teaspoon pepper
1 cup mayonnaise (homemade, if possible)
1 teaspoon lemon juice

Squeeze all juice out of thawed spinach. Mix with remaining ingredients. Serve with fresh vegetables such as cauliflower, broccoli, celery, carrots and cucumber.

This should be made 4 to 5 hours ahead for seasonings to be absorbed by spinach.

Hot Pecan Spread

Serves 6 to 8

2 tablespoons milk
8 ounces cream cheese
1 (2½ ounce) jar dried beef, shredded
2 tablespoons onion flakes
¼ teaspoon pepper

¼ cup bell pepper, finely chopped
⅛ teaspoon garlic powder
½ cup sour cream
2 tablespoons butter
½ cup pecans, chopped

Blend cream cheese with milk. Add beef, onion flakes, seasonings and bell pepper. Fold in sour cream. Spread in shallow oven-proof dish. Heat pecans in butter and sprinkle over cheese mixture. Bake at 350°F for 30 minutes. Serve with Melba rounds.

Bleu Cheese Biscuits

Yields Approximately 3 Dozen

1 cup bleu cheese, softened
½ cup butter, softened
1 cup flour

½ cup nuts, coarsely chopped
½ cup nuts, finely chopped

Cream cheese and butter. Add flour and coarsely chopped nuts. Take teaspoons of mixture and form into balls. Roll in finely chopped nuts and bake at 350°F for 15 to 17 minutes.

Cheese Snaps

Yields 6 Dozen

½ cup butter
2 cups sharp cheese, grated
2 cups flour

Red pepper and salt, to taste
½ cup pecans, chopped

Cream butter and cheese. Add flour, pepper, salt, pecans and mix well. Form into small rolls and wrap in foil. Refrigerate until firm enough to slice. Bake at 350°F for 10 to 15 minutes—watch closely.

These may be frozen in the rolls.

Cocktail Cheese Biscuits
Yields 4 Dozen

½ cup butter (no substitute)   ½ teaspoon cayenne pepper
1 cup sharp New York State   1 cup flour
   cheese, grated   Pecan halves
1 teaspoon salt

Cream butter, cheese, salt and pepper. Add flour and work in-to smooth, large ball. Roll into small balls and press half pecan on each ball to flatten. Place on cookie sheet and bake 15 minutes in 350°F oven.

Hot Cheese Tidbits
Yields 4½ Dozen

8 ounces cream cheese   Dash cayenne pepper
½ cup butter   American or Cheddar cheese,
1 cup flour   cut in small pieces
¹/₈ teaspoon salt   (about ½ " x ¼ ")

Cream butter and cream cheese. Add flour, salt and cayenne pepper. Mix and shape into a ball. Chill. Roll thin. Cut in two inch squares. Put a piece of cheese in each square. Fold in triangle. Press edges with a fork. Freeze. Baking time FROZEN—450°F 5 to 7 minutes.

Plains "Special" Cheese Ring   Serves 10

1 pound sharp Cheddar
  cheese, grated
1 cup pecans, chopped
1 cup (scant) mayonnaise

1 small onion, grated
Black pepper, to taste
Dash cayenne
Strawberry preserves

Mix all ingredients except preserves. Mold into desired shape (a ring mold is good). Place in refrigerator until chilled. When ready to serve, fill center with strawberry preserves.

This may be served as an appetizer or with the main course.

Steak Tartare   Serves 12

1 pound sirloin, ground
  (with fat removed before
  grinding)
2 ounces anchovies, diced
  fine
2 tablespoons capers,
  drained

1 medium onion, grated
Seasoned salt and pepper, to
  taste
½ teaspoon Worcestershire
  sauce
1 egg, beaten
Sliced olives, for garnish

Mix all ingredients well before adding meat. Mold together in shape of an oval, flattened on top. Score top to form diamonds and garnish with sliced olives in each square.

Serve cold as an appetizer with a fork, or serve with crackers or small rounds of bread.

Oysters and Artichokes   Serves 6

9 ounces frozen artichoke
   hearts
1 pint oysters with their
   water
½ cup butter
2 tablespoons flour

1 small bunch green onions
1 clove garlic, crushed
Salt and pepper, to taste
¼ teaspoon thyme
2 tablespoons fresh parsley

Cook and drain artichoke hearts. Boil oysters in their own water until plump and firm. Remove oysters and save liquid. Brown the butter, add flour and stir, making a roux. Add onions and garlic, salt, pepper and thyme. Add 2 cups oyster water. Cook very slowly until thick. Add oysters and artichoke hearts. Cook slowly 15 minutes over low heat. Add fresh parsley and serve on small plates with hunks of French bread and forks.

Oysters Savannah ~ Pirates' House   Serves 6 to 8

1 pound bacon
1 cup green peppers,
   chopped
4 ounces canned pimentos,
   drained and chopped

1 teaspoon salt
½ teaspoon pepper
1 tablespoon paprika
1 quart oysters
Rock salt

Chop uncooked bacon fine, add peppers, pimentos, salt, pepper and paprika. Fill natural oyster shells with oysters. Cover with bacon mixture. Heat rock salt on steel platter or broiler pan covered well with aluminum foil. Place filled oysters on heated rock salt and cook under broiler until golden brown on top.

If oyster shells are not available, this can be made in a 1½ quart casserole, alternating layers of oysters and bacon mixture ending with bacon mixture on top. Bake 350°F about 40 minutes.

A specialty of The Pirates' House restaurant.

Artichokes Stuffed With Crab   Serves 8

2 tablespoons butter
3 tablespoons bread crumbs
6½ ounces crab meat
Few drops Tabasco
Dash cayenne
¼ cup mayonnaise

¼ cup water chestnuts, sliced
1 scallion, finely minced
1 teaspoon Dijon mustard
Salt and pepper, to taste
2 (14 ounce) cans artichoke
   bottoms

Melt butter and stir into bread crumbs. Combine remaining ingredients except artichoke bottoms. Stir in bread crumb mixture. Stuff artichoke bottoms with crab mixture. Place on a buttered baking dish and bake at 350°F for 25 to 30 minutes. Serve hot. Artichoke bottoms may be quartered or halved before serving.

Mushrooms Stuffed With Cheese   Serves 6

12 large fresh mushrooms
2 tablespoons onion, finely
   chopped
3 tablespoons butter or
   margarine
1 tablespoon parsley,
   minced

¼ cup fine fresh bread crumbs
1½ tablespoons bleu cheese,
   crumbled
1 tablespoon lemon juice
½ teaspoon salt
Dash paprika

Remove stems from mushrooms and mince. Sauté stems and onions in butter; add parsley, bread crumbs, cheese, lemon juice and salt. Fill caps with mixture and place in shallow baking dish. Sprinkle with paprika. Bake at 450°F for 5 minutes; then broil 3 minutes until delicately brown.

Clams Casino

Serves 4 to 6

2 dozen clams

Open clams and wash well in cold water. Remove clams and drain juice; set aside. Place shells in a 15 x 10-inch pan filled with coarse salt (approximately ¼ inch deep). Make sure clams do not tip.

¼ cup butter   1 tablespoon anchovy paste

Blend thoroughly and spoon small amount into each clam shell. Cover with clams. Sprinkle clams with lemon juice and spoon the following mixture over clams:

¼ cup green pepper,   ¼ cup onion, chopped
   minced   2 teaspoons pimento, chopped

Season with salt and pepper. Cut 3 slices of bacon into fine pieces. Top each clam with bacon. Bake at 450°F for 15 to 20 minutes or until bacon is crisp.

Crabmeat Mornay

Serves 8

½ cup butter   1 pint half-and-half
1 small bunch green onions,   ½ pound Swiss Cheese, grated
   chopped   1 tablespoon sherry
½ cup parsley, finely   Red pepper, to taste
   chopped   Salt, to taste
2 tablespoons flour   1 pound white crab meat

Melt butter in heavy pot and sauté onions and parsley. Blend in flour, cream and cheese until cheese is melted. Add remaining ingredients and gently fold in crab meat. May be served in chafing dish with Melba toast or in patty shells.

Mushrooms Stuffed With Escargots

Serves 4

½ cup butter (no substitute)
12 large, fresh mushroom
  caps
¼ teaspoon salt
2 cloves garlic, minced
2 medium shallots, minced

1 dozen escargots, drained
2 tablespoons parsley, chopped
1 tablespoon vermouth or dry
  white wine
½ tablespoon lemon juice
1 loaf French bread

In large skillet with a lid, melt butter, add mushroom caps and sprinkle with salt, garlic and shallots. Sauté for 15 minutes over low heat, uncovered, turning occasionally. Remove mushrooms and add escargots and remaining ingredients except bread; simmer, covered, for 30 minutes. Place one escargot in each mushroom cap and place in baking-serving dish and pour butter over all. Bake at 400°F just until bubbly, 5 to 10 minutes. Serve with French bread (to be dipped in butter).

Marinated Mushrooms

Serves 6

1 pound fresh mushrooms
¾ cup olive oil
⅓ cup red wine vinegar
2 tablespoons lemon juice
1 tablespoon chives,
  chopped

1 teaspoon tarragon
1 small clove garlic, chopped
1 teaspoon salt
½ teaspoon sugar

Wash and trim mushrooms. Mix remaining ingredients together and pour over mushrooms. Chill for 2 or 3 hours.

Tomato Stuffed Mushrooms

Serves 10
Allowing 2 Per Person

20 large mushrooms
Dash salt
2 tablespoons butter
2 tablespoons oil
1 medium onion, finely
    chopped
2 garlic cloves, minced

Dash thyme
Dash pepper
1 large ripe tomato, peeled,
    seeded and chopped
3 eggs yolks, well beaten
¼ cup Parmesan cheese

Break mushroom caps off stems and place caps bottom side up in skillet. Sprinkle with salt. Melt 1 tablespoon butter and combine with 1 tablespoon oil. Sprinkle over mushroom caps. Cover and cook over low heat for 10 minutes. Put caps on tray and refrigerate. Chop stems fine. Add rest of oil and butter to skillet and sauté with stems and onion for 3 minutes, stirring constantly. Add garlic, thyme, pepper and tomato. Bring to a boil and simmer 12 minutes. Cool slightly, then gradually beat in egg yolks. Bring to boil and cook 1 minute, stirring constantly. Remove from heat and cool. Stuff caps with mixture and sprinkle with cheese. Place on baking sheet and bake at 375 °F for 25 to 30 minutes.

Vegetable Mousse

1 envelope unflavored gelatin
1 cup cold water
1 cup sour cream
½ cup mayonnaise
8 ounces sharp cheese,
    shredded
2 tablespoons green pepper,
    chopped

2 tablespoons pimento,
    chopped
1 tablespoon onion,
    chopped
1 tablespoon Worcestershire
    sauce
¼ teaspoon salt

Sprinkle gelatin over cold water. Place over low heat. Stir 3 to 4 minutes until dissolved. Combine remaining ingredients and stir. Chill mixture slightly and stir again. Pour into a four cup mold and congeal.

Mushrooms Stuffed With Sausage

Serves 6

24 large, fresh mushrooms	1 pound hot sausage meat
1 tablespoon butter	½ cup bread crumbs
¼ cup oil	1 egg
1 onion, chopped	Salt and pepper, to taste

Separate mushroom caps and stems. Chop stems and brown with butter, oil, onions and sausage. Mix in bread crumbs and egg. Add salt and pepper to taste. Stuff mixture into mushroom caps. Heat in 300°F oven before serving. Cayenne pepper can be added if hotter flavor is desired.

Low Country Stuffed Mushrooms

Fresh mushrooms, large	Salt and pepper, to taste
Butter	Fresh oysters, small
Shallots, grated	Parmesan cheese, grated
Parsley, finely chopped	Small toast rounds

Choose as many large mushrooms as desired. Peel and stem. Cook minced stems in a little butter along with a little grated shallots, 1 tablespoon chopped parsley for each 12 mushrooms and salt and pepper, to taste. Broil mushroom caps dipped in olive oil until tender. Fill bottom of each cap with a little of the stem mixture. Lay on this a small fresh oyster, dipped in lemon juice and butter. Cover with freshly grated Parmesan cheese. Brown under broiler until cheese bubbles. Serve hot on small rounds of toast.

Red Caviar Soup   Serves 8

4 cans madrilene consommé   2 tablespoons fresh parsley,
1 cup red caviar   chopped
1 cup sour cream

Jell the madrilene by placing in refrigerator for 12 hours. Put 2 teaspoons red caviar and 1 tablespoon sour cream in the bottom of each of 8 bouillon cups. Cover with jelled madrilene. Stir. Garnish with chopped parsley. Serve very cold.

Vichyssoise   Serves 6

2 cups green onions, thinly   1 quart chicken stock
   sliced (use white parts   2 teaspoons salt
   only)   2 cups light cream
1 medium onion, chopped   ¼ teaspoon white pepper
2 tablespoons butter   1 cup heavy cream
4 medium potatoes, peeled   Dash Tabasco
   and thinly sliced

In a deep kettle, soften onions in butter. Add the potatoes, stock and salt. Simmer for 30 minutes. Puree in blender or food processor. Warm the light cream and add to the pureed mixture. Blend again. Season to taste with white pepper. Let mixture cool to room temperature. Chill. Thoroughly mix in the heavy cream just prior to serving.

Cold Tomato Cream   Serves 4

2½ cups tomato or   ½ cup sour cream
   vegetable juice   3 tablespoons chives
½ teaspoon seasoned salt   Dash Tabasco

Mix all ingredients in blender. Chill and serve.

Cold Cucumber Soup

Yields 6 cups

2 large or 4 small
  cucumbers, seeded, pared
  and thinly sliced
1 cup water
1 small onion, thinly sliced
½ teaspoon salt

2 shakes pepper
4 tablespoons flour
2 cups chicken stock
¾ cup heavy cream,
Chives, chopped

Cook cucumbers, onions, salt and pepper in water until soft. Cool. Puree in blender; strain and set aside. Blend flour and chicken stock until smooth. Add cucumber puree and stir over heat about 1 minute. Correct seasonings and cool. Add heavy cream and refrigerate.

Serve cold with chopped chives on top.

Zippy Gazpacho

Yields 1 Quart

3 cups vegetable juice
1 cucumber, halved and
  peeled
1 small onion, chopped
1 clove garlic, crushed
1½ tablespoons
  Worcestershire sauce
⅛ teaspoon salt

¼ cup olive oil
¼ cup wine vinegar
4 scallions or green onions
1 tomato
1 cup garlic croutons
Lemon wedges, optional
Sour cream, optional

In blender combine juice, ½ cucumber, onion, garlic, Worcestershire and salt; blend until smooth. Blend in vinegar and oil. Chill well. Dice ½ cucumber, scallions and whole tomato. Pour into chilled bowls, top with diced vegetables, croutons, lemon wedges or sour cream.

Herbed Cucumber Soup

Serves 4

2 tablespoons butter
¼ cup onion, chopped, or 1
  leek, sliced and cubed
2 cups cucumber, unpeeled
  and diced
1 cup watercress leaves
½ cup raw potatoes, diced
2 cups chicken broth

2 sprigs parsley
½ teaspoon salt
¼ teaspoon pepper
¼ teaspoon dry mustard
1 cup heavy cream
Chopped chives and cucumber,
  to garnish

Melt butter and cook onion in it until transparent. Add remaining ingredients except cream and garnishes. Bring to boil. Simmer for 15 minutes or until potatoes are tender. Puree in blender or food processor. Correct seasonings and chill. Before serving, add cream. Garnish with chopped chives and cucumber.

Cold Strawberry Bisque

Serves 4

2 (10 ounce) packages
  frozen strawberries, thawed

1 cup milk or light cream
½ cup sour cream

Puree all ingredients in blender until smooth. Serve cold.

Cold Asparagus Soup

Serves 6

14 ounces chicken broth
10 ounces canned
  asparagus, drained
2 cups sour cream

Dash cayenne pepper
Salt, lemon juice, curry powder,
  to taste
One cucumber, peeled, optional

Puree all ingredients in blender. Strain to remove strings. Chill and serve.

Chicken Caviar Soup
Serves 8

1½ quarts clear, congealed
  chicken stock, skimmed of
  fat

1 (4 ounce) jar black caviar
½ cup sour cream
2 teaspoons chives, finely cut

Put 2 teaspoons caviar and 1 tablespoon sour cream in bottom of each of 8 soup cups. Divide jellied stock into cups. Stir well, sprinkle with chopped chives and serve.

Cold Beet Soup
Serves 4

16 ounces canned beets,
  drained
2 cups vegetable juice
¼ cup French dressing (oil
  and vinegar base) or ¼
  cup Italian dressing

½ teaspoon salt
¼ teaspoon pepper
4 heaping tablespoons sour
  cream
½ cucumber, thinly sliced
Chives, chopped

Blend all ingredients in blender until beets are minced. Serve with thin slices of cucumber and/or chopped chives.

Lemon Soup
Yields 16 Cups

2 quarts chicken broth
5 celery stalks, chopped
1 carrot, chopped
1 large onion, chopped

Salt and pepper, to taste
3 egg yolks
Juice of 1 lemon
Lemon slices

Simmer broth, celery, carrot and onion for 1 hour. Add salt and pepper to taste. In double boiler (do not let liner of double boiler touch hot water), beat egg yolks and slowly add lemon juice; beat. Strain broth and add to egg mixture while both are still warm, stirring quickly. Serve with a slice of lemon on top. Good hot or cold.

Cream of Cauliflower Soup

Yields 2 Quarts

1 medium cauliflower, cut
  in flowerets
1 cup onion, chopped
½ cup celery, chopped
2½ cups chicken broth
½ cup water

½ teaspoon Worcestershire
  sauce
1 teaspoon salt
½ teaspoon white pepper
1½ cups half-and-half
1 cup cheese, grated (optional)

Combine all ingredients except cream and cheese. Bring to a boil. Reduce heat, cover and simmer for 15 minutes or until vegetables are tender. Pour 1 cup at a time in blender and puree until smooth. Return to a large pan, add cream and cheese and heat 2 to 4 minutes, or until hot. Serve hot or cold.

Cream of Spinach Soup

Serves 6

3 tablespoons green onions,
  sliced
3 tablespoons butter
3 tablespoons flour
2 cups milk
1 cup cream
Salt, to taste

Pepper, to taste
Dash nutmeg
2 cups spinach, cooked [2
  packages (10 ounce) frozen
  spinach equal 2 cups cooked
  spinach]
Paprika

Sauté onions in butter. When onions are soft, add flour and stir until smooth. Mix in slowly hot milk and cream. Stir until sauce becomes thick; add salt, pepper and a dash of nutmeg. Mash spinach through a sieve (or put in food processor) and mix with the cream sauce. Reheat and garnish with paprika.

Cream of Peanut Soup   Serves 8

2 stalks celery, chopped	1 cup milk
1 small onion, chopped	1 cup light cream
¼ cup butter	1 cup peanut butter
2 tablespoons flour	Salt and pepper, to taste
2 cups chicken broth	Watercress, for garnish

Brown celery and onion in butter. Stir in flour and gradually add chicken broth. Add milk and cream; strain. Stir in peanut butter and simmer for 5 minutes. Season with salt and pepper. Garnish with chopped peanuts and sprig of watercress.

Spanky's Clam Chowder   Serves 8

3 small onions, diced	¼ cup margarine
1 green pepper, diced	2 teaspoons salt
2 potatoes, diced	½ teaspoon white pepper
Slice of ham, diced	½ teaspoon celery salt
24 ounces clams, drained and diced	Tabasco, to taste

Combine all ingredients and cook for 20 minutes.

Roux:

4 tablespoons margarine	5 cups milk
5 tablespoons flour	

Melt margarine, add flour; stir until flour is well cooked. Add flour mixture to clam mixture. Add milk; cook slowly, stirring occasionally until chowder is hot and potatoes are tender, approximately 15 minutes. If a thinner chowder is desired, add more milk.

A specialty of Spanky's restaurant.

Onion Soup Gratinée

Serves 6

4 to 5 large onions, minced
3 tablespoons butter or
  margarine
¼ teaspoon pepper
1 tablespoon flour
4 cups beef broth

1½ cups water
1 bay leaf
6 to 8 slices French bread,
  toasted
½ cup Swiss cheese, grated

Sauté onions in butter; add pepper. Cook until onions are lightly browned. Sprinkle onions with flour, cook 1 minute, stirring constantly. Add beef broth, water and bay leaf. Simmer 30 to 40 minutes; discard bay leaf. Taste and correct seasonings if necessary. Turn soup into an oven proof tureen or individual oven proof dishes. Place toast on top and sprinkle with cheese. Place under broiler or in 400°F oven until cheese is golden.

Vegetable Beef Soup

Serves 12

4 to 6 beef soup bones
4 beef bouillon cubes
2 garlic cloves, pressed
1 bay leaf
2 stalks celery, chopped
1 tablespoon Worcestershire
  sauce
Good dash oregano, thyme,
  savory
Small dash tarragon

2 (14½ ounce) cans tomatoes
  with juice
2 medium onions, chopped
  coarsely
Salt and pepper, to taste
1 pound ground beef, cooked
  and drained
2 pounds mixed vegetables
½ cup rice, uncooked

Cover soup bones with water. Let cook for ½ hour. Skim occasionally. Add other ingredients up to the ground beef. Let simmer for an hour. Add remaining ingredients. Taste for adjustment to seasonings and let cook for 45 minutes to 1 hour longer. Remove soup bones, cut meat off bones and add meat to soup.

Dugger's Holiday Gumbo

Serves 8 to 10

¼ cup butter
½ pound cooked ham, diced
2 cups cooked turkey or chicken, diced
1 pound fresh okra
2 cups onion, diced
1 green pepper, seeded and diced
1 or 2 cloves garlic, minced
28 ounces canned tomatoes
2½ cups chicken broth
1 pint oysters or cooked shrimp, peeled
1½ teaspoons salt
⅛ teaspoon red pepper

Melt butter in heavy saucepan over medium heat. Add ham and cooked chicken or turkey. Cook 2 minutes, stirring frequently. Add okra, onion, and green pepper and cook for 5 minutes. Add garlic, tomatoes, chicken broth, liquid from oysters, salt and pepper. Bring to a boil. Simmer for 45 minutes or longer. Add oysters or shrimp and cook for 1 minute. Season to taste.

Okra Gumbo

Serves 12 to 15

1½ to 2 pounds beef shanks with meat
2 pounds fresh okra or 4 (10 ounce) packages frozen okra
2 (14½ ounce) cans tomatoes
1 large onion, chopped
1 large bell pepper, chopped
6 ounces canned tomato paste
Salt, pepper, Tabasco, Worcestershire, to taste

Cover soup bones with cold water, about 1½ quarts, and boil slowly for at least two hours. Cool and refrigerate overnight. The next day, remove all grease which has congealed on top of stock. Take bones out, cut up and reserve meat. Add to stock the cut up okra, onion, bell pepper and tomatoes with juice. Cook for two hours. Add tomato paste during last ½ hour. Season to taste. Add chopped soup meat last. Serve over rice or in soup bowls.

Vegetarian Vegetable Soup   Serves 4

16 ounces canned stewed
   tomatoes, chopped
1¼ cups beef broth
1 cup cucumbers, peeled
   and chopped

1 cup celery, chopped
1 cup onion, sliced
2 tablespoons lemon juice
1 small clove garlic, pressed
Pepper, to taste

Combine all ingredients in saucepan. Simmer for 10 minutes.
Chill. Top with sour cream.

Minestrone   Serves 8 to 10

14½ ounces chicken broth
14½ ounces beef broth
2 cups water
3 slices bacon, cut into small
   pieces
½ small green cabbage,
   shredded
½ small onion, chopped
1 clove garlic, crushed
2 carrots, diced
2 stalks celery, chopped
1½ teaspoons salt

½ teaspoon pepper
10 ounces frozen chopped
   spinach
10 ounces frozen peas
10 ounces navy beans
⅓ cup thin pasta (macaroni,
   shells or vermicelli)
¼ teaspoon each marjoram,
   thyme and basil
1 cup Parmesan cheese, freshly
   grated

Prepare all the vegetables. Bring broth to simmering point in a
large heavy pot. Add bacon, cabbage, onion, garlic, carrots, celery,
salt and pepper. Simmer until vegetables are almost tender, about
15 to 20 minutes. Add spinach, peas, beans, macaroni and herbs to
broth. Simmer for 8 minutes until macaroni is tender. Taste for
seasoning, adding more salt and pepper if necessary.

Serve hot, sprinkled generously with Parmesan cheese.

Fresh Mushroom Soup   Serves 6

4 tablespoons butter
1 pound fresh mushrooms,
   chopped
1 medium onion, chopped
2 tablespoons flour
2½ cups beef broth
2½ cups water

¾ cup half-and-half
½ teaspoon salt
¼ teaspoon pepper
2 teaspoons Worcestershire
   sauce
½ cup sherry

In a large saucepan, melt butter. Sauté mushrooms and onion until softened. Stir in flour. Add beef broth and water and cook until thickened, about 5 minutes. Puree mixture in blender or food processor. Add half-and-half, salt, pepper and Worcestershire sauce. Stir in sherry. Blend thoroughly. Heat but do not allow to boil.

Curry Soup   Serves 8

3 cups tomatoes
1 onion, chopped
4 sprigs parsley
4 peppercorns
1 stalk celery, chopped
3 tablespoons flour
2 tablespoons butter
2 cups milk

1 cup chicken stock or 1
   chicken bouillon cube
   dissolved in 1 cup boiling
   water
2 teaspoons curry powder
½ cup heavy cream
Salt, to taste

Simmer tomatoes, onion, parsley, peppercorns and celery for 30 minutes. While this is cooking, make a cream sauce with flour, butter and milk. When sauce is smooth and thick, add stock, curry powder and cream. Strain tomato mixture and add to cream sauce. Reheat and serve.

Cheddar Soup

Yields 2 Quarts

5 slices bacon
½ cup carrot, grated
½ cup celery, finely
  chopped
½ cup onion, finely
  chopped
½ cup green pepper, finely
  chopped
¼ cup flour
4 cups chicken or beef
  broth

3 cups sharp Cheddar cheese,
  shredded
2 cups milk
2 tablespoons dry sherry
5 ounces pimento-stuffed
  olives, chopped
Salt, to taste
Ground pepper, to taste
Parsley, to garnish

In large pan, cook bacon until crisp. Drain and reserve. Sauté carrots, celery, onion and green pepper in bacon drippings until tender. Do not brown. Blend in flour and gradually add broth. Cook over low heat until mixture thickens and boils. Cook about 5 minutes. Add cheese and stir until melted. Stir in milk, sherry and olives; simmer 10 minutes. Season to taste. Serve garnished with crumbled bacon and parsley.

Spanky's Chili

Serves 4 to 6

1 pound ground beef
2 small onions, diced
1 green pepper, diced
2 tablespoons chili powder
1 teaspoon cumin

1 teaspoon salt
1 teaspoon black pepper
16 ounces whole tomatoes
8 ounces tomato sauce
16 ounces kidney beans

Brown ground beef; pour off fat. Add remaining ingredients and cook over low heat for an hour, stirring often. This recipe is very hot.

A specialty of Spanky's restaurant.

Black Bean Soup

Serves 8

1 pound black beans
2 tablespoons olive oil
1 medium ripe tomato
1 bay leaf

½ medium onion
½ medium green pepper
1 garlic clove, unpeeled and
  crushed

½ cup olive oil
½ medium onion, chopped
½ green pepper, chopped
1 garlic clove, minced
1 level teaspoon crushed
  oregano

¼ teaspoon cumin
2 tablespoons wine vinegar
1 tablespoon salt

½ teaspoon hot sauce

2 tablespoons dry sherry

Wash beans and discard imperfect ones. Place in a deep bowl and cover with water 2 inches above beans. Soak overnight.

Next day, pour beans into a 3 to 4 quart kettle with the same soaking water. If necessary, add more water so that beans will be covered one inch above. Add to the beans 2 tablespoons olive oil, whole tomato, bay leaf, ½ onion, ½ green pepper, crushed garlic clove. Bring to a boil then lower heat to moderate, cover and cook until beans are tender, about 1 hour. Use only a wooden spoon for stirring. Remove the bay leaf and what is left of the half onion, tomato, pepper and garlic.

In a skillet, heat ½ cup olive oil and sauté the chopped onion and green pepper until transparent. Add the garlic, crushed oregano, cumin, wine vinegar and salt. Stir to mix well and cook 2 minutes longer, then add to beans. Stir in hot sauce, cover and cook for a good half hour. Correct seasonings, and add sherry. Serve hot with cooked long grain white rice and raw chopped onions.

Leek and Potato Soup   Serves 8

2 onions
2 bunches leeks or spring
  onions
5 tablespoons butter
1½ quarts chicken stock or
  broth

3 raw potatoes, chopped
  Salt and pepper, to taste
3 tablespoons butter
1½ cups light cream

Chop together onions and leeks. Sauté in butter until soft. Add chicken stock, potatoes, salt and pepper. Cook until potatoes are soft; remove from heat and mash through a coarse strainer. While still warm, stir in 3 tablespoons butter and cream. Garnish with paprika. Serve hot.

Curried Crab Soup   Serves 6

3 tablespoons butter
½ cup onion, chopped
1 clove garlic, minced
½ cup apple, peeled and
  diced
1 tablespoon curry powder
3 tablespoons flour

½ cup tomato, chopped
2½ cups chicken broth
Salt and pepper, to taste
¾ pound white crab meat
1 cup light cream
Tabasco

Melt butter in saucepan and sauté onion until wilted. Add garlic and apple. Stir and add curry powder and flour. Add tomato and chicken broth, stirring with wire whisk. When thickened and smooth, add salt, pepper and crab meat. Simmer 10 minutes. Add dash of Tabasco and cream and bring to a boil. Serve immediately.

Oyster Stew Herb River

Serves 4

2 or 3 stalks celery, diced
1 small onion, minced
½ cup butter
1 pint oysters
½ teaspoon salt

⅛ teaspoon pepper
Fresh parsley, chopped
⅛ teaspoon mace
1 pint half-and-half

Sauté celery and onions in butter until soft. Add oysters including liquid. Add salt, pepper, parsley and a little mace. Simmer until oysters curl. Add half-and-half. Heat until bubbles form around the edges, but do not boil. Remove from heat and serve.

Crab Soup With Sherry

Serves 4

1 pound crab meat
2 tablespoons butter
3 cups half-and-half
1 teaspoon salt
½ tablespoon Worcestershire
   sauce

1 tablespoon flour
2 tablespoons onion, grated
3 to 4 tablespoons sherry

Heat all ingredients except crab and flour in double boiler. Do not boil. Mix flour with a little milk and add with crab to milk mixture. Reduce heat and simmer ½ hour, stirring frequently.

Seafood Stew

Serves 4 to 6

Fry in 2 tablespoons olive oil for 5 minutes:

1 large onion, chopped

2 garlic cloves, chopped

3 tablespoons parsley, chopped

1 green pepper, chopped

½ cup mushrooms, chopped

Add and simmer 1 hour, covered:

1 bay leaf

½ teaspoon saffron

2 cloves

⅛ teaspoon celery seed

1 teaspoon pepper

1 teaspoon salt

Dash cayenne

15 ounces canned stewed tomatoes

1 cup red wine

Add and cook 15 minutes:

1½ cups liquid (seafood stock made by boiling shrimp shells, tomato juice, etc. or combination, strained)

Cubed ocean fish (at least one type)

Shelled shellfish (at least one type, lobster, shrimp, crab, oysters)

Serve in bowls over thick slices of buttered toast.

"Miss Rosa" Barbee's Terrapin Soup   Serves 16

5 terrapin
Bouquet garni, consisting of
   8 bay leaves, 3 dozen
   cloves, 1 teaspoon whole
   thyme
1 tablespoon salt
2 cups butter

16 egg yolks, hard-cooked and
   grated
4 heaping tablespoons flour
4 cups half-and-half
Salt and cayenne pepper to
   taste
Madeira

Simmer terrapin in a quart and a half of water to which a tablespoon of salt has been added. Add the *bouquet garni*. Let simmer, skimming off the scum, until the meat is just tender enough to fall from the bones. For frozen meat, this will take approximately 45 minutes to an hour. Remove seasonings. Remove terrapin from the stove, break off the head at the neck, remove meat from the back of the head and throw the rest of the head away. Let meat and stock cool; store in refrigerator. This can be done several days ahead.

Cream together butter, grated egg yolks and flour. Place in a large saucepan and add 4 cups terrapin stock and 4 cups half-and-half. Cook, stirring, until sauce is creamy. Season to taste with salt and cayenne, then add the meat. Heat, but do not scald or boil. Pour soup in hot bowls to which a teaspoon of Madeira has been added.

Serve with Melba toast and a glass of vintage Madeira, and an extra plate for the bones!

Shrimp Bisque
Serves 6 to 8

1 pound shrimp, boiled and
   peeled
4 tablespoons butter
4 to 5 tablespoons flour
1 quart milk
2 teaspoons salt

3 teaspoons lemon juice
½ teaspoon Tabasco
Dash white pepper
Sherry
Lemon slices

Grind shrimp in blender or food processor. Combine butter and flour in saucepan. Add milk and salt and stir until thickened. Add lemon juice, Tabasco and pepper. Add shrimp and sherry (approximately 2 tablespoons per serving).

Serve hot with lemon slice floating on top.

Oyster Stew
Serves 4

½ cup water
1 small white onion,
   chopped
½ cup celery, chopped
1 pint stewing size oysters

½ teaspoon salt
¼ teaspoon pepper
2 tablespoons butter
1 pint half-and-half

Pour ½ cup water into medium size saucepan. Add onions and celery and boil until slightly tender. Add oysters and cook until oysters curl. Add ½ teaspoon salt and ¼ teaspoon pepper. Reduce heat and add butter. Pour in 1 pint of half-and-half.

Crab Stew

Serves 4 to 6

6 tablespoons butter
1 pound lump crab meat
2 tablespoons onion, grated
2 eggs, hard-cooked and
    mashed

3 cups milk or 2 cups milk and
    1 cup half-and-half
½ teaspoon white pepper
½ teaspoon salt
2 tablespoons sherry

Melt butter in a large saucepan. Add crab meat, eggs and onion. Heat thoroughly. Add milk and seasonings. Simmer for 20 minutes without allowing mixture to boil.

THE PURSUIT OF CULTURE

The Pursuit of Culture

It is said that the early 1800's boasted a few quiet intellectuals who cherished and collected books, who traveled abroad to learn, and who cultivated their professions with distinction. But much of early Savannah society was too busy building the city and establishing itself commercially to engage in the serious pursuit of culture.

It was not until the 1830's that Savannah began to enjoy a fuller cultural life. And it was not until the 1870's and '80's that the Telfair sisters laid the foundation for widespread arts appreciation with the building of Hodgson Hall for the Georgia Historical Society and the creation of the Telfair Academy of Arts and Sciences.

In 1834, John James Audubon secured from Savannah businessman William Gaston three subscriptions to his forthcoming publication, *The Birds of America.*

The same year two groups of young men founded the Young Men's Debating Society and the Savannah Lyceum, both of which sponsored public lectures. Also in 1834 Lyceum Hall was built at Bull and Broughton streets. There or at the Savannah Theatre, built in 1819, one could find a variety of popular cultural amusements ranging from concerts and plays to circus performances.

By the 1870's and '80's Savannah was hosting many of the better actresses and actors of the times. Lectures and debates were held almost weekly at the Historical Society, and opera troupes often could count on a two-week stay.

By then, however, everyone was getting into the act. A local dramatic group, the Garrick Club, was formed in 1884 and gave five plays a season which were considered "delightful social affairs."

By the 1890's Savannah always was ready to "go dramatic," according to one writer. Plays were given constantly in private houses and small halls, some for ladies only, and one amateur entertainment taxed to overflowing the Guards' Hall when 700 tickets were sold. As it was observed, "A number of belles, beaux and beauties were in the cast, and everyone else was in the audience."

Salads and Dressings

Gazpacho Salad Mold

Serves 8

3 envelopes unflavored
gelatin
18 ounces canned tomato
juice
⅓ cup red wine vinegar
1 teaspoon salt
Tabasco, to taste
2 medium tomatoes, peeled
and diced (1¼ cups)
1 large cucumber, pared
and diced (1½ cups)

1 medium green pepper, diced
(¾ cup)
¼ cup red onion, finely
chopped
1 tablespoon chopped chives
3 large ripe avocadoes
Lemon juice
½ cup bottled oil and vinegar
dressing
Watercress, for garnish

In medium saucepan, sprinkle gelatin over ¾ cup tomato juice to soften. Place over low heat, stirring constantly until gelatin is dissolved. Remove from heat. Stir in remaining tomato juice, vinegar, salt and a few drops of Tabasco. Set in a bowl of ice, stirring occasionally, until mixture is consistency of unbeaten egg white, about 15 minutes.

Fold in tomatoes, cucumber, green pepper, onion and chives until well blended. Pour into 1½ quart mold that has been rinsed in cold water. Refrigerate until firm, at least 8 hours.

To unmold, run a small spatula around edge of mold. Just before serving, peel and slice avocado. Brush with lemon juice. Arrange around salad and pour dressing over it. Garnish with watercress.

Tomato Aspic With Artichoke Hearts   Serves 6

2 tablespoons unflavored gelatin	Few celery leaves
¼ cup cold water	2 teaspoons salt
4 cups tomato juice	2 teaspoons sugar
1 bay leaf	1 tablespoon lemon juice
1 small onion, thinly sliced	14 ounces canned artichoke hearts

Soften gelatin in cold water. Combine tomato juice with seasonings. Heat to boiling. Simmer 20 minutes. Strain and add softened gelatin. Stir until well dissolved. Add lemon juice. Pour a small amount of mixture into a mold that has been rinsed in cold water. Chill until firm. Cut artichokes in half and place in mold. Add remaining mixture and refrigerate.

Artichoke Mousse   Serves 8

8 medium size fresh artichokes	2 tablespoons gelatin
3 tablespoons salt	1 cup warm water
Water to cover above	1 cup homemade mayonnaise
1 large lemon	Pinch cayenne
	Salt and white pepper, to taste

Slightly over-boil the artichokes in salted water, covered. Let cool but do not drain. In a large shallow dish, scrape all leaves with a spoon reserving liquid. Remove choke and discard; chop hearts of artichoke and mix with scrapings. Reserve a few fine leaves for garnish. Add juice of 1 lemon immediately to artichoke meat. Soften gelatin in warm water. Stir into artichoke meat: mayonnaise, softened gelatin, cayenne, salt and pepper.

Turn into 8-inch ring mold which has been lightly greased with oil. Refrigerate, covered, for at least 3 hours. Turn out onto round platter. Fill center with choice of either shrimp, crab or chicken salad, or watercress dressed with French dressing; i.e., oil, vinegar, salt and pepper. Garnish platter with mixed salad greens. Garnish mousse with reserved artichoke leaves.

Cold Broccoli Mold With Anchovy Dressing

Serves 6 to 8

3 ounces cream cheese

2 (10 ounce) packages frozen, chopped broccoli, cooked and drained

1 envelope unflavored gelatin

10½ ounces chicken broth

1 cup mayonnaise

2 eggs, hard-cooked and finely chopped

Tabasco, to taste

Dice cream cheese and soften at room temperature. Combine cream cheese and broccoli, stirring until cream cheese melts. Soften gelatin over half the chicken broth in a small saucepan, stirring over low heat to dissolve. Add gelatin/broth mixture to cream cheese and broccoli. Stir in the following, one at a time: mayonnaise, eggs, Tabasco and remaining broth. Refrigerate in a 6-cup mold.

Top with mayonnaise, sour cream, ranch dressing, or preferably the following:

Anchovy Dressing:

2 tablespoons scallions, minced

1 tablespoon anchovies, chopped

2 tablespoons lemon juice

½ cup mayonnaise

1 cup sour cream

2 tablespoons white wine vinegar

⅜ teaspoon dried, crushed tarragon

Combine all ingredients and chill.

Avocado Mousse

Serves 6

1 envelope unflavored
gelatin
3 tablespoons lemon juice
1 heaping cup avocado,
mashed
½ cup sour cream

½ cup mayonnaise
¼ teaspoon salt
⅛ teaspoon pepper
Dash cayenne, dill and onion
salt (use up to ¼ teaspoon)
1 cup small shrimp, optional

Lightly oil 1½-quart ring mold. Soften gelatin in ¼ cup cold water. Add 1 cup boiling water and 1 tablespoon lemon juice. Chill until slightly thickened. Puree avocado in blender. Blend sour cream and mayonnaise. Add avocado, remaining lemon juice and seasonings. Combine with gelatin. Fold in shrimp and pour into mold. Chill until set. Unmold on serving dish covered with greens. Shrimp can be reserved until serving time and used to fill center of mold.

Mandarin Orange and Red Onion Salad

Serves 6

6 cups lettuce, torn (red
tipped is nice for color)
1 red onion, thinly sliced in
rings

11 ounces canned mandarin
oranges, drained

Dressing:
6 tablespoons oil
2 tablespoons tarragon
vinegar

1 teaspoon paprika
1 teaspoon salt
1 teaspoon sugar

Mix dressing. Toss with fruit and vegetables. Serve immediately.

Note: Pink grapefruit can be substituted for the oranges. Also, the exact proportions are not important, more or less onion and lettuce may be used.

Grapefruit Salad   Serves 12

3 large or 4 small grapefruit   1 teaspoon sugar
2 (3 ounce) packages lemon   1 teaspoon salt
  gelatin   4 scant cups liquid juice from
8¼ ounces canned crushed   pineapple and grapefruit.
  pineapple   Add water, if necessary.

Cut grapefruit into halves the wrong way. Scoop out fruit with a spoon. Drain off juice and use it mixed with pineapple juice and water to make the 4 cups of liquid. Heat liquid and dissolve gelatin, sugar and salt. Let cool until it begins to set. Add grapefruit sections and crushed pineapple. Put mixture in grapefruit shells and chill.

To serve, cut each half into two wedges and spoon on Fruit Salad Dressing (recipe follows).

Dressing:

⅔ cup sugar   Juice of 1 orange
2 tablespoons flour   ½ cup pineapple juice
2 egg yolks, beaten slightly   ½ cup heavy cream, whipped
Juice of 1 lemon

Combine sugar, flour and egg yolks. Add fruit juices and cook in double boiler, stirring constantly until thick. Take off heat and set aside to cool. Fold in whipped cream and serve on grapefruit wedges.

Ginger Pear Salad   Serves 4 to 6

2 ripe pears, peeled, cored   1 head Boston lettuce, torn into
  and sliced   bite-size pieces
1 cup seedless grapes

Dressing:

6 tablespoons oil   ¼ cup crystallized ginger,
2 tablespoons lime juice   chopped
1 teaspoon sugar   Salt and pepper, to taste

In a bowl, put pears, grapes and lettuce. Mix ingredients of dressing. Add dressing to fruit and toss.

Gingered Fruit

4 grapefruit
2 cups honeydew melon
2 cups cantaloupe
4 plums
4 nectarines or peaches
½ pound seedless grapes
½ pint strawberries

½ cup lime juice, strained
⅓ cup preserved ginger,
  including syrup
5 teaspoons superfine
  granulated sugar
Lime rind, grated

Trace a rick-rack design around the middle of each grapefruit. With a sharp knife, follow the design inserting knife into center of the fruit as it is cut and pull halves apart. Section grapefruit, detaching each segment from the membrane with a grapefruit knife and reserve segments; chill. With a spoon, scrape out and discard any pulp remaining in the shells and chill shells, covered.

Cut enough honeydew melon and cantaloupe into ¾ inch pieces to measure 2 cups of each and combine them in a bowl with plums and nectarines or peaches, pitted, and cut into ¾ inch pieces. Combine with seedless green grapes, halved, and strawberries which have been hulled and quartered.

In a blender or food processor fitted with steel blade, combine lime juice, preserved ginger including syrup and sugar; blend mixture until ginger is finely minced. Pour sauce over fruit in bowl, combine mixture well and chill, covered, for at least 2 hours.

Put each grapefruit shell in a glass bowl on a plate. Divide reserved grapefruit segments among each shell and top with fruit mixture. Pour any juices remaining in bowl over fruit in each shell and top each serving with grated lime rind.

Orange Jelly   Serves 6

1½ envelopes unflavored   Pinch salt
   gelatin   1 cup orange segments
2 cups fresh orange juice   (Mandarin oranges may be
3 tablespoons sugar   used)

Place gelatin, orange juice, sugar and salt in a saucepan over moderate heat. Stir until gelatin is dissolved. Chill and when slightly thick, stir in orange segments. Pour into small mold and chill until set.

Mushroom Salad   Serves 6

1 pound fresh mushrooms   1 teaspoon chopped chives
Salt, to taste   Juice of 1 lemon
Pepper, freshly ground   2 to 4 tablespoons mayonnaise
4 tablespoons olive oil   Romaine lettuce
4 tablespoons oil

Wash and slice mushrooms. Place in bowl and sprinkle with salt and freshly ground pepper. Combine oils, chives, lemon juice and mayonnaise. Mix well and pour over mushrooms. Chill 30 minutes. Serve on a bed of Romaine lettuce and sprinkle with chives and parsley.

Bleu Cheese Potato Salad   Serves 10 to 12

8 potatoes   ½ cup slivered almonds,
2 tablespoons parsley,   toasted
   chopped   ¼ teaspoon white pepper
3 green onions with tops,   8 ounces bleu cheese
   chopped   ¼ cup wine vinegar
2½ teaspoons salt   3 eggs, hard-cooked
1 cup sour cream   Bacon, crumbled, for garnish

Boil and peel potatoes. Cool and dice. Add remaining ingredients. Garnish with crumbled bacon.

Stuffed Lettuce

Serves 4 or More

1 small head iceberg lettuce
3 ounces cream cheese
½ pound bleu cheese
2 tablespoons milk

1 tablespoon chives, chopped
1 (2 ounce) jar pimentos,
  chopped
French dressing

Hollow out center of lettuce, leaving a 1 inch thick shell. Beat cheeses and milk together until smooth. Add chives and pimentos and mix thoroughly. Fill lettuce hollow with cheese and chill in refrigerator until cheese is solid.

When ready to serve, cut in crosswise slices about ¾ inch thick and serve with French dressing.

Hearts of Palm Salad With Dijon Dressing

Serves 6 to 8

¼ teaspoon each basil,
  tarragon and thyme
2 tablespoons cider vinegar
½ teaspoon salt
⅓ cup olive oil
1 tablespoon Dijon mustard
½ teaspoon pepper,
  coarsely ground

1 clove garlic, crushed
14 ounces canned hearts of
  palm
3 cups watercress
2 cups romaine lettuce, torn
  into bite-size pieces
1 cup iceberg lettuce, torn into
  bite-size pieces

Soak basil, tarragon and thyme for 1 hour in vinegar. Dissolve salt in the seasoned vinegar. Add olive oil, mustard, pepper and garlic. Shake well.

Drain hearts of palm and cut in serving pieces. Combine hearts of palm with watercress, romaine and iceberg lettuce. Place the greens in a large bowl and toss with dressing.

Marinated Asparagus   Serves 10

3 (15 ounce) cans white
  asparagus, drained
1 teaspoon tarragon
1 teaspoon garlic salt
Black pepper, freshly
  ground

1 cup Italian dressing
½ cup tarragon vinegar
Salt, to taste

Lay asparagus in shallow pan. Sprinkle with tarragon leaves, garlic salt and pepper. Pour dressing and vinegar over all. Refrigerate overnight. To serve, arrange on Boston lettuce and top with mayonnaise mixed with some of the remaining marinade.

Hearty Salad Ring   Serves 6 to 8

1 tablespoon unflavored
  gelatin
½ cup cold water
2 tablespoons lemon juice
2 teaspoons horseradish
2 teaspoons prepared
  mustard

1 cup mayonnaise
½ teaspoon salt
2 cups chicken, cooked and
  cubed
1 cup celery, diced
2 tablespoons onion, minced

Soften gelatin in cold water. Dissolve over hot water. Add lemon juice, horseradish, mustard, mayonnaise and salt. Mix thoroughly. Add remaining ingredients and mix well. Pour into oiled 8-inch ring mold and chill until firm. Unmold on crisp lettuce.

Ham, tuna, shrimp or salmon may be substituted for chicken.

Cabbage Soufflé Salad   Serves 6 to 8

1 (3 ounce) package lemon
    gelatin
1½ cups hot water
1½ cups mayonnaise
2 tablespoons cider vinegar
2 tablespoons sugar
¼ teaspoon salt

1 cup cabbage, chopped
½ cup celery, chopped
¼ cup radishes, chopped
3 tablespoons green pepper,
    chopped
1 tablespoon onion, chopped

Dissolve gelatin in water; add the next four ingredients, blend well. Refrigerate until partially jelled. Add remaining ingredients; blend well. Pour into ring or individual molds and chill until firm.

Mattie's Chicken Salad   Serves 8

8 large chicken breasts
Few celery leaves
1 onion, sliced
Few sprigs parsley
Juice of 1 large lemon
1 cup celery hearts,
    chopped fine

1 cup homemade mayonnaise
1 tablespoon Durkee's dressing
1 heaping teaspoon sugar
Salt, to taste
Capers and large black olives
    or, green grapes and
    almonds

Wash chicken breasts and place in heavy soup pot with celery leaves, sliced onion and parsley. Add water to cover and add salt. Simmer until well done. Cool and remove meat from bones and cut into small pieces with kitchen scissors. Squeeze juice of a large lemon over cut chicken.

Mix celery, mayonnaise, Durkee's, sugar and salt. Toss gently with fork. Chill. Serve with capers and large black olives or with green grapes and toasted almonds.

Shrimp Lutèce   Serves 6

6 heads Bibb lettuce (one
  small head per serving)
16 ounces canned artichoke
  hearts, drained and
  halved

2 avocados, sliced
2 pounds large, raw shrimp in
  shell, cooked and peeled
4 hard-cooked eggs, quartered

Wash and dry lettuce; gently separate leaves. Combine with other ingredients and toss lightly.

Dressing:
¾ teaspoon salt
White pepper, to taste
½ teaspoon prepared
  mustard
½ clove garlic, crushed
¼ cup tarragon vinegar

1 egg yolk
1 cup oil
½ teaspoon sugar
1 tablespoon Worcestershire
  sauce
¼ cup chili sauce

Make a paste of salt, pepper, mustard, garlic and small amount of vinegar. Blend in egg yolk until smooth. Start adding oil very slowly until dressing is consistency of mayonnaise. (May use blender or rotary beater.) Continue adding oil alternately with remaining vinegar. Beat in sugar and Worcestershire sauce; fold in chili sauce and chill thoroughly.

Shrimp Savannah   Serves 6 to 8

¾ cup oil
3 tablespoons prepared
  mustard
6 tablespoons cider vinegar
1½ teaspoons salt
¾ teaspoon pepper

2 pounds shrimp, cooked and
  diced
4 green onions with tops, sliced
¾ cup celery, chopped
Lettuce, shredded

Make a dressing using oil, mustard, vinegar, salt and pepper. Add shrimp, onions and celery. Marinate for two hours. Drain and serve mixed with lettuce or on bed of lettuce.

Spinach Salad Lafayette   Serves 8

2 pounds spinach, cleaned
  and stems removed
8 ounces fresh mushrooms,
  sliced
4 green onions, sliced

4 eggs, hard-cooked and
  chopped fine
Bacon bits
Walnuts
Bean sprouts, optional

Dressing:
6 tablespoons sugar
1 teaspoon salt
1 teaspoon dry mustard

1 teaspoon onion, grated
½ cup lemon juice
1 cup oil

Place salad dressing ingredients in blender and blend well. Pour over spinach just before serving and toss with mushrooms, green onions, eggs, bacon bits, walnuts and bean sprouts.

Special Spinach Salad   Serves 12

2 pounds fresh spinach
1 to 2 cups water chestnuts,
  sliced thin
4 eggs, hard-cooked and
  chopped fine
1 large red onion, sliced in
  rings

16 ounces canned bean sprouts,
  drained
1 pound bacon, fried, drained
  and crumbled

Dressing:
1 cup oil
¾ cup sugar
½ cup cider vinegar

2 teaspoons salt
⅓ cup catsup

Mix together dressing early in the day. Set aside. Wash spinach, add other ingredients and top with dressing when ready to serve.

Spinach Salad

Serves 4

1 pound fresh spinach,
  washed and drained
2 apples, peeled and diced
8 slices bacon, fried and
  crumbled

½ cup almonds, slivered and
  sautéed in bacon grease
2 green onions, sliced

Dressing:
1 cup oil
3 tablespoons sugar
2⅔ teaspoons dry mustard

5 tablespoons plus 1 teaspoon
  cider vinegar

Blend dressing thoroughly and toss lightly over salad.

Wilted Spinach Salad

Serves 4

1 pound fresh spinach
8 ounces fresh mushrooms
6 slices bacon
2 tablespoons wine vinegar

1 tablespoon lemon juice
¼ teaspoon black pepper,
  coarsely ground
½ teaspoon salt

Wash spinach and discard stems. Dry and tear into bite-size pieces; return to refrigerator until ready to toss. Wash and slice mushrooms. Fry bacon until crisp; reserve drippings. Combine vinegar, lemon juice, pepper and salt in pan with drippings.

When ready to serve, combine spinach, mushrooms and crumbled bacon in bowl. Heat drippings to boiling, pour over spinach and toss until all leaves are coated and slightly wilted. Serve at once in individual salad bowls.

Marinated Green Salad   Serves 6

9 ounces frozen artichoke
  hearts
10 ounces frozen peas
1 cup celery, sliced
  diagonally
½ cup pitted green olives

½ cup oil
¼ cup cider vinegar
1 teaspoon salt
½ teaspoon sugar
¼ teaspoon black pepper

Cook artichoke hearts; drain. Put peas in collander, pour boiling water over them and drain thoroughly. Rinse with cold water; drain well. Combine all ingredients; Refrigerate at least 1 hour or overnight, if possible. Serve on Romaine lettuce.

Caesar Salad   Serves 4

Romaine salad greens
1 clove garlic, minced
Generous amount salt and
  pepper
Pinch thyme and oregano
2 teaspoons lemon juice
1 tablespoon German
  mustard
½ tablespoon steak sauce

½ tablespoon Worcestershire
  sauce
1 egg
6 tablespoons olive oil
1 tablespoon wine vinegar
½ cup Parmesan cheese, grated
1 cup croutons
1 ounce anchovies

Rinse lettuce and dry leaves well.

Mix next 10 ingredients; pour over lettuce and toss. Top with Parmesan cheese, croutons and anchovies.

Fruit Salad Dressing   Yields 1½ Cups

1 teaspoon celery seed   1 teaspoon onion juice
1 teaspoon dry mustard   ½ cup sugar
1 teaspoon paprika   ¼ cup cider vinegar
1 teaspoon salt   1 cup oil

Mix dry ingredients well. Add onion juice and vinegar. Beat in oil slowly. Put in jar. Refrigerate. Keeps well.

Italian Salad Dressing   Yields ½ Cup

6 tablespoons olive oil   ¼ teaspoon salt
3 tablespoons cider vinegar   ⅛ teaspoon pepper
1 garlic clove, crushed   ⅛ teaspoon dry mustard

Mix all ingredients thoroughly. Shake well. Make ahead of time and let stand before using. Shake well each time dressing is used.

Mayfair Dressing   Yields 1 Quart

1 clove garlic   ½ teaspoon sugar
1 rib celery   2 tablespoons prepared
½ medium onion   mustard
2 ounces canned anchovies   1 tablespoon lemon juice
1 teaspoon black pepper   3 eggs
1 heaping teaspoon   2 cups oil
  monosodium glutamate

Add all ingredients except eggs and oil; blend for a few seconds in blender. Add eggs; blend. Add oil slowly.

Brown mustard or horseradish is a good substitute for the prepared mustard. This makes about 1 quart and keeps well for about two weeks in the refrigerator.

Celery Seed Dressing

Yields 1½ Cups

⅓ cup sugar
1 teaspoon dry mustard
1 teaspoon salt
1 teaspoon paprika
1 teaspoon onion, finely
    grated

1 heaping teaspoon celery seed
1 teaspoon cider vinegar
1 cup oil
3 tablespoons cider vinegar

Put first 7 ingredients in blender and mix well. Add alternately the oil and 3 tablespoons vinegar, beating well in between additions. Beat until smooth. Refrigerate in blender. Blend again before serving.

Serve over fresh, chilled grapefruit sections on a bed of lettuce. May be made ahead.

The Chart House Bleu Cheese Dressing

Yields 2½ Cups

¾ cup sour cream
½ teaspoon dry mustard
½ teaspoon black pepper
½ teaspoon salt, scant
⅓ teaspoon garlic powder,
    scant

1 teaspoon Worcestershire
    sauce
1⅓ cups mayonnaise
4 ounces Danish bleu cheese

Blend all ingredients except mayonnaise and bleu cheese at low speed for 2 minutes. Add mayonnaise and blend ½ minute at low speed, then blend 2 minutes at medium speed. Crumble and add bleu cheese; blend at low speed no longer than 4 minutes.

Must sit 24 hours before serving.

A specialty of The Chart House restaurant.

SAVANNAH HOSPITALITY

Savannah Hospitality

In 1831, a Savannah woman boasted in a letter to a Rhode Island friend, ". . . in other places you will find one or two Lady Bountifuls, but here they are all bountiful." A look at how Savannah has entertained some of its more important visitors makes one feel Savannahians are very generous, indeed.

When President Taft once visited the William W. Gordons, he downed a complete breakfast and then seven entire waffles made from a 100-year-old recipe. According to a Gordon descendant it was the all-time record for waffle-eating at his grandfather's household.

President McKinley apparently had eaten just as well on his visit to Savannah in December, 1898. At a banquet in his honor he was served, besides celery, olives, cheese and crackers, a sumptuous meal of oysters on the half shell, green turtle soup, salmon, beef tenderloin, sweetbreads, Georgia terrapin, roasted Chatham County partridge, asparagus, potatoes, DeSoto punch, coffee and crème de menthe followed by cigars and cigarettes.

President Monroe's visit to Savannah in 1819 was greeted with no less gusto. In between the dedication of Independent Presbyterian Church and a jaunt down to Tybee on the new *Savannah,* about to become the first steam vessel to cross the Atlantic, he was entertained lavishly.

One fête involved a riverfront dinner complete with toasts punctuated by cannon firings from the nearby revenue cutter *Dallas.* A ball was held in Johnson Square in a specially constructed and festooned pavilion designed by the young English architect William Jay.

All this was preceded by a reception given Monroe by the William Scarbroughs at their brand-new home, designed by Jay, on West Broad Street.

One of the merchant princes of the city and the prime mover behind the *Savannah,* Scarbrough also was a celebrated host who on occasion had entertained more than 300 persons in his previous home on Broughton Street, taking down the beds to allow more room for dancing.

In 1856, the Charles Greens entertained 700 guests at a ball in their Gothic Revival home that is now the Parish House of St. John's Episcopal Church.

The occasion was a commercial convention being held in Savannah, and a correspondent for a Petersburg, Virginia newspaper praised what he called the exquisite music, the nimble and graceful dancing, the vast collection of cakes, confections and champagne bottles and the home itself with its unsurpassed furniture and dome lit by ninety-eight gas jets.

In summing up that and a number of other parties given for the convention, another observer wrote, ". . . we feel proud of the ancient city of Oglethorpe. She has long plodded her way with an old fogy tread, but she has shaken off her lethargy and now marches with proud steps, to take her position alongside the greatest cities of the Union. One thousand cheers for Savannah."

Deviled Eggs With Shrimp
Serves 6

¾ pound fresh shrimp
6 eggs, hard-cooked
¼ teaspoon dry mustard
½ teaspoon salt
½ cup mayonnaise
½ teaspoon curry powder

½ teaspoon paprika
a) 6 slices dried toast or,
b) 10 ounces frozen broccoli
   spears,
c) ½ cup sautéed bread crumbs

Sauce:
4 tablespoons butter
4 tablespoons flour
2 cups half-and-half
1 cup sharp Cheddar
   cheese, grated

1 tablespoon onion, grated
½ teaspoon dry mustard
½ teaspoon Worcestershire
   sauce

Cook shrimp in boiling, salted water until pink and tender, about 3 minutes.

Make deviled eggs by mashing yolks of cooked eggs and add mustard, salt, mayonnaise, curry powder and paprika; blend well. Stuff mixture into whites of egg.

Sauce:
Melt butter; add flour, cook, stirring for 3 minutes. Gradually add half-and-half. Stir until thickened. Add remaining ingredients and stir until melted and blended. Add shrimp.

a) Dry 6 pieces buttered toast in oven at 250°F for 1 hour. Arrange deviled eggs over them and pour heated shrimp on top. Or,

b) Arrange broccoli (defrosted but not cooked) in casserole, with deviled eggs on top and cover with shrimp mixture. Cover with ½ cup sautéed bread crumbs and bake at 350°F for 25 minutes. Or,

c) Combine in casserole deviled eggs and cover with shrimp mixture. Top with ½ cup sautéed bread crumbs and bake at 350°F for 25 minutes.

Bruncheon Eggs

Serves 6 to 8

6 eggs
2 cups milk
1 teaspoon salt
1 teaspoon dry mustard
1 pound sausage, mild or
  hot

3 or 4 slices French bread,
  cubed and sautéed in melted
  butter
1 to 1½ cups sharp cheese,
  grated

Beat eggs, milk, salt and mustard. Sauté and drain sausage. Layer bread, cheese and sausage in greased 9 x 13 inch dish. Pour milk and egg mixture over all. Refrigerate overnight. Bake at 350°F for 45-50 minutes.

Davenport Brunch

Serves 6

¾ pound sharp cheese
½ teaspoon dry mustard
½ teaspoon paprika
1 teaspoon salt

¾ cup sour cream
1 pound hot sausage, cooked
  and drained
10 eggs

In a 10 x 6 x 2 inch dish, slice half the cheese to cover the bottom. Mix seasonings with sour cream. Pour half of sour cream mixture over cheese. Add crumbled sausage, spreading evenly over sour cream mixture. Break whole eggs on top of sausage. Sliced, hard-cooked eggs may be used, if desired. Spread remaining sour cream mixture and top with remaining grated cheese.

Bake at 325°F for 30 to 40 minutes.

To check for doneness of eggs, test in corner — if eggs are firm, casserole is done.

Eggs Scarborough
Serves 8

¼ cup butter
2 large shallots, sliced
½ pound fresh mushrooms,
  sliced
⅓ cup flour
1½ cups chicken stock, hot
¾ cup cream, hot
2 tablespoons white wine

2 egg yolks, beaten
1 tablespoon lemon juice
½ teaspoon salt
¼ teaspoon pepper
9 eggs, hard-cooked and
  sectioned
2 tablespoons minced parsley
½ cup buttered bread crumbs

In a heavy, large saucepan, sauté mushrooms and shallots in butter. Add flour and cook, stirring about 3 minutes. Add heated stock, cream and wine, stirring constantly until thickened. Remove from heat. Stir in egg yolks, beat well, add lemon juice, salt and pepper. Pour over sectioned eggs in a casserole dish. Top with bread crumbs and parsley. Bake at 350°F for 15 minutes.

Serve from casserole dish, over toast points or in pastry shells.

Eggs With Asparagus And Ham
Serves 6

Butter
Salt
White pepper

12 eggs
2 1/2-inch slices baked ham
30 asparagus spears

Brush 6 1-cup timbale molds with butter and chill for 5 minutes. Sprinkle molds lightly with salt and pepper. Cut ham into ½ inch strips the height of the mold (need approximately 60 strips).

Steam the asparagus, drain and lightly butter. Cut the tender part of the stalks with tips still attached the height of the mold. Line mold with asparagus and ham, using alternately 1 piece of asparagus and 2 slices of ham. Place 2 eggs into each mold with yolks unbroken. Place the molds in a pan of boiling water and cook eggs, covered, for 10 minutes or until whites are set. Unmold and serve.

Baked Eggs and Cheese   Serves 8

8 eggs, hard-cooked
¼ cup butter
¼ cup flour
1 cup milk
1 cup heavy cream

½ teaspoon salt
¼ teaspoon white pepper
¼ teaspoon dry mustard
1 cup Gruyère cheese, grated
½ cup Parmesan cheese, grated

Place eggs which have been halved, cut side down in a buttered baking dish. Make sauce by melting butter, add flour and cook, stirring constantly for 2 to 3 minutes. Add milk gradually, stirring until thickened. Add cream and seasonings. Melt in Gruyère cheese and pour sauce over eggs. Sprinkle top with Parmesan cheese.

Bake at 450°F for 25 minutes or until heated through, bubbling and browned lightly on top.

Plantation Eggs   Serves 12

8 slices bacon
¼ cup butter or margarine
½ cup flour
1 quart milk

Pepper
1 (4 ounce) jar dried beef,
    diced
½ cup mushrooms, sautéed

Fry bacon until crisp, drain and discard fat. Melt butter in large frying pan, add flour, pepper and milk. Cook until smooth; add diced beef, mushrooms and crumbled bacon. Set aside.

¼ cup butter or margarine
16 eggs

1 cup evaporated milk
¼ teaspoon salt

Blend eggs with milk and salt. Scramble eggs in melted butter until soft. Layer eggs with sauce in large casserole dish beginning and ending with sauce. Bake 1 hour, covered, at 275°F. Add 15 minutes if casserole has been in refrigerator. May be frozen.

Eggs In Tomatoes

Serves 6

6 ripe tomatoes
Salt
6 teaspoons butter
6 slices bacon

6 eggs
6 tablespoons fresh bread
 crumbs
Parmesan cheese, optional

Cut the tops from tomatoes and remove pulp. Salt insides lightly and invert to drain. Put 1 teaspoon butter into each tomato and bake at 400°F for 10 minutes.

Fry bacon until crisp, drain and crumble one piece of bacon into each tomato. Break an egg into each tomato and salt lightly. Bake tomatoes, covered loosely, for 10 minutes or until egg whites are set. Top each egg with 1 tablespoon bread crumbs, a little butter and Parmesan cheese, if desired. Place under broiler and heat until crumbs are golden brown or until cheese melts.

Eggs Parmesan

Serves 8

¼ pound cooked ham,
 chopped fine
¾ cup Parmesan cheese,
 grated
Butter

8 eggs
Salt and pepper
4 English muffins, halved
Hollandaise sauce, see *Index*

Mix chopped ham with Parmesan cheese. Butter 8 custard cups well. Break 1 egg into each cup; add salt and pepper and cover with mixture of ham and cheese. Place cups in a pan of hot water, in 350°F oven for 25 minutes.

Toast English muffins. Turn eggs out on muffins and arrange on platter. Mask each egg with lightly heated hollandaise sauce.

Bacon And Eggs
Serves 6 to 8

4 tablespoons butter
1½ tablespoons flour
1 cup half-and-half
½ teaspoon salt
¼ teaspoon pepper

4 ounces sharp cheese
8 eggs, hard-cooked and sliced
12 slices bacon, crumbled
Cracker crumbs

Make a cheese sauce by melting butter and slowly stirring in flour. Gradually add half-and-half and cook over low heat until thickened, about 10 to 15 minutes. Add seasonings and cheese.

In a 9 x 9 inch pan, layer 4 eggs, half the bacon and half the cheese sauce. Repeat. Top with cracker crumbs and bake at 350°F for 20 minutes.

Country Ham Soufflé
Serves 6

6 tablespoons butter
6 tablespoons flour
1½ cups milk
⅛ teaspoon paprika

1 tablespoon lemon juice
1½ cups country ham, ground
6 medium eggs, separated

Melt butter in heavy saucepan. Stir in flour and cook 2 to 3 minutes. Add milk and stir until a thick, smooth cream sauce develops. Add paprika, lemon juice and ham. Allow to cool slightly. Add beaten egg yolks, then fold in beaten egg whites.

Pour into buttered 1½-quart soufflé dish and bake at 400°F for 40 to 45 minutes.

Hollandaise sauce may be added.

Classic Cheese Soufflé

Serves 6

Butter	½ teaspoon dry mustard
Parmesan cheese, grated	1½ cups milk
⅓ cup butter	1½ cups Cheddar cheese,
⅓ cup flour	shredded
1 tablespoon onion, minced	6 eggs, separated

Butter bottom and sides of a 2½-quart soufflé dish and dust with Parmesan cheese. In medium saucepan, melt ⅓ cup butter, then blend in flour, onion and mustard. Cook and stir over medium-high heat until mixture is smooth and bubbly. In a separate saucepan, heat milk until near boiling, then pour into flour mixture all at once. Stir until smooth and thick. Stir in Cheddar cheese until melted and remove from heat. Beat egg yolks at high speed for about 5 minutes. Into yolks, blend the hot mixture a little at a time, then combine the two mixtures thoroughly. Beat the egg whites in a copper bowl until stiff, then fold into the yolk mixture. Carefully pour into prepared dish. For the classic "top hat", hold a spoon upright and circle mixture along the rim of the dish about 1 inch deep. Bake in preheated 350°F oven 35 to 40 minutes until puffy and lightly browned. Serve immediately.

Garlic Cheese Grits

Serves 8 to 10

1 cup grits, uncooked (regular, not quick)	6 ounces rolled garlic cheese
4 cups water	8 ounces sharp cheese, grated
1 tablespoon salt	2 tablespoons Worcestershire
½ cup butter	sauce
	Paprika

Cook grits in salted water. When cooked, add butter, cheeses and Worcestershire. Stir until butter and cheese have melted. Place in greased casserole and sprinkle with paprika. Bake in preheated 350°F oven for 15 to 20 minutes.

Cheese Custard
Serves 4 to 5

4 eggs
4 tablespoons milk
½ teaspoon salt
2 tablespoons butter
8 ounces Jarlsberg cheese,
  grated

2 slices ham, cut into long, thin
  strips
2 tablespoons leeks, finely
  sliced

Whisk the eggs lightly with milk and salt. Heat butter in a pan until golden brown. Pour in egg mixture. Sprinkle all the cheese over egg mixture and top with finely sliced leeks and ham. Cover the pan and cook over moderate heat for 5 to 6 minutes. Custard should be firmly set and puffed when done.

Cheddar Cheese Quiche
Serves 4

4 slices bacon
1 medium onion, sliced
¾ cup milk
2 eggs, beaten
½ cup Cheddar cheese,
  grated
½ teaspoon salt

¼ teaspoon pepper
2 tablespoons parsley, chopped
Pinch sugar and nutmeg
Dash red pepper
Dash paprika
1 9-inch pie shell, unbaked

Fry bacon until crisp; crumble. Drain and reserve drippings. Cook onion in drippings until transparent. Combine milk, eggs, ¼ cup cheese, salt, pepper, parsley, sugar, nutmeg and red pepper in mixing bowl. Stir in bacon and onion. Pour into pie shell and sprinkle with remaining cheese, then with paprika.

Bake at 350°F for 25 to 35 minutes.

Leek And Cheese Tarts   Serves 6

4 leeks
1 bouillon cube (chicken)
4 tablespoons butter
½ medium onion, finely
  chopped
4 tablespoons flour
1 cup cream
3 ounces Gruyère cheese,
  cubed

3 tablespoons Parmesan cheese,
  grated
Salt and ground peppercorns,
  to taste
Parmesan cheese
Butter
6 tart shells

Remove the tough outer layers and tops from leeks. (If leeks are
not available, 2 bunches of spring onions may be substituted.) Cut
them into pieces 1 inch long and boil in very little water until
tender. Drain and set aside water in which they are cooked. Dissolve bouillon cube in a cup of leek water. In another pan, sauté
onion in butter until soft. Add flour; cook. Add bouillon and water
mixture, stirring constantly. When mixture is smooth, stir in
cream, Gruyère and Parmesan cheese, salt and ground peppercorns. Stir over low heat until smooth. Add cooked leeks and fill
tart shells which have been baked for 10 minutes in a hot oven
(375°F to 400°F). Remove tarts from tins. Sprinkle with Parmesan
cheese and dot with butter. Bake at 350°F for 20 minutes or until
brown on top.

Swiss Pie
Serves 4 to 6

1 cup cracker crumbs, finely crushed
4 tablespoons butter, melted
6 slices bacon
1 cup green onion, chopped
8 ounces Natural Swiss cheese, grated

2 eggs, slightly beaten
¾ cup cottage cheese or sour cream
½ teaspoon salt
Pepper, to taste
½ cup sharp processed American cheese, grated

Combine cracker crumbs and butter. Press into bottom and sides of an 8-inch pie plate.

Cook bacon until crisp; drain and crumble. Pour off all but 2 tablespoons of bacon drippings. Add onion to drippings and sauté. Combine crumbled bacon, onion, Swiss cheese, eggs, cottage cheese or sour cream, salt and pepper. Pour into pie shell. Sprinkle with American cheese. Bake at 375°F for 25 to 30 minutes or until knife inserted off-center comes out clean. Let stand 5 to 10 minutes before cutting.

Onion Quiche
Serves 6

1 cup saltines, rolled into crumbs
1 cup butter, divided and melted
4 cups sweet or Vidalia onions, thinly sliced

4 eggs, lightly beaten
1½ cups milk
¾ cup Cheddar cheese, grated

Mix ½ cup butter with cracker crumbs and pat into 9-inch pie plate. Sauté onions in ½ cup butter. Put onions into pie shell. Slowly add milk to beaten eggs. Pour over onions. Sprinkle top with grated cheese.
Bake at 350°F about 30 minutes or until cheese is brown.

Artichoke Quiche

Serves 6

1 9-inch deep dish pie shell
9 ounces frozen artichoke
  hearts, cooked and
  chopped
½ cup ham, chopped
3 slices bacon, cooked and
  crumbled
¾ cup Swiss cheese, grated

3 eggs
1 cup half-and-half
1 tablespoon flour
½ teaspoon salt
¼ teaspoon pepper
¼ cup Spanish onions, minced
1 tablespoon Dijon mustard

Line pie shell with artichoke hearts, ham, bacon and grated cheese. Blend remaining ingredients in blender and pour over mixture in pie shell. Bake at 375°F for 40 minutes, or until toothpick comes out clean.

Mushroom Quiche

Serves 5

1 cup Swiss cheese
½ cup Parmesan cheese
8 ounces mushrooms,
  sliced
1 tablespoon butter
1 10-inch pie shell
3 eggs

1 cup heavy cream
White pepper, to taste
½ teaspoon monosodium
  glutamate
¼ teaspoon salt
1½ teaspoons Worcestershire
  sauce

Grate cheeses. Sauté mushrooms in butter. Place cheese and sautéed mushrooms in the bottom of a 10-inch pie shell. Beat eggs slightly; add cream and seasonings. Pour egg mixture over mushrooms and cheese. Bake at 350°F for 35 to 40 minutes.

CULINARY DELIGHTS

Culinary Delights

From almost the beginning of the colony Savannahians ate well. Besides what could be grown in the way of vegetables and fruits, the local waters yielded shrimp, crab, oysters and fish. And the port attracted ships bearing foods from abroad—pickled herring and mackerel, salmon, prunes, citron, ginger, wines, cheeses and sugar as well as coffee and tea.

In the nineteenth century, most Savannahians still ate abundantly, if simply. Features of the everyday Southern dinner included pilau, or boiled chickens on a bed of rice with a large piece of bacon between the chickens; hoppin' john, or cow peas with bacon; okra soup; shrimp and prawn pie; crab salad; pompey head (a stuffed filet of veal); roast quail, snipe and, during the winter, shad—boiled, broiled or baked.

Ward McAllister celebrated the barnyard-fed turkey, such a staple on Savannah tables, that he noted, "It was turkey hot and turkey cold, turkey tender and turkey tough, until at grace, one would exclaim, 'I thank ye, Lord, we've had enough.' "

Rice birds, plump from stealing rice from the plantation fields, were considered quite a delicacy. Planters favored good friends with bushel baskets filled with the birds, and a big silver platter of them served on toast was said to be a supper dish for royalty.

The most acclaimed favorite that appears over and over on Savannah menus, however, was that made from the terrapin. The turtle was found in the ditches of the rice fields and was the most valued delicacy of the South. It could be caught only in July and August and in its rarity commanded a high price.

Ward McAllister called Southern terrapin soup with plenty of eggs in it "a dish for the gods and a standard dinner party dish in the days when a Savannah dinner was an event to live for."

Another of Savannah's turtle-loving gourmets was Dr. Richard Arnold, a nineteenth century mayor of the city. In recounting to his wife a dinner party in 1845, he said, "A very good vegetable soup rather dampened me, for I had somehow or other made up my mouth 'turtle fashion.' " Dr. Arnold's spirits soared again, however, when his host served a "most capacious dish of real green turtle stew." He described it as composed entirely of the green fat of the turtle with forced meat balls made of turtle. The only additions were some mild spices and claret and Madeira which mingled with the natural juices to form a rich gravy.

Asparagus In Artichokes

Serves 4

4 large artichokes
4 tablespoons lemon juice
40 stalks asparagus
2 tablespoons butter

Salt and pepper
½ cup margarine
2 egg yolks

Wash the artichokes thoroughly. Cut off the stem and tough outer leaves. Cut artichokes 1½ to 2 inches above the base and cut off any prickly tops that remain. Place in a deep pan with 1 to 1½ inches boiling salted water. Add 2 tablespoons lemon juice to the water. Boil artichokes in a covered pan for 30 minutes or until tender. (Artichokes can be steamed for 25 to 30 minutes until tender.) Drain upside down and remove the center (choke) with a teaspoon. Rub the artichoke with butter, leaving a bit in the center. Snap off the lower part of the asparagus stalks and remove scales from upper portion. Cover and cook the tips in boiling salted water for 10 to 15 minutes or steam for 8 minutes until tender. Drain and toss in 2 tablespoons butter. Season with salt and pepper. The asparagus and artichokes should be kept warm until serving or reheated in butter.

Chill thoroughly the margarine, egg yolks and remaining 2 tablespoons of lemon juice. Mix and cook over low heat until thickened. Fill artichokes with this hollandaise sauce and place 10 tips of asparagus into each artichoke.

Artichoke Squares

Serves 6 to 8

14 ounces canned artichoke
   hearts, drained
½ pound sharp cheese,
   grated
1 scallion, chopped

4 eggs
6 saltine crackers, crushed
Salt and pepper
2 dashes Tabasco

Cut artichoke hearts in small pieces. Sauté chopped scallion in small amount of oil. Beat eggs. Place scallion and other ingredients in bowl and mix. Grease 9-inch square pan. Pour mixture into pan and bake at 350°F for 20 to 30 minutes or until firm. Can be cut into smaller squares and used as an hors d'oeuvre.

Artichokes In Cheese Sauce

Serves 6

2 (9 ounce) packages frozen
   artichoke hearts
4 tablespoons butter
3 tablespoons flour
½ cup light cream

Salt and pepper, to taste
2 ounces Swiss cheese, grated
½ clove garlic, chopped fine
4 tablespoons dried bread
   crumbs

Cook artichokes according to package directions; drain and reserve liquid. Measure liquid and add enough water to measure 1 cup. Cook flour in 3 tablespoons butter; stir in artichoke liquid until thickened and bubbly; add enough cream to make sauce the consistency of heavy cream. Season with salt and pepper; add cheese and stir. Put artichokes in baking dish; pour sauce over them. Mix garlic with bread crumbs and sprinkle over artichokes and sauce. Dot with remaining butter. Heat in 350°F oven until hot and bubbly.

Artichokes And Peas

Serves 6

16 ounces canned young
   green peas
14½ ounces canned
   artichoke hearts, drained
   and quartered

3 tablespoons butter or
   margarine
¼ pound bleu cheese,
   crumbled
Cashews, chopped (optional)

Heat peas and artichokes through; drain well. Combine quickly in casserole dish with butter and cheese (both should thoroughly melt). Serve sprinkled with chopped cashews, if desired.

Beets With Orange Sauce

Serves 4

½ cup sugar
⅛ teaspoon salt
2 tablespoons cornstarch
1 tablespoon butter, melted

1 cup orange juice
16 ounces canned tiny whole
   beets, drained
Orange slices for garnish

Combine sugar, salt, cornstarch, butter and orange juice. Cook until thick. Place drained beets in casserole dish and pour sauce over. Reheat in oven before serving if necessary.

Garnish with orange slices.

Broccoli Ring

Serves 6

1 cup mayonnaise
1 cup heavy cream or
   evaporated milk
3 eggs
1 tablespoon butter, melted

1 tablespoon flour
½ teaspoon salt
2 cups chopped broccoli,
   cooked and cooled

Combine and mix all ingredients. Pour into buttered ring mold or baking dish. Set in pan of water and bake at 350°F until firm on top, about 30 to 40 minutes. Can bake about 10 to 15 minutes longer, if desired.

Butter Crumb Broccoli
Serves 4

½ cup sweet butter
1 tablespoon dried parsley
  flakes
2 teaspoons onion, minced
1½ teaspoons dill weed
½ teaspoon salt

10 ounces frozen broccoli,
  thawed and drained
2 tablespoons pimento, sliced
  and drained
1 cup croutons

In 2-quart saucepan, melt butter over medium heat. Add parsley, onion, dill, salt and broccoli. Cover and cook until tender, about 5 to 6 minutes. Remove cover and add pimento and croutons. Toss to coat. Serve at once.

Sesame Seed Broccoli
Serves 6

1 bunch fresh broccoli
2 tablespoons oil
2 tablespoons red wine
  vinegar

2 tablespoons soy sauce
1 teaspoon sugar
2 tablespoons sesame seeds,
  toasted

Clean and prepare broccoli for steaming. Steam to desired tenderness. While broccoli is steaming, toast sesame seeds. Heat other ingredients and pour sauce over broccoli immediately before serving. Top with sesame seeds.

Glazed Buttered Carrots
Serves 8

2 pounds carrots, cut into
  julienne slices
¼ teaspoon salt
Water
⅔ cup butter

½ cup water
1 teaspoon sugar
½ teaspoon salt
⅛ teaspoon white pepper

Cover the carrots with salted water and let boil for 3 minutes. Drain immediately and rinse with cold water. Return to pan and toss carrots in butter until they are well-coated. Add water, sugar, salt and pepper, and cook, uncovered, until the liquid evaporates.

Carrots With Orange Sauce

Serves 8

3 cups water
1 cup sugar
Grated rind and juice of 1
   orange
3 tablespoons cornstarch
   dissolved in ¼ cup water

2 large bunches carrots
1 tablespoon butter, melted
½ teaspoon orange extract

Heat water, sugar, grated orange rind and juice in a saucepan until sugar is dissolved. Stir in cornstarch mixture and boil sauce, stirring continuously until sauce is thickened. Add orange extract. Peel and slice carrots. Cook in salted water until tender. Drain and add melted butter. Cover carrots with heated orange sauce.

Sauce can be made ahead and refrigerated.

Olde Pink House Spiced Carrots With Mock Hollandaise Sauce

Serves 6
Using 12 Large Carrots

Peel amount of carrots desired to serve. Slice each carrot diagonally in 3 to 4 pieces. Place in saucepan and cover with water. Add salt, several cloves, a dash of cinnamon and the rind of a lemon. Bring to boil and cook until carrots are tender. Pour off part of the water leaving enough for a glaze. Add ¼ cup brown sugar, ¼ cup butter for approximately 12 large carrots and enough cornstarch (1 tablespoon cornstarch and 1 tablespoon water) for a good glaze. Reheat until carrots are glazed thoroughly. Add a dash of sherry, if desired.

Sauce:

2 cups mayonnaise
Juice of 1 lemon

¼ cup sugar
¼ cup prepared mustard

Mix thoroughly and warm in a double boiler. Serve glazed carrots with sauce on top and sprinkle with diced coconut, raisins, sliced almonds and chopped parsley.

A specialty of The Pink House Restaurant and Tavern.

Sunday Cabbage
Serves 6 to 8

1 small to medium head of
cabbage
3 eggs, hard-cooked
2 cups milk
2 tablespoons flour

½ cup margarine
4 ounces Cheddar cheese
Worcestershire sauce, to taste
Seasoned salt, to taste
Salt and pepper, to taste

Pour milk in small saucepan; bring to a boil. Make flour paste by adding a little milk to the flour. Add boiling milk until it becomes a thick white sauce. Add ¼ cup margarine, seasoned salt, pepper and cheese. Cut cabbage in wedges and boil until tender, 5 to 7 minutes. Drain cabbage, salt it and toss with remaining ¼ cup margarine. Place half of the cabbage in a 1-quart dish, dice 1½ eggs over top and cover with half of cheese sauce. Top with buttered bread crumbs; repeat second layer in same order. Bake at 350°F for 30 minutes or until bubbly.

Crunchy Creamed Celery
Serves 6

4 cups celery, cut in 1 inch
pieces
¼ cup margarine
1½ tablespoons flour
1 cup milk, warmed
5 ounces canned water
chestnuts, drained and
thinly sliced

¼ cup pimentos, chopped
¼ teaspoon celery salt
¼ teaspoon salt
½ cup bread crumbs, toasted
2 tablespoons butter, melted
½ cup slivered almonds

Cook celery in boiling water 8 minutes; drain. Melt butter, add flour slowly, then milk, stirring constantly to form a fairly thick cream sauce. In 1-quart greased casserole, combine celery, water chestnuts, cream sauce, pimentos and seasonings. Top with mixture of bread crumbs, butter and almonds. Bake at 350°F, uncovered, for 20 minutes.

Summer Corn Soufflé

Serves 6

6 to 8 ears fresh corn,
  grated (2 cups)
½ cup butter
6 eggs, beaten
½ teaspoon salt

½ teaspoon black pepper
¼ teaspoon cayenne
1 tablespoon sugar
1 pint half-and-half

Melt butter in large saucepan. Stir in corn. Fold in beaten eggs; add seasonings and half-and-half. Place in a warmed 2-quart casserole. Put casserole in oven in a pan of hot water and cook at 325°F for 1 hour. This casserole should set like a custard and can be tested with a knife blade.

Cauliflower With Mushroom Cheese Sauce

Serves 6

1 medium head cauliflower
1½ cups mushrooms, sliced
2 tablespoons butter
2 tablespoons flour
¼ teaspoon salt

Dash white pepper
1 cup milk
1 cup sharp cheese, grated
1 teaspoon prepared mustard
1 tablespoon parsley, snipped

Steam whole head of cauliflower in basket for 15 minutes until crisp-tender. Cook fresh mushrooms in butter until tender (about 4 minutes). Blend flour, salt and white pepper into butter. Add milk; cook, stirring constantly until thickened. Stir in cheese and mustard. Heat until cheese melts. Place cauliflower on platter; spoon sauce over and serve remaining sauce. Sprinkle with parsley.

Cauliflower Milanese
Serves 6

2 heads cauliflower
1 teaspoon salt
½ teaspoon sugar
Boiling water

4 tablespoons butter, melted
½ cup Parmesan cheese, grated
Ground white pepper

Wash cauliflower and break into flowerets. Place in saucepan with salt and sugar, adding boiling water to a depth of ½ inch. Bring to a boiling point and cook uncovered for 5 minutes. Cover and cook 10 minutes until barely tender. Place drained flowerets in buttered shallow baking dish. Cover with melted butter and sprinkle with cheese and pepper. Bake in a preheated 450°F oven until slightly brown, about 10 to 15 minutes.

Ham Stuffed Eggplant
Serves 2 to 4

1 medium eggplant
¼ cup ham, chopped or in
  strips
¼ cup onion, minced
¼ cup mushrooms, sliced

3 tablespoons butter
Salt and pepper, to taste
¼ to ½ cup sour cream
Parmesan cheese, grated

Cut eggplant in half lengthwise. Remove pulp, leaving ¼ inch pulp in shell. Sprinkle shells with salt and invert on paper towel. Chop eggplant pulp as small as possible and sauté with ham, onion and mushrooms in butter until onion, mushrooms and eggplant pulp are soft. Add salt and pepper to taste. Remove from heat and stir in sour cream (enough to make mixture moist, but not runny.) Spoon mixture in eggplant halves and sprinkle Parmesan cheese over top. Bake in 350°F oven for 30 minutes or until hot and bubbly.

Stuffed Eggplant

Serves 8

2 large eggplants, unpeeled
1 onion, sliced
1 tomato, chopped
1 clove garlic, chopped
½ green pepper, chopped
6 tablespoons fine bread
  crumbs

2 eggs
½ teaspoon salt
½ teaspoon pepper
Parmesan cheese, grated

Cook eggplants in boiling water for 20 minutes. Drain. Cut in half lengthwise. Scoop out pulp, leaving ¼ inch thickness to the shells. Chop eggplant pulp in a wooden bowl and drain all surplus water. Add onion, tomato, garlic, green pepper and bread crumbs. Add eggs, salt and pepper. Mix thoroughly. Refill eggplant shells with mixture. Sprinkle thickly with grated Parmesan cheese, dot with butter and bake for 20 minutes in a 375°F oven.

Serve on platter garnished with parsley.

Fresh Snap Beans With Shallots

Serves 6 to 8

3 pounds fresh snap beans
4 tablespoons butter

2 tablespoons shallots, minced
Salt

Snap beans and drop, a handful at a time, into rapidly boiling, salted water. (Use approximately 7 quarts of water for 3 pounds of beans.) Return water to boil and cook beans, uncovered, for 10 minutes. Should be crunchy when done.

While beans are boiling, sauté shallots in 1 tablespoon butter until tender, about 3 to 5 minutes. Drain beans and toss immediately with shallots and remaining 3 tablespoons butter.

Creamed Green Beans   Serves 6

½ cup onion, finely sliced
1 tablespoon parsley,
   minced
2 tablespoons butter
2 tablespoons flour
1 teaspoon salt
½ teaspoon pepper
½ teaspoon lemon peel,
   grated

1 cup sour cream
5 cups green beans, cooked and
   drained (should be French-
   sliced)
½ cup mushrooms, sautéed
½ cup sharp Cheddar cheese,
   grated
½ cup bread crumbs
2 tablespoons butter, melted

Cook onion and parsley in butter until tender, but not brown. Add flour, salt, pepper and lemon peel. Add sour cream and mix well. Stir in beans and mushrooms. Place in a 7 x 11 inch casserole. Top with grated cheese. Combine bread crumbs and melted butter and sprinkle on top of green beans. Bake at 350°F for 30 minutes.

Baked Beans With Sausage   Serves 20

3 (32 ounce) cans pork and
   beans
2 pounds sausage links,
   cooked and diced
2 medium onions, sliced
1 cup brown sugar

4 tablespoons prepared
   mustard
2 teaspoons Worcestershire
   sauce
3 teaspoons dry mustard
1 cup dark corn syrup

Mix all ingredients together. Bake in a 350°F preheated oven for 1 hour.

Casserole of Black Beans, Topped With Sour Cream

Serves 8

1 pound dried black beans
(Frijoles Negros)
1½ cups onion, coarsely
chopped
2 large cloves garlic, minced
3 stalks celery, coarsely
chopped
1 medium carrot, scraped
and coarsely chopped
1½ tablespoons salt

½ teaspoon black pepper,
freshly ground
2 bay leaves
¼ teaspoon oregano
1 tablespoon parsley, chopped
Dash cayenne
4 tablespoons butter or
margarine
1 to 2 ounces dark rum
(optional)

Rinse beans and pick over. Place in large kettle, add water to cover. Cover and bring quickly to full boil. Remove from heat and let stand, covered, for 1 hour. Add next 9 ingredients and more water to cover, bring back to a boil and simmer, covered, over low heat for 2 hours, stirring occasionally. Correct seasoning and if desired, a bit of cayenne can be added.

Remove bay leaves and turn bean mixture into a 3 quart casserole. Stir in butter or margarine and 2 ounces dark rum, if desired. Mix thoroughly. Cover and bake in preheated 350°F oven for 1 hour or more, until beans are thoroughly tender. Remove from oven and stir in 2 ounces dark rum, if desired. Serve with side dish of sour cream as topping.

Good served with baked ham, smoked tongue or turkey and a large salad of greens. Freezes beautifully.

Mushroom Newburg

Serves 4 to 6

¼ cup butter
1½ pounds medium size
  mushrooms
3 tablespoons onion,
  chopped
½ cup sherry
¾ cup non-dairy creamer

3 tablespoons flour
1½ cups boiling water
Pinch salt, cayenne, nutmeg
2 egg yolks
2 tablespoons water
Parsley
Paprika

In a skillet, melt butter until foamy; add whole mushrooms and chopped onions. Cook until almost tender. Add sherry and simmer 1 to 2 minutes. Combine non-dairy creamer and flour; blend into mixture in skillet. Add boiling water and seasonings. Cook, stirring constantly, until mixture thickens.

Beat egg yolks and 2 tablespoons water together; blend into skillet mixture and cook an additional minute. Serve piping hot in a chafing dish, garnished with parsley and paprika. Ladle over toast points.

Shrimp may be substituted for the mushrooms.

The use of non-dairy creamer instead of cream prevents the possibility of curdling.

Gourmet Onions

Serves 5 to 6

3 tablespoons butter
½ teaspoon sugar
¼ teaspoon salt
¼ teaspoon pepper

¼ cup sherry
10 to 12 small white onions,
  peeled, cooked and drained
¼ cup Parmesan cheese

Melt butter in saucepan. Stir in sugar, salt, pepper and sherry. Add onions and beat quickly (about 5 minutes), stirring frequently to avoid burning. Turn into a serving dish and sprinkle with cheese.

Baked Stuffed Mushrooms   Allow 4 Per Person

Mushrooms (large)
Butter
Salt and pepper
White-fleshed fish or
  chicken

Garlic, minced
Parsley, chopped
Egg
Bread crumbs

Cut ends of stems and remove from caps. Chop the stems finely and sauté in butter over very low heat. Remove and season with salt and pepper. Chop finely enough fish or chicken to equal the amount of stems. Mix and flavor to taste with finely minced garlic and chopped parsley. To each cup of mixture, add one egg. Blend well and heap mushrooms cap high. Sprinkle with bread crumbs and place a tiny piece of butter on each mound. Bake in moderate oven (350°F) for 15 minutes.

Baked Vidalia Onions
In Sherry Cream Sauce   Serves 6

3 cups Vidalia (or sweet)
  onions, precooked
⅓ cup sherry
1 cup light cream
½ teaspoon salt
½ teaspoon pepper
2 eggs, beaten

2 tablespoons pimentos,
  chopped
4 ounces mushrooms, sliced
3 tablespoons butter
⅓ cup sharp Cheddar cheese,
  grated

Drain onions and arrange in shallow baking dish. Combine sherry, cream, salt, pepper, eggs, pimentos and mushrooms. Pour over onions; dot with butter. Sprinkle with grated cheese, cover and bake at 350°F for 20 minutes.

Sour cream can be used in place of light cream.

Ratatouille Filling For Crêpes

Serves 5

Sauce: (Make one day ahead)

3 tablespoons oil
1 cup onion, chopped
¼ cup dried parsley

¼ cup sauterne
15 ounces canned tomato sauce
1 cup water

Sauté onion in oil, cooking until the onions are limp and golden. Add parsley, sauterne, tomato sauce and water. Simmer, cooking down until thickened. Refrigerate.

Filling:

1½ cups mushrooms, sliced
3 green onions with tops,
   sliced
2 tablespoons butter
2 medium zucchini, sliced
½ cup bell pepper, chopped
½ cup Parmesan cheese
¼ teaspoon marjoram

¼ teaspoon thyme
½ teaspoon basil
1 tomato, skinned, seeded and
   chopped
1½ tablespoons Swiss cheese,
   grated
1½ tablespoons Monterey Jack
   cheese, grated

Sauté mushrooms and onions in butter, cooking until the juice evaporates. Add the zucchini and bell pepper and cook for 10 minutes. Add remaining ingredients, except cheeses. Place ¼ cup of the above mixture on each of 10 crêpes. Sprinkle with 1½ tablespoons of grated Swiss cheese. Roll up the crêpes and place seam side down in an oiled 13 x 9-inch pan. Cover and bake for 30 minutes at 350°F.

Heat sauce. Cover crêpes with sauce and sprinkle with grated Monterey Jack cheese.

Frying Pan Potatoes   Serves 6

4 medium-sized potatoes   ¾ teaspoon salt
  (about 2 pounds)   ¼ teaspoon pepper
4 slices bacon   ¼ teaspoon thyme leaves
¼ cup butter or margarine   2 medium-sized tomatoes,
1 medium-sized onion,   peeled and diced
  thinly sliced   2 tablespoons parsley, chopped
1 clove garlic, minced

Peel the potatoes and cut into slices about ¼ inch thick; set aside. In a large, heavy frying pan, fry bacon slowly until browned and crisp; remove bacon from pan. Drain and crumble. Add butter to drippings in pan and sauté onion and garlic over medium heat until golden, about 5 minutes. Add potatoes, salt, pepper and thyme; continue cooking, turning with a wide spatula until potatoes are lightly browned, about 10 minutes. Sprinkle diced tomatoes over potatoes, reduce heat to low, cover, and cook until potatoes are tender, about 20 minutes. Turn occasionally.

Serve garnished with parsley and crumbled bacon.

Sweet Potato Soufflé   Serves 6

3 cups sweet potatoes,   3 eggs
  cooked and mashed   1 cup sugar
¼ cup butter, melted   ¼ teaspoon salt
½ cup evaporated milk

Mix the above ingredients well. Pour into a buttered baking dish. Top with the following:

¼ cup self-rising flour   ½ cup light brown sugar,
2 tablespoons butter,   tightly packed
  melted   ¼ cup pecans, chopped

Blend these ingredients by hand using a pastry blender until a coarse, crumb-like mixture. Sprinkle on top of the sweet potato mixture. Bake uncovered at 350°F until brown, approximately 15 to 20 minutes.

Spinach And Artichoke Hearts   Serves 6 to 8

8 ounces cream cheese
½ cup butter
Juice of 1 lemon
2 (10 ounce) packages
  chopped, frozen spinach,
  cooked and drained

14 ounces canned artichoke
  hearts, drained and sliced

Soften cream cheese and butter with lemon juice in top of double boiler. Add chopped spinach. Place artichoke slices in a greased casserole and pour spinach mixture over artichokes. Bake at 350°F for 15 minutes.

Spinach Pie   Serves 6

1 pastry pie shell
2 (10 ounce) packages
  frozen chopped spinach
½ teaspoon salt
4 eggs

1 cup sour cream
1½ cups coarse bread crumbs
6 tablespoons butter, melted
½ cup cheese, shredded

Precook pie shell until lightly browned. Cook spinach according to instructions on package. Drain well and add salt to spinach. Place drained spinach in pie shell and cover with eggs. Lightly whip sour cream to make it spreadable and cover the eggs with it. Toss bread crumbs in butter and shredded cheese and sprinkle over sour cream. Bake in a preheated 350°F oven 20 to 30 minutes. The eggs should be set like poached eggs. Do not overcook.

Use one package of spinach for a deep dish pie shell; use 2 packages for a quiche pan.

Spinach Timbale

Serves 6 to 8

½ cup onions, finely
    chopped
5 tablespoons butter
⅔ cup plus 2 tablespoons
    bread crumbs
½ cup Gruyère or Swiss
    cheese, grated
½ teaspoon salt

⅛ teaspoon nutmeg
Cayenne, to taste
5 eggs
1 cup milk
3 cups spinach, chopped and
    cooked
3 eggs, hard-cooked

Cook onions in 1 tablespoon butter over low heat for 10 minutes. Do not let them color. Combine onions with ⅔ cup bread crumbs, cheese, salt and freshly grated nutmeg and cayenne, to taste.

Beat in 5 eggs, one at a time and gradually add milk heated with remaining butter until milk is hot and the butter melted. Fold in spinach and pour mixture into a buttered 1½-quart mold. Sprinkle with 2 tablespoons bread crumbs. Set the mold in a pan of boiling water and bake it in a moderately slow oven at 325°F for 35 to 45 minutes, depending on the depth of the mold, or until a knife inserted in the center comes out clean.

Remove the mold from the water and let it stand for 5 minutes. Run a small knife around the edge to loosen it and turn out timbale on a serving platter. Cover the top with chopped, hard cooked eggs and surround timbale with sections of egg.

Serve with a sauceboat of melted butter and lemon juice.

Spinach Custard With Hollandaise Sauce

Serves 6

1 cup chopped spinach,
    cooked

3 eggs, well beaten
1½ cups milk
Hollandaise Sauce, see *Index*

Combine all ingredients and bake in a buttered casserole at 350°F for an hour or less, until set. Pour Hollandaise Sauce over custard.

Spinach With Sour Cream Sauce   Serves 6 to 8

2 (10 ounce) packages   ½ teaspoon salt
  chopped, frozen spinach   Pinch dry mustard
½ pound mushrooms   Dash red pepper
6 tablespoons butter   16 ounces canned artichoke
1 tablespoon flour   bottoms or 9 ounces frozen
½ cup milk   artichoke hearts, drained

Sour Cream Sauce:
½ cup sour cream   2 tablespoons lemon juice
½ cup mayonnaise

Cook spinach according to directions, drain and mash. Cut crowns from mushrooms, sauté in butter, remove and set aside. Reserve stems. Add flour to melted butter and cook until bubbly. Blend in milk. Add seasonings, chopped mushroom stems and spinach. Butter 2-quart casserole. Put artichokes on bottom of casserole and cover with spinach mixture. (If using frozen artichoke hearts, cook according to directions.) Mix ingredients for sour cream sauce and pour over spinach. Arrange mushroom crowns over sauce. Heat 30 minutes in 350°F oven.

Squash Ring   Serves 6 to 8

4 cups squash, cooked and   ½ cup sharp cheese, grated
  finely mashed   1½ teaspoons salt
½ cup onion, minced   ½ teaspoon pepper
3 eggs, beaten   1 teaspoon basil
¼ cup margarine, melted   ¼ cup bread crumbs

Mix above ingredients in order listed. Pour into a greased 2-quart ring mold and set in pan of hot water. Bake at 350°F for 30 to 45 minutes. Unmold on platter and fill center with buttered French green beans.

Spinach Mornay

Serves 8

3 (10 ounce) packages
  frozen, chopped spinach
4 tablespoons butter
3 tablespoons flour
Salt, to taste
Dash cayenne

2 teaspoons Dijon mustard
1 cup milk
3 tablespoons Swiss cheese,
  grated
½ cup Parmesan cheese, grated
4 tablespoons light cream

Cook spinach without adding any water; drain thoroughly and set aside. Melt butter; remove from heat and add flour, stirring well. Season with salt, cayenne and mustard. Return to heat and add milk, stirring constantly until mixture boils. Add cheeses and light cream. Simmer 5 minutes. Combine with spinach and refrigerate or freeze. To serve, bring to room temperature. Bake at 350°F for 15 to 20 minutes. Can also be baked in tomato cases.

Baked Butternut Squash

Serves 6

2 cups butternut squash
3 eggs
1 cup sugar

½ cup margarine, melted
¼ to ½ teaspoon powdered
  ginger

Bake squash at 350°F for approximately 50 minutes, or until it can be forked easily. Discard seeds, scoop out and reserve pulp. Combine pulp and remaining ingredients. Beat at high speed of electric mixer until squash is thoroughly blended. Pour into a greased loaf dish (4½ x 8½ x 2½ inches). Bake at 350°F until casserole is set, about 45 minutes.

Stuffed Guinea Squash

Serves 4 to 6

1 large eggplant
6 tablespoons butter or
  margarine
½ cup onion, minced
1 cup mushrooms, sliced

2 cups Cheddar cheese, grated
1 cup soft bread crumbs
Salt, to taste
Pepper, to taste

Cut eggplant in half lengthwise and scoop out interior leaving ¼ inch shell. Cut up scooped out portion and sauté in 4 tablespoons butter. Cook until tender. Remove from pan. Use rest of butter to sauté onions and mushrooms; return eggplant pieces to pan and add grated cheese, crumbs, salt and pepper. Stuff filling into shells and sprinkle with grated cheese. Bake, covered, 20 to 25 minutes at 375°F. Cut in halves or thirds to serve.

Squash With Tomatoes

Serves 8

3 cups yellow squash (use
  fresh only)
1 large onion
3 fresh tomatoes
Salt and pepper, to taste

Buttered bread crumbs,
  optional
Butter, optional
Parmesan or Cheddar cheese,
  optional

Clean and slice squash. Slice onion paper thin. Peel and slice tomatoes. Layer vegetables in a buttered casserole adding salt and pepper to taste ending with a squash layer. Top with buttered bread crumbs and/or cheese. Bake in 350°F oven for 45 to 50 minutes or until hot and bubbly.

Casserole may be made without topping.

Sautéed Zucchini
Serves 4 to 6

3 to 4 medium zucchini
¼ teaspoon ground white
pepper

¼ teaspoon salt
Parmesan cheese, grated

Peel zucchini; grate or julienne and drain on paper towels, squeezing out excess moisture. In non-stick pan, sauté zucchini 2 to 4 minutes, stirring over medium flame, until heated through. Toss with salt, pepper and season with Parmesan cheese to taste (at least ¼ cup). Serve immediately.

Zucchini can be sautéed with ¼ cup margarine. Also, ½ cup sour cream can be added just before serving.

Zucchini Canoes
Serves 6 to 8

3 slices bacon
6 medium or 8 small
zucchini
1 egg, slightly beaten
¼ cup heavy cream
1 cup Swiss cheese,
shredded

⅛ teaspoon nutmeg
Salt and pepper, to taste
2 tablespoons dry bread crumbs
Boiling water

In skillet, cook bacon until crisp. Drain, crumble and set aside, reserving fat in skillet. With teaspoon, hollow out zucchini in canoe shapes, reserving pulp. Blanch canoes in water for 2 minutes. Drain and set aside.

Chop reserved pulp and sauté in bacon fat until crisp-tender, combining with bacon and remaining ingredients, except for bread crumbs. Sprinkle one teaspoon bread crumbs into each canoe and fill with zucchini mixture. Place in a shallow baking dish and pour one inch hot water into dish. Bake in 350°F oven 30 minutes or until knife inserted in zucchini mixture comes out clean.

Tomatoes and Artichokes

Serves 6 to 8

1 pint cherry tomatoes
2 teaspoons salt
½ teaspoon black pepper
¼ teaspoon sugar
2½ teaspoons sweet basil

14 ounces canned artichoke
  hearts, drained and rinsed
6 tablespoons butter
1 cup bread crumbs, fresh
½ cup Parmesan cheese, grated

Cut tops off cherry tomatoes (only a thin slice). Combine salt, pepper, sugar and sweet basil. Cover each tomato with spice mixture. Alternate tomatoes and artichoke hearts in a buttered 10 x 6 x 2 inch baking dish. Melt 2 tablespoons butter, toss in bread crumbs and toast slightly. Dice remaining butter and place on top of artichoke and tomatoes. Combine bread crumbs and Parmesan cheese. Sprinkle half of bread and cheese mixture over artichokes and tomatoes. Bake at 400°F for 3 to 5 minutes. Remove from oven and sprinkle with remainder of bread and cheese mixture. Broil on middle rack for 2 to 3 minutes or until golden brown. Serve hot.

This may be removed from casserole dish and used to garnish a meat platter.

Baked Stuffed Tomatoes

Serves 12

6 large tomatoes
¼ teaspoon salt
⅛ teaspoon pepper
8 tablespoons shallots, finely
  minced
½ teaspoon garlic powder

2 tablespoons basil
4 tablespoons minced parsley
¼ teaspoon sugar
¼ teaspoon thyme
1 cup fresh bread crumbs
Olive oil

Cut tomatoes in half. Leave skins on, but seed and squeeze. Sprinkle lightly with salt and pepper and place them in a buttered, shallow pan. Toss together shallots, spices and bread crumbs. Fill tomatoes and drizzle with olive oil. Bake at 400°F for 10 minutes.

Dugger's Hoppin' John

Serves 8

1½ cups dried cow peas,
   soaked overnight
1 cup celery, chopped
2 medium onions, chopped

¾ pound hog jowl, chopped
   very fine
Rice

Combine all ingredients except rice in heavy pot and cook in plenty of water until peas are done, approximately 2 to 3 hours.

Fold in raw rice, the amount depending on amount of liquid in pot. (Use 1 cup rice to 2 cups liquid). Cook until rice is done.

Wild Rice With Mushrooms

Serves 6

½ pound wild rice
¼ pound butter
2 to 3 tablespoons flour
1 cup heavy cream
½ cup sherry
¾ pound fresh mushrooms,
   sliced

2 ounces slivered almonds,
   toasted
Salt to taste
Buttered crumbs

Wash, soak, and scrub wild rice. Cook in boiling, salted water until tender (about 30 minutes). Drain and steam dry. Meanwhile, sauté sliced mushrooms in butter. Add flour and cream, stirring constantly. Add cooked rice and stir in sherry. Do not overcook. Add almonds and stir. Put in well-greased casserole and top with buttered crumbs. Bake at 350°F until heated through and light brown on top.

If dish is to be reheated, add more cream or sherry. This may be done on top of stove, adding buttered crumbs before serving.

Savannah Red Rice

Serves 8

¼ pound bacon
½ cup onion, chopped
½ cup celery, chopped
¼ cup green pepper, seeded
   and chopped
2 cups rice, uncooked

2 (16) ounce cans tomatoes,
   puréed
3 teaspoons salt
¼ teaspoon pepper
1 teaspoon sugar
⅛ teaspoon Tabasco

In a large frying pan, fry bacon until crisp; remove from pan. Crumble and reserve. Sauté onions, celery and green pepper in bacon grease until tender. Add rice, tomatoes, crumbled bacon, and seasonings. Cook on top of the stove for 10 minutes. Pour into large, greased casserole dish, cover tightly and bake at 350°F for 1 hour.

Herbed Rice Stuffing

Serves 10 to 12

6 ounces long grain and
   wild rice
1½ cups celery, chopped
1½ cups mushrooms, sliced
½ cup butter
8 ounces packaged herb
   seasoned stuffing

1 cup hot water
1 (2 ounce) jar pimentos, sliced
   and drained
½ cup parsley, chopped

Cook rice as directed. While rice is cooking, sauté celery and mushrooms in butter. Add hot water to stuffing mix and add mix to cooked rice, along with celery and mushrooms. Add pimentos and parsley. Bake at 350°F for 20 to 30 minutes.

Use as stuffing for turkey or prepare as a side dish.

Almond Curry Rice

Serves 6

1 cup rice
¼ cup butter
1 onion, diced
1 bell pepper, diced
½ cup slivered almonds,
    toasted

1 cup white raisins
2 cups chicken broth
1 teaspoon curry powder
1 teaspoon orange rind, grated
2 tablespoons chutney
1 tablespoon pimento, chopped

Sauté rice in butter until white. Add seasoning, vegetables and liquid. Cover after coming to a boil. Cook over low heat for 45 minutes.

Add heated chutney and toasted almonds.

Spaghetti With Spinach

Serves 4 to 5

¼ cup oil
¼ cup butter
1 medium onion, diced
2 garlic cloves, minced
1 pound fresh spinach,
    cleaned with stems
    removed

1 teaspoon basil
½ teaspoon salt
¼ teaspoon pepper
½ cup Parmesan cheese, grated
4 ounces vermicelli or
    spaghetti, cooked according
    to package directions

Heat oil and butter. Add onion, garlic and spinach; cook 10 minutes. Add spices and cheese; cook 5 additional minutes. Serve with slotted spoon immediately over hot spaghetti. Pass additional Parmesan cheese.

Good side dish for veal.

Noodles Romanoff

Serves 12

2 (8 ounce) packages fine
noodles
3 cups small curd cottage
cheese
3 cups sour cream
8 ounces cream cheese
2 cloves garlic, crushed

2 green onions, finely chopped
2 tablespoons Worcestershire
sauce
3 tablespoons horseradish
1½ cups Parmesan cheese,
grated
Salt and pepper, to taste

Cook noodles in salted water according to package directions. Blend together first three cheeses, garlic, onions, Worcestershire sauce, horseradish and 1 cup Parmesan cheese. Mix well. Add salt and pepper to taste. Blend cheese mixture with cooked noodles. Sprinkle remaining ½ cup Parmesan cheese over top. Bake at 350°F for 25 minutes, until bubbling.

Can add buttered bread crumbs to ½ cup Parmesan cheese before baking. One-half pound sliced, cooked and crumbled bacon may be blended into mixture before baking.

Delicious Noodles

Serves 6

1 (6 ounce) package small
egg noodles
1 cup cottage cheese
1 cup sour cream
¼ cup onion, finely
chopped
¼ cup Parmesan cheese,
grated

1 clove garlic, minced
1 teaspoon salt
½ to 1 teaspoon pepper
2 eggs, well beaten
¼ cup dry vermouth

Cook noodles in boiling water until tender. Drain. Mix remaining ingredients and add noodles to this mixture. Place in a greased 1½-quart casserole and bake for 30 minutes at 350°F.

THE CITY MARKET

The City Market

From almost the beginning Savannah has offered its residents a variety of places to shop. Some of the city's older citizens still remember Ferber's, a confectionery that dispensed Savannah tradition in the form of ribbon candy.

Recalled one Savannahian, "No party I ever went to lacked those enticing coils in pink, green or white which decorated the refreshment table. But I never saw anybody eat any!"

Lyons' Grocery was another institution fondly remembered for its great cans of crackers well within reach of junior customers and for its formidable coffee counter. Shoppers could specify their own personal formula—¼ Mocha, ¾ Java, for example—and the clerk would dip the roasted beans from the big brass bunkers and grind them on the spot.

When it comes to marketing, however, the one memory that dims all others is that of the City Market. It was established on Ellis Square in 1763 and remained there, housed in various structures, until 1954 when the latest building was demolished and replaced by a parking garage. The market's fate was one of the factors that gave rise to the historic preservation movement in Savannah.

According to Emily Burke, a Northern schoolteacher who visited Georgia in the 1840's, the market was largely a roof supported by pillars and covering a brick floor. In the middle were a pump that supplied water and a bell that was rung at the ten o'clock closing time.

The building was fitted out with stalls rented to purveyors who sent produce there to sell. Gaily dressed servant women manned the stalls for their masters, and it was a generally held business principle that the gaudier the dress the better the sales.

The market was often surrounded by wagons driven to town by country people—barefoot men and bonneted women—with their own produce to sell. By day, quilts pieced together from farm clothing shielded the wagons from the sun, and by night, these very same quilts were taken down and used as bedcovers.

Fruits, vegetables, meats, poultry and seafood comprised the staples of the market trade, but it was a good place to give a visitor a first taste of sugar cane or to sample some local delicacy like benne seed candy made by an enterprising market woman.

In some Savannah families, it was the man of the house who stopped by the market on his way to the office to select the family's meat and poultry and have it sent home by a servant. Then the mistress or her cook might select vegetables and seafood from the many colorful men and women who traversed the streets calling in lilting tones, "Here swimp, here crab," or "Hyah corn, Hyah okra goin' by yer."

One of the favorites among these vendors was an ice cream seller known as Old Man Green who attracted many customers with his catchy chant:

"Ice cream,
Made in the shade, sold in the sun,
If you haven't got a nickel, you can't get none."

Baked Ogeechee Shad

Serves 6 to 8

1 large Ogeechee roe shad
  (5 to 6 pounds)
Salt
Pepper

1 large Bermuda onion
4 strips bacon, or more
1 quart milk

Have roe shad cleaned and head removed. This recipe does not call for using the roe, so prepare the roe as you wish.

Season shad well with salt and pepper inside and out. Slice Bermuda onion and place on rack in the bottom of a covered roaster. Salt and pepper the onion. Place shad on top of onion and place strips of bacon on top of shad. Pour milk in bottom of roaster. Do not pour over shad. Cover roaster, making sure it is airtight. Cook at 250°F for 7 to 7½ hours. Do not open oven until cooking time is complete.

Remove cover and brown shad under broiler if desired. All shad bones will have dissolved.

Shad And Roe

Serves 4 to 6

1 shad, filleted
2 pairs shad roe
Juice from half of lemon
Seasoned salt

Paprika
Butter
Bacon

Drizzle lemon juice over shad and sprinkle with seasoned salt and paprika. Dot with butter. Sprinkle roe with seasoned salt. Let bacon soften for a few minutes so that you may wrap completely around roe. Secure with toothpicks. Place in greased baking pan and bake in a preheated 400°F oven for 10 minutes. Baste with pan juices and broil until browned. Remove fish from pan and continue broiling the roe until bacon is crisp, turning once when needed.

The bacon-wrapped roe may be cooked separately in a frying pan in a small amount of cooking oil.

Baked Stuffed Shad
Serves 6

2 pieces shad,
   approximately 3½ to 4
   pounds together
1 pair shad roe
2 tablespoons parsley
   chopped
2 tablespoons onion,
   chopped

1 tablespoon butter
½ cup soft bread crumbs
Salt and pepper, to taste
Flour
Butter
White wine
Lemon wedges

Make a stuffing by boiling roe in water 2 minutes. Drain and split roes. Mix with parsley, onion, butter, bread crumbs, salt and pepper.

Place one piece of shad in a greased baking pan. Cover with stuffing. Lay other piece of shad on top. Sprinkle with flour. Dot with butter and add a little dry white wine. Bake at 400°F for 30 minutes, basting frequently.

Serve with melted butter and lemon wedges.

Baked Trout Amandine
Serves 10 to 12

6 trout fillets
Salt and pepper
Flour
¼ cup olive oil

½ cup butter, melted
½ cup blanched, slivered
   almonds
Juice of 1 lemon

Season fillets with salt and pepper. Dredge with flour. Sauté in olive oil until browned on both sides. Arrange in large, shallow baking dish.

Combine butter, almonds and lemon juice and pour over fillets. Bake at 400°F for 5 to 10 minutes or until almonds are nicely browned and fish flakes easily with a fork.

Baked Fillets St. Catherine   Serves 6

6 fillets of sole or flounder   ½ cup white wine
6 celery tops   ½ pound mushrooms, sliced
2 bay leaves   Butter
Parsley   ½ cup sherry
Pinch thyme   Salt and white pepper, to taste
1 small onion, chopped   1 cup white sauce

Trim edges and skin from fish, cover trimmings with water to make a fish broth. Strain. Add celery tops, parsley, bay leaves, thyme, onion and white wine to broth. Cook, covered, until herbs are done. Strain.

Place fish, skin side down, in buttered pan. Pour broth over and bake in 350°F oven approximately 15-20 minutes, depending on thickness of fillet. Sauté mushrooms in butter. Add sherry, salt and pepper; mix and add to white sauce. Pour sauce over fish when ready to serve.

Baked Fish Parmesan   Serves 4

2 to 3 pounds fillet of fish   Salt, pepper and paprika, to
¼ pound butter   taste
¼ cup lemon juice   Parmesan cheese, grated
½ cup dry white wine

Preheat oven to 500°F.

Place butter in shallow baking dish (9 x 13 inch) and place in oven until browned. Reduce heat to 400°F. Place fillets in dish, flesh side down, and return to oven for 5 to 10 minutes, depending upon thickness of fish. Remove from oven. Turn carefully and baste with pan juices. Mix lemon juice and white wine and pour over fish. Sprinkle with salt, pepper, paprika and Parmesan cheese. Return to oven until done, approximately 10 minutes, until flakes easily when forked. Baste once or twice with pan juices. Serve in sauce.

Baked Fish
With Spinach Stuffing

Serves 6 to 8

Stuffing:

4 tablespoons butter
3 tablespoons shallots or
   scallions, finely chopped
½ cup cooked, fresh
   spinach, finely chopped
   and squeezed dry, or, 10
   ounces frozen (thawed,
   but not cooked) spinach,
   squeezed dry

2 cups bread crumbs
2 to 4 tablespoons heavy cream
¼ teaspoon lemon juice
½ teaspoon salt
Pepper, freshly ground

Fish:

4 to 5 pounds fish, cleaned,
   scaled and boned but with
   head and tail left on
   (snapper, flounder, trout)
6 tablespoons butter, melted

1 cup dry white wine
1 tablespoon butter, softened
Watercress or parsley
Decoratively cut lemons

Stuffing Preparation:

Melt butter and cook shallots until soft. Add spinach and cook for 2 to 3 minutes to evaporate moisture. Transfer to bowl and add bread crumbs, cream, lemon juice, salt and pepper; mix.

Fish Preparation:

Preheat oven to 400°F. Wash fish thoroughly and dry with paper towel. Fill with stuffing mixture and lace closed with small skewers and criss-crossed string. Brush 2 tablespoons melted butter on bottom of shallow baking and serving dish. Place fish in dish and brush top with 2 tablespoons melted butter, then salt and pepper fish. Combine rest of melted butter with wine and pour around fish. Bake, uncovered, on middle rack of oven, basting every 5 to 7 minutes. If wine evaporates, add up to ¾ cup more. Bake 40 to 50 minutes until fish is just firm. Transfer juices to small pan and reduce over high heat until syrupy. Remove from heat, stir in 1 tablespoon soft butter and pour sauce over fish.

Garnish with parsley or watercress and lemon halves with top and edge cut zig-zag. Serve with hollandaise sauce on the side.

Sole Fillets In White Wine Sauce   Serves 6

6 fillets of sole
1 cup water or fish stock
Salt and pepper
6 tablespoons butter
2 shallots, chopped or 1
   small onion

½ cup dry white wine
1 tablespoon flour
½ cup cream

Halve fillets lengthwise and roll each half. Fasten with toothpicks and place in a skillet. Add water or fish stock, salt, pepper, 3 tablespoons butter, shallots and wine. Bring to a boil, reduce heat and simmer until fish is white in center, about 12 to 15 minutes. Remove to hot platter and keep warm.

Reduce liquid in pan to one-third. Add flour blended with cream. Add remaining butter. Heat, stirring until smooth. Strain and pour over fish.

Skewered Fish Mediterranean   Serves 4 to 6

¼ cup lemon juice
¼ cup lime juice
¼ cup olive oil
1 clove garlic, minced
1 teaspoon basil
1 teaspoon oregano
1 teaspoon salt

¼ teaspoon pepper, freshly
   ground
2 pounds fish fillets, 1½ inches
   thick
2 bell peppers, seeded and cut
   in 1 inch pieces
2 oranges, cut in chunks

Combine lemon and lime juices in 2-quart glass bowl. Whisk in oil and spices. Cut fish in 1½ inch cubes; add cubes to marinade and toss well. Let stand at room temperature 2 hours; stir occasionally. Drain fish and reserve marinade.

Heat oven to 550°F or broil. Thread fish cubes alternately with green pepper and orange chunks on skewers. Place skewers on rack in 15 x 10 x 1 inch pan. Broil 4 to 5 inches from heat; turning a quarter turn 3 times and basting with marinade about 6 to 8 times. Heat remaining marinade and serve with fish.

Baked Red Snapper In Tomato Sauce   Serves 6

1 red snapper, 4 to 5
  pounds

Salt and pepper, to taste
2 tablespoons butter

Sauce:

3 slices bacon
2 large onions, finely
  chopped
2 (16 ounce) cans tomatoes
1 sprig parsley, chopped

¼ teaspoon thyme
2 bay leaves
Salt and pepper, to taste
Lemon slices
Parsley

Rub inside and out of snapper with salt and pepper. Put in 9 x 13 inch baking dish and dot with butter. Bake at 400°F for 15 minutes before covering with sauce.

Sauce:

Fry bacon in skillet. Remove bacon and sauté onions in grease. When onions are brown, add tomatoes. Cook a few minutes and add parsley, thyme, bay leaves, chopped bacon, salt and pepper. Let cook until water from tomatoes has evaporated. Add sauce to fish in oven after 15 minutes, lowering temperature to 350°F. Bake about 45 minutes, basting fish with sauce. Add a little water if necessary.

Garnish with lemon slices and parsley.

Baked Red Snapper
Serves 4

3 to 5 pounds red snapper
½ cup butter
Flour
Fresh dill
Salt

Coarsely ground black pepper
3 tablespoons white wine
Cucumber slices
Paprika

Have the fishmonger butterfly a red snapper, leaving head and tail on, so that it is gutted, gilled and open down middle.

Wipe fish dry and brush inside and out with melted butter, reserving some. Lightly dust inside and out with flour, then sprinkle liberally with salt and freshly ground black pepper. It is important to dust inside and out with flour and spices. Place fresh dill weed inside. Close fish.

Place in buttered baking dish along with white wine. Bake in preheated 400°F oven for 35 minutes. Baste at least once with reserved butter. Lower oven temperature to 350°F if butter becomes too dark. Be sure to keep liquid in bottom of pan.

Remove dill to serve; place split pimento stuffed olives in eye socket. Decorate with slices of cucumbers and paprika. Serve with new potatoes, sour cream and dill weed.

Grilled Salmon Steaks
Serves 8

8 salmon steaks, ¾ inch
   thick
¾ cup dry vermouth
¾ cup oil
1½ tablespoons lemon juice
¾ teaspoon salt
Dash black pepper, freshly
   ground

¼ teaspoon thyme
¼ teaspoon marjoram
1/8 teaspoon sage
1 tablespoon parsley, finely
   chopped

Place salmon steaks in large pan. Mix remaining ingredients and pour over salmon. Let stand 3 to 4 hours in refrigerator, turning once. Preheat broiler. Remove fish, reserving marinade. Place fish on greased broiler rack and broil until brown. Turn carefully and brown other side. Cook about 15 minutes until fork tender, brushing frequently with marinade.

Salmon Florentine   Serves 4

2 cups salmon, cooked or
   canned
Milk
¼ cup butter
¼ cup flour
½ teaspoon dry mustard

¼ teaspoon salt
¼ teaspoon Tabasco
1½ cups mild cheese, grated
2 cups spinach, cooked and
   drained

Preheat oven to 425°F.

Drain and flake salmon, reserving liquid. Add enough milk to salmon liquid to make 1½ cups. In saucepan, melt butter and add flour; stir until blended. Bring milk mixture to a boil and add to flour and butter, stirring briskly until smooth and thick. Season with mustard, salt, Tabasco and 1 cup cheese. Place spinach in four individual greased casseroles, top with salmon, sauce and remaining cheese. Bake, uncovered, for 15 minutes.

Salmon Timbales   Serves 4-6

16 ounces canned red
   salmon
½ cup heavy cream
½ teaspoon salt
⅛ teaspoon pepper
¼ cup green onion,
   chopped

1 tablespoon parsley
½ teaspoon lemon juice
4 eggs, separated
Hollandaise sauce, see *Index*

Preheat oven to 400°F.

Drain salmon, remove bones and skin. Flake and mash with fork. Add cream, salt, pepper, onions, parsley and lemon juice. Beat egg yolks and add to salmon mixture. Beat egg whites until they form soft peaks and carefully fold into mixture.

Grease 6 4-ounce ramekins or 4 6-ounce ramekins and pour in salmon mixture. Place in pan with 2-inch sides; pour in 1 inch of boiling water. Bake 15 to 20 minutes, longer for large ramekins. Unmold, arrange on platter and top with Hollandaise sauce.

Salmon Mousse

Serves 8 to 10

1 envelope unflavored
  gelatin
¼ cup cold water
½ cup boiling water
½ cup mayonnaise
1 tablespoon lemon juice
1 tablespoon onion, grated
½ teaspoon Tabasco
½ teaspoon paprika
1 teaspoon salt

2 cups red salmon, drained
  and flaked
1 tablespoon capers, chopped
½ cup heavy cream, whipped
Olives, sliced
Eggs, hard-cooked and sliced
Pimento
Lemon slices or watercress
  for garnish

Soften gelatin in cold water. Add boiling water and stir until gelatin is dissolved. Cool. Add mayonnaise, lemon juice, onion, Tabasco, paprika and salt; mix well. Chill until consistency of unbeaten egg whites. Add salmon and capers; beat well. Fold in whipped cream.

Garnish bottom and sides of oiled 2-quart fish or other mold with sliced olives, hard-cooked eggs and pimento. Pour mousse carefully into mold and chill. Unmold and garnish with lemon slices or watercress. Serve with dill sauce.

Dill Sauce:

1 teaspoon salt
Pinch pepper
Pinch sugar
4 teaspoons lemon juice
1 teaspoon onion,
  grated

2 tablespoons dill weed, finely
  cut or 1 tablespoon dry dill
  weed
1½ cups sour cream
½ cup cucumber, peeled,
  seeded and grated

Mix all ingredients together. Stir and chill. Serve with Salmon Mousse.

Poached Fish With Wine And Capers

Serves 4 to 6

2-3 pounds fish fillets
2 celery stalks, chopped
½ onion, sliced
1 to 2 bay leaves
1 lemon, sliced very thin

Dash salt
Ground white pepper
2 cups water
1 cup white wine

Caper Sauce:
2 tablespoons butter
2 tablespoons flour

1½ cups liquid
4 tablespoons capers, drained

Place celery, onion, bay leaves and lemon slices in bottom of shallow pan (or fish poacher). Lay fish on top; season with salt and pepper. Pour water and wine over; poach on top of stove for 20 minutes (liquid should be hot enough to bubble, not a rolling boil) or until fish flakes easily. When done, remove fish to warm platter.

Remove bay leaves and grind all solids and liquid in food processor or blender.

Sauce:

Make a roux with flour and butter; add liquid mixture and stir until thickens. Add capers and serve over fish. Reserve some sauce to pass at table.

Crabmeat Ogeechee

Serves 4 to 6

½ cup butter, melted
4 shallots or scallions, finely
  chopped
¼ cup cider vinegar
½ teaspoon salt

Dash Tabasco
Dash white pepper
1 tablespoon parsley, chopped
1 pound lump crab meat

Sauté shallots in butter until transparent. Add vinegar, salt, Tabasco, pepper and parsley and simmer a few minutes. Add crab meat. Stir mixture carefully so that it remains in lump form. Pour into oven-proof ramekin or pie plate.

Broil 3 inches from heat for about 8 minutes or until just browned. Serve with rice to absorb the delicious juices.

Fish Fillets Bonne Femme
Serves 4

2 shallots, chopped or 1
  small onion
¾ cup fresh mushrooms,
  sliced
½ teaspoon salt
¼ teaspoon black pepper,
  freshly ground

2 pounds fish fillets
1 cup dry white wine
2 tablespoons white sauce
¼ cup heavy cream
1 tablespoon butter
1 tablespoon chives, chopped
1 tablespoon parsley, chopped

Preheat oven to 350°F.

Butter oblong baking dish; arrange shallots and mushrooms on bottom of dish and sprinkle with salt and pepper. Place fish on top. Add wine and cover with buttered wax paper or foil. Bake approximately 15 minutes until fish flakes easily with fork.

Drain juices into a saucepan. Cook until reduced by one-half. Add white sauce and cream and cook until sauce thickens slightly. Add butter, a little at a time. Pour over fish and sprinkle with chives and parsley.

White Sauce:
1 tablespoon butter
1 tablespoon flour

½ cup milk
Salt and pepper, to taste

Make a roux of butter and flour. Add milk, stirring constantly. Season with salt and pepper.

Deviled Crabs
Serves 6

1 cup cracker crumbs
1 egg, beaten
2 tablespoons oil
1 tablespoon Dijon mustard
1 tablespoon Worcestershire
  sauce

Salt and pepper, to taste
2 tablespoons onion, chopped
2 tablespoons green pepper,
  chopped
1 pound crab meat

Moisten cracker crumbs with a little water; add beaten egg. Add remaining ingredients and mix with crab meat. Put in crab shells. Brush with a little oil. Bake at 350°F for about 20 minutes.

Crab Cakes

Serves 6

1 pound white crab meat
1 cup green onion, chopped
1½ cups fresh bread
  crumbs
2 eggs
¼ cup milk
1 teaspoon Worcestershire
  sauce

½ teaspoon salt
⅛ teaspoon pepper
1 tablespoon Dijon mustard
¼ cup oil
Tartar sauce

Mix crab, onions and ¾ cup of bread crumbs. In another bowl, beat eggs and add milk, Worcestershire sauce, salt, pepper and mustard. Pour this over crab mixture and mix. Shape into round cakes. Dredge them in the remaining bread crumbs. Heat oil in skillet to medium high. Fry cakes, turning once (about 5 minutes per side). Drain and serve hot with tartar sauce.

Crab And Rice In Sea Shells

Serves 8

1 cup rice, cooked
1 pound crab meat
5 eggs, hard-cooked and
  chopped
1½ cups mayonnaise
½ teaspoon salt
¼ teaspoon cayenne pepper
Dash black pepper
⅛ teaspoon crushed
  tarragon

1 tablespoon minced parsley
2 teaspoons onion, finely
  chopped
5 ounces canned evaporated
  milk
8½ ounces canned water
  chestnuts, drained and sliced
½ cup Cheddar cheese, grated

Combine first 3 ingredients. Blend together remaining ingredients except cheese. Combine with first mixture until well blended. Fill 8 buttered sea shells or ramekins. Sprinkle with cheese. Bake at 350°F for 20 minutes or until hot and cheese is melted.

Royal King Crab Casserole
Serves 6

1 pound king crab meat	Dash of grated nutmeg
1½ cups half-and-half	½ teaspoon salt
2 rounded tablespoons flour	1 tablespoon parsley, chopped
4 tablespoons butter	1 teaspoon lemon juice
1 clove garlic	4 tablespoons dry sherry
Rind of half lemon, grated	Bread crumbs

Make extra thick cream sauce, melting butter with bud of garlic (remove bud before adding crab). Stir in flour. When well mixed and a thick paste, slowly add hot milk, parsley, lemon rind, nutmeg, salt and pepper.

When well thickened and smooth, add sherry and lemon juice, then add crab meat. Pour into individual buttered ramekins and cover with fine bread crumbs.

Heat in 350°F oven until sauce bubbles. Serve with a quarter of lemon nestled in a sprig of parsley.

Baked Seafood With Artichokes
Serves 8

3 tablespoons butter	1 tablespoon sherry
3 tablespoons flour	1 cup sharp Cheddar cheese, grated
1 pint half-and-half	
1 teaspoon Worcestershire sauce	1 pound crab meat
1 teaspoon paprika	2 pounds shrimp, cooked
1 tablespoon lemon juice	14 ounces canned artichoke hearts, diced
2 tablespoons catsup	Bread crumbs
Salt and pepper, to taste	

Make cream sauce of butter, flour and cream. Add Worcestershire sauce, paprika, lemon juice, catsup, salt and pepper. Add sherry and cheese. In a greased 11 x 7 inch baking dish, place seafood, artichokes and cream sauce in layers, ending with cream sauce. Sprinkle bread crumbs over top and bake in 400°F oven for 20 minutes.

Crab Imperial

Serves 6

1 pound fresh crab meat
(lump preferred)
½ cup butter
2 tablespoons onion, finely
chopped
1 tablespoon green pepper,
finely chopped
2 tablespoons flour
¼ teaspoon salt
½ teaspoon celery salt
½ teaspoon white pepper

1 cup milk or half-and-half
2 tablespoons dry sherry
Dash Tabasco
1 egg
1 tablespoon fresh parsley,
chopped
1 pimento, chopped
¼ teaspoon orange peel, grated
1 cup soft bread crumbs
2 tablespoons butter, melted
Paprika

Heat oven to 350°F. Check crab meat carefully and remove any shells, making sure to keep crab in large pieces. Melt butter in saucepan over moderate heat. Add onion and green pepper and cook until tender. Blend in flour, salt, celery salt and white pepper. Gradually add milk or half-and-half and cook until thickened, stirring constantly. Remove from heat and stir in sherry and Tabasco. Beat egg slightly in a medium-size bowl; gradually add cream sauce to beaten egg. Fold in crab meat, parsley, pimento and orange peel.

Spoon crab mixture into 6 well-buttered scallop shells or 5-ounce custard cups. Toss bread crumbs with melted butter and sprinkle over crab mixture. Sprinkle with paprika. Bake 20 to 25 minutes or until crumbs are slightly browned.

Nice served with avocado and grapefruit salad.

Crab Au Gratin   Serves 6

1 pound crab meat	Salt, to taste
2 tablespoons butter	¼ cup Parmesan cheese, grated
1 tablespoon cornstarch	¼ cup Swiss cheese, grated
1 cup half-and-half	Paprika
1 egg yolk	

Sauté crab in butter for 3 minutes. Mix cornstarch, half-and-half, egg yolk and salt; stir into crab until thickened.

Mix in cheese and pour into buttered 2-quart baking dish. Heat at 350°F for 20 minutes. Serve on avocado, toast or in pastry cups. Sprinkle paprika on top for color.

Baked Seafood Salad   Serves 6

1 small green pepper, chopped	1 cup mayonnaise
1 small onion, chopped	½ teaspoon salt
1 cup celery, chopped	Pepper
1 pound crab meat	1 teaspoon Worcestershire
1 pound raw shrimp, peeled and deveined	sauce
	1 cup bread crumbs, buttered

Cook shrimp. Mix all ingredients in casserole; sprinkle buttered bread crumbs on top. (Grated cheese may also be added to crumb topping.) Bake 30 minutes at 350°F. Do not overbake.

Shrimp Orleans   Serves 6 to 8

½ cup butter	1 teaspoon Worcestershire
3 to 4 tablespoons flour	sauce
1 cup sour cream	½ pound mushrooms, chopped
1 cup milk	2 pounds raw shrimp,
½ teaspoon pepper	peeled and deveined
½ cup catsup	Rice, cooked

Cook shrimp. Make cream sauce of butter, flour and milk. Add other ingredients, stirring to blend. Heat well and add shrimp. Serve over hot rice.

Shrimp Creole
Serves 8

1 tablespoon shortening
1 tablespoon flour
2 onions, chopped
2 cloves garlic, minced
1 large bell pepper,
  chopped
2 teaspoons parsley,
  chopped fine
28 ounces canned tomatoes
⅛ teaspoon red pepper
  (optional)

½ teaspoon salt
2 bay leaves
½ teaspoon celery seed
¼ teaspoon powdered thyme
2 pounds raw shrimp, peeled
  and deveined
2 teaspoons Worcestershire
  sauce

In heavy skillet or pot, melt shortening and stir in flour. Add onions, garlic, bell pepper and parsley. Stir until onions become transparent then add tomatoes. Season with red pepper, salt, bay leaves, celery seed and thyme. Add shrimp and cook slowly, covered, for an hour. Add Worcestershire sauce after 30 minutes.
Serve over rice.
This is better prepared a day ahead.

Shrimp Scampi
Serves 4

½ cup butter, melted
3 cloves garlic, crushed
2 tablespoons olive oil
24 large or jumbo shrimp,
  peeled and deveined

2 tablespoons parsley, chopped
2 tablespoons dry white wine
1 tablespoon lemon juice
Salt and pepper, to taste

Heat butter, garlic and olive oil in a large skillet. Add shrimp and sauté on both sides until done (about 5 minutes).

Pour off pan drippings into a small saucepan. Add the remaining ingredients. Cook over high heat 1 minute. Pour sauce over shrimp and serve with rice to absorb the juices.

Ocean Springs Shrimp

Serves 4

1 pound shrimp, cooked,
   peeled and deveined
Salt and pepper, to taste
½ pound mushrooms, sliced
3 tablespoons butter
1 tablespoon flour

1 cup sour cream
5 tablespoons butter, well
   softened
1 teaspoon soy sauce
¼ cup Parmesan cheese, grated
1 teaspoon paprike

Place the shrimp in a buttered shallow baking dish just large enough to hold them in one layer. Sprinkle with salt and pepper. In a skillet, sauté mushrooms in butter until they are browned and transfer to a bowl. Toss the mushrooms with flour and stir in sour cream, softened butter, soy sauce and salt and pepper, to taste.

Pour sauce over shrimp and sprinkle with Parmesan cheese and paprika. Bake in a preheated 400°F oven for 10 minutes.

Whitemarsh Island Shrimp

Serves 6

1½ pounds raw, large
   shrimp, peeled and
   deveined
¼ cup butter
½ cup olive oil
8 shallots, chopped very
   fine (about ¾ cup)

4 cloves garlic, chopped fine
1 cup stewed tomatoes
½ cup fresh mushrooms, sliced
1 teaspoon salt
Dash pepper
⅓ cup lemon juice
¼ cup parsley, chopped

Butterfly shrimp. In hot butter and oil, sauté shallots, mushrooms and garlic while stirring 3 minutes. Add tomatoes and cook, stirring 5 minutes longer. Add salt, pepper, lemon juice, 2 tablespoons parsley and shrimp. Toss to mix. Divide shrimp mixture into 6 individual baking dishes and broil 4 to 5 inches from heat for 10 minutes or just until shrimp are tender and coral-colored. Garnish with remaining parsley.

Low Country Shrimp Boil

Serves 12 to 14

6 pounds raw shrimp
  (headed), in shells
1 pound butter, (reserve ¾
  pound for serving with
  corn)

½ cup salt
Tabasco sauce
16 ears of corn, broken in half
5 pounds smoked sausage links
  or sweet Italian sausage

Sauce:
3 cups catsup
1 teaspoon horseradish, or
  to taste

Dash lemon, to taste
Dash Worcestershire sauce, if
  desired

Wash and rinse shrimp. Cut sausage in 2 to 3 inch lengths. Fill one 8 to 10-quart pot (or two smaller ones) half full of water. Add ½ cup butter and salt to water and bring to boil. Add Tabasco to taste.

Put corn in water and boil 5 minutes. Add sausage to water and boil 2 to 3 minutes. Add shrimp to water and boil 3 minutes or until shells begin to separate from shrimp. Drain and serve from one large bowl, serving butter with corn and sauce with shrimp.

This is great cooked outdoors if you have a gas burner. In the low country, this is often served poured in a heap on newspapers spread on tables—no plates . . . no forks.

Shrimp Luncheon Pie

Serves 4

One 9-inch pie shell,
  unbaked
4 ounces Swiss cheese,
  grated
8 ounces shrimp, cooked,
  peeled and deveined
4 eggs, beaten

¾ cup milk
½ teaspoon salt
¼ teaspoon pepper
Dash Tabasco
¼ cup onion, chopped
¼ cup green pepper, chopped

Line pie shell with half of the cheese. Top with cooked shrimp and cover with remaining cheese. Combine eggs, milk, salt, pepper, Tabasco, onion and green pepper and beat well. Pour into pie shell and bake at 375°F for 45 minutes.

Sherried Scallops

Serves 4

¼ cup flour
½ teaspoon salt
1 pound scallops
2 tablespoons butter

⅓ cup dry sherry
¼ teaspoon tarragon
Lemon wedges

Combine flour and salt. Coat scallops with flour. Sauté in melted butter 5 to 7 minutes, or until scallops are done. Remove to heated dish. Add sherry and tarragon to skillet; stir 1 minute. Pour sauce over scallops and serve.

Scallops In Tomato Sauce

Serves 4 to 6

2 tablespoons butter
1½ pounds sea scallops
Sauce:
⅔ cup chili sauce
⅓ cup catsup
1 tablespoon horseradish
1 tablespoon Worcestershire
  sauce

Parsley, finely chopped

1 tablespoon lemon juice
2 teaspoons prepared mustard
⅛ teaspoon garlic salt

Combine ingredients for sauce and set aside.

Sauté scallops in butter until brown and tender, 5 to 8 minutes. Pour sauce around scallops and heat just to boiling. Sprinkle with parsley and serve.

Scallops Rumaki

Serves 6

Boiling water
12 slices bacon
24 sea scallops

24 whole water chestnuts
2 tablespoons soy sauce
½ cup dry white wine

Pour boiling water over bacon. Let stand 5 minutes, then drain. Stretch bacon as much as possible. Cut each slice in half. Wrap bacon piece around scallop and a water chestnut and fasten with toothpick. Cover with soy sauce and wine in shallow pan. Marinate for several hours. Remove from marinade and put in 350°F oven until bacon is cooked, approximately 1 hour.

La Médiatrice
(Peace Maker's Oyster Loaf)

Serves 6

1 (15 inch) loaf French
  bread
6 tablespoons butter
2 dozen oysters
½ cup half-and-half

¼ teaspoon garlic powder
2 tablespoons celery, chopped
1 tablespoon parsley, snipped
1 teaspoon salt
3 drops Tabasco

Slice off top of loaf and set aside to use as cover. Remove soft bread, leaving a shell of crust. Melt 2 tablespoons butter in pan, add soft bread and stir over low heat until lightly browned. Remove from pan and set aside. Drain oysters, reserving liquid for basting. Heat 2 tablespoons butter in same pan; add oysters and sauté lightly only until edges curl.

Add cream, garlic, celery, parsley, salt and Tabasco. Fill bread shell with mixture, cover with bread pieces, replace top of loaf and brush with remaining butter. Place in greased shallow pan (9 x 11 inch) and bake in 375°F oven for 5 minutes, then baste in oyster liquid. Bake about 25 minutes in all, basting two more times. Slice 1 inch thick and serve hot.

Good with asparagus for light lunch or dinner.

Oysters Casino

Serves 2 or can be served as appetizer

24 oysters on half shell
½ cup butter, softened
⅓ cup shallots, finely
  chopped
¼ cup parsley, finely
  chopped

¼ cup green pepper, finely
  chopped
Juice of 1 lemon
2 teaspoons pimento, chopped
24 one inch squares of partially
  cooked bacon

Preheat oven to 450°F. Place the oysters in shallow pans of rock salt (ice cream salt). Cream the butter, shallots, parsley and green pepper. Spoon equal portions of the mixture over the oysters and top with lemon juice, chopped pimento and bacon squares.

Bake until the oysters are heated through and the bacon is brown, about 6 minutes.

Creole Oysters

Serves 4

⅓ pound butter
3 tablespoons green onion, chopped
3 tablespoons parsley, minced
½ teaspoon Tabasco

1 teaspoon Worcestershire sauce
¼ pound bacon
4 slices bread, crumbled
1 pint oysters, washed and drained

Combine butter, onion, parsley and sauces; cook slowly until onions are done. Fry bacon until crisp; drain well and crumble. Sauté bread crumbs in bacon drippings until toasted. Put a layer of oysters in baking dish and coat with butter paste. Crumble bacon on top and add some bread crumbs. Continue layering until all oysters are used, ending with bread crumbs. Bake at 450°F for 15 to 20 minutes.

Can be served as a casserole or on toast rounds.

The Mayor's Shrimp And Oyster Pilaf

Serves 6 to 8

2 cups onion, chopped
1 cup butter
15 ounces canned tomato sauce
16 ounces canned whole tomatoes, mashed

5 cups chicken broth
2 cups rice
1 pound raw shrimp, peeled and deveined
1 pint oysters, drained
Salt and pepper, to taste

Place onion in 4 quart pot, brown slightly with ½ cup butter. Add tomato sauce and whole tomatoes. Let simmer 30 minutes.

Add chicken broth, salt and pepper and simmer another 30 minutes. Bring to a boil; add rice, shrimp and oysters. Reduce heat immediately to very low, cover pot and cook 20 minutes without removing lid. Remove lid, stir well and cook 10 minutes at same heat.

Place ½ cup butter in skillet and burn until *black*. Pour hot burned butter in pot with shrimp mixture, stir again and serve.

Baked Oysters And Wild Rice

Serves 4

1 cup oysters
½ cup wild rice, raw
½ cup butter, melted
2¼ cups cracker crumbs

⅛ to ¼ teaspoon Tabasco
3 tablespoons butter, melted
Chicken broth

Drain oysters thoroughly and reserve liquid. Precook wild rice until it begins to open.

Combine ½ cup melted butter, cracker crumbs and Tabasco. Arrange in layers in buttered casserole in this order: ½ crumb mixture, ½ wild rice, ½ oysters; repeat. Top with 3 tablespoons melted butter. Add enough chicken broth to oyster liquor to make 1½ cups and pour in casserole. Top with remaining crumbs.

Bake in covered casserole 30 to 40 minutes at 350°F. Uncover and bake 15 minutes or until light brown.

Oyster And Wild Rice Casserole

Serves 8

3 cups wild and long grain
   rice
½ cup onion, chopped
2 cups celery, chopped
¼ cup butter
½ cup milk
3 tablespoons flour

½ teaspoon salt
¼ teaspoon sage
¼ teaspoon thyme
⅛ teaspoon pepper
1 pint oysters, drained
½ cup butter, melted
Cracker crumbs

Cook rice according to package instructions. Brown onion and celery in ¼ cup butter. Remove from heat and add milk, flour and spices. Add drained rice to mixture. Pour into a greased 2-quart casserole.

Drain oysters and let soak in melted butter 5 to 10 minutes. Pour over rice mixture, spreading oysters evenly. Top with cracker crumbs. Bake at 350°F for 45 minutes.

Oyster Fritters

Serves 8

1 quart oysters
¾ cup yellow cornmeal
¾ cup flour
1½ teaspoons baking
   powder
½ teaspoon salt

Pinch cayenne pepper
2 eggs
1 cup milk
Vegetable oil
Lemon wedges

Drain oysters; reserve 2 tablespoons liquor. Combine cornmeal, flour, baking powder, salt and cayenne pepper in large bowl. Beat eggs and milk in small bowl and stir into cornmeal mixture. Add oysters and 2 tablespoons oyster liquor.

Pour ¼ inch oil in skillet over medium heat. Spoon 6 fritters, using 1 oyster and about 1 rounded tablespoon batter each, into oil. Fry, turning once, until browned, about 3 minutes. Remove to paper towel-lined plate. Keep warm. Serve fritters with lemon wedges and tartar sauce.

Scalloped Oysters

Serves 4

2 cups coarse toast crumbs
¼ cup butter or margarine,
   melted
2 dozen raw oysters,
   drained well
¼ cup oyster liquid
2 tablespoons half-and-half

¼ teaspoon pepper
¼ teaspoon salt
1 teaspoon Worcestershire
   sauce
Dash cayenne
1 tablespoon sherry

Preheat oven to 425°F.

Combine crumbs and butter and line bottom of well greased, flat baking dish with half of crumbs. Arrange all oysters on crumbs. Combine remaining ingredients and spoon over oysters. Top with remaining crumbs.

Bake, uncovered, for 30 minutes.

THE SPORTING LIFE

The Sporting Life

It is said that early life in Savannah did not promote athletic activities as much as it did barroom brawls and the compulsion to defend one's honor according to the Code Duello. Fortunately, there did develop some sporting pastimes less damaging to one's health than drinking at the City Hotel and dueling on Hutchinson Island.

The Savannah Golf Club claims to be not only one of the oldest sports clubs in Savannah, but the earliest golf club in the nation as well. According to a notice in the city's first newspaper, *The Georgia Gazette,* the club celebrated an anniversary in 1796. Club officials are not sure which anniversary it was, but they believe that it was two years earlier that Savannahians first played golf here on a course laid out for that purpose.

The Savannah Jockey Club was organized in 1832, one year after horse racing was banned from public highways, and the locals staged annual horsing events at the Bonaventure track four miles from the city.

A rifle club also was active in the 1830's as was the "Coit Club," composed of some of the town's leading citizens. The members met on Saturday afternoons near Fairlawn Plantation where Gaston Street now intersects East Broad to play quoits, a game similar to horseshoes.

Today sailing ranks as a popular pastime with the boating crowd, but in the 1830's boat racing meant rowboats. A group of young planters from south of Savannah introduced the sport. At first, husky servants served as oarsmen and the spectators busied themselves with betting on the outcome, but in time the gentry themselves took over the oars.

A tennis club was organized in the latter part of the nineteenth century and played its games on a parade ground that now is the site of the DeSoto Hilton Hotel. The ladies wore wide hats and skirts that touched the ground, while the men donned pinstriped trousers and gaily colored loose flannel blazers.

The winter of 1886 brought a new sport to Savannah when the thermometer dipped to seven degrees below zero. Boys who had learned to skate at school in the North telegraphed for skates, and throngs of spectators lined the solidly frozen Ogeechee Canal to watch them and others perform figure eights.

Perhaps the sport about which many Savannahians feel most passionate, however, is shooting—at wildlife in general and at waterfowl in particular.

Ward McAllister chose the shooting party as one of the means of entertaining visiting English nobility. His brother-in-law sent his ten-oared boat, *The Rice Bird,* to Savannah to transport the group to his plantation. There they reportedly shot snipe over the rice fields, and, according to McAllister, lunched "elaborately" at the house, returning home in the cool of the day.

Another Englishman did not fare quite so well when he was sent shooting with one of Savannah's legendary hunters named Ward Allen.

Edinburgh-educated, and a Shakespearean scholar to boot, Allen retired at an early age to a houseboat on the Savannah River where he made his living as a market hunter supplying fowl to local restaurants and private clientele.

A crusty character whose dogs even knew to walk three feet behind, Allen became enraged at the complaints of this particular Briton who was dressed like a dandy and carried a fancy gun. Before the visitor knew what was happening, he was put out of the boat at a railroad trestle and told to walk back to Savannah.

Brandied Chicken Breasts
Serves 6

4 whole chicken breasts,
  halved, skinned and
  boned
Brandy
1 teaspoon salt
1 teaspoon pepper
1 teaspoon marjoram
6 tablespoons margarine

½ cup dry sherry
4 egg yolks
2 cups half-and-half
Salt, pepper and nutmeg, to
  taste
½ cup Swiss cheese, grated
½ cup buttered bread crumbs

Rub breasts with brandy and let stand a few minutes. Season with salt, pepper and marjoram. Heat margarine and sauté chicken 6 to 8 minutes on each side. Remove to an ovenproof platter and keep warm. Add sherry to remaining butter in pan and simmer over low heat until liquid is reduced by half.

Beat egg yolks into cream and add to liquid in pan, stirring constantly. Season with salt, pepper and nutmeg. Stir and cook until slightly thickened. Pour sauce over chicken breasts and sprinkle with Swiss cheese and crumbs. Run under broiler for a few minutes to brown topping.

Lemon Drumsticks
Serves 12

½ cup cider vinegar
2 tablespoons cracked
  pepper
1 teaspoon salt

¼ cup brown sugar
¼ cup lemon juice
2 cups oil
18 drumsticks

Bring vinegar, pepper, salt and sugar to a boil. Remove from heat and add lemon juice and oil. Marinate drumsticks several hours. Place on a rack over broiler pan and broil, basting with marinade, about 10 minutes on each side. Serve with soy sauce, if desired.

Poulet Bonne Femme
Serves 4 to 6

1 3 to 3½ pound chicken (or
    3 whole chicken breasts)
4 tablespoons margarine
12 small onions or whole
    shallots
6 slices bacon, diced
2 tablespoons flour

4 ounces button mushrooms,
    drained
⅝ cup white wine
⅝ cup water
1 chicken bouillon cube
1½ tablespoons Bouquet Garni
Salt and freshly ground pepper

Cut up chicken. Melt margarine in a large saucepan and sauté chicken until golden brown. Remove chicken and drain off margarine. Add onions and bacon and cook until softened. Drain bacon fat. Add flour and mushrooms and stir well. Add water, wine, bouillon cube, Bouquet Garni, salt and pepper, to taste. Bring to a boil and add the chicken. Simmer for 25 to 30 minutes. Serve chicken in a heated dish with sauce.

Sour Cream Chicken
Serves 6

3 whole chicken breasts,
    halved and boned
Butter
Flour
Egg batter (1 cup milk, 1
    tablespoon flour, 1 egg,
    ½ teaspoon salt)

½ cup mushrooms, sliced
1½ cups sour cream
½ cup chives

Split the long way of the breast and insert a pat of butter in each slit. Roll up tightly and fasten with toothpick. Roll in flour and dip in egg batter. Roll in flour again and fry in butter until brown and tender. Drain off fat left in the pan and add the mushrooms. Simmer 1 minute; add sour cream and chives. Simmer until it starts to boil. Place breasts in casserole and pour the mushroom sauce over them and bake at 350°F, covered, until thoroughly heated.

Chicken Piccata
Serves 3 to 4

2 whole chicken breasts,
  skinned, boned, and cut
  into strips
4 tablespoons flour
Salt and pepper, to taste
5 tablespoons olive oil

Juice of 2 lemons
⅓ cup white wine
1 teaspoon pepper, freshly
  ground
⅓ cup fresh parsley, chopped

Flour chicken and season with salt and pepper. Heat olive oil until fragrant. Brown chicken strips for approximately 3 minutes in olive oil. Sprinkle with lemon juice, wine, pepper and parsley. Simmer for 3 minutes.

Serve immediately with seasoned rice.

Almond Chicken Bourbon
Serves 4

2 whole chicken breasts,
  halved and boned
Salt and pepper, to taste
3 tablespoons butter
½ teaspoon salt
¼ teaspoon pepper

6 ounces canned frozen orange
  juice concentrate, thawed
½ cup salted almonds, toasted
  and chopped
2 tablespoons bourbon

Season chicken with salt and pepper, to taste; brown in butter over medium heat. Reduce heat to low. Add orange juice, ½ teaspoon salt and ¼ teaspoon pepper. Cover and cook until chicken is done — 20 to 30 minutes; spoon sauce over chicken while cooking. Remove chicken from pan and sprinkle with almonds. Keep warm. Reduce liquid over high heat and stir until slightly brown. Add bourbon and stir. Pour over chicken and serve over rice.

Day Ahead Chicken
Serves 4

2 to 3 whole chicken
  breasts, halved
½ cup honey

½ cup Dijon Mustard
1 tablespoon curry powder
2 tablespoons soy sauce

Chicken may be skinned, if preferred. Place chicken snugly in baking dish, skin side down. Mix honey, mustard, curry and soy sauce. Pour over chicken and refrigerate for 6 hours or overnight, covered. Turn chicken skin side up. Cover with foil and bake 1 hour at 350°F. Baste well with sauce and continue baking, uncovered, for 15 minutes. Spoon sauce over chicken and serve.

Imperial Chicken
Serves 4

2 whole chicken breasts,
  halved and boned
½ cup fine dry bread
  crumbs
⅓ cup Parmesan cheese,
  grated
2 tablespoons parsley,
 ·minced

1 teaspoon salt
⅛ teaspoon pepper
½ cup butter, melted
½ clove garlic, crushed
Juice of 1 lemon
Dash paprika

Blend bread crumbs, cheese, parsley, salt and pepper. Set aside. Combine melted butter and garlic. Roll each chicken breast half into a firm roll, skewer with a toothpick. Dip chicken into butter mixture, then roll in bread crumb mixture. Arrange in a baking pan or glass casserole dish. Pour lemon juice over chicken and drizzle with any remaining butter. Sprinkle with paprika. Place in a 350°F preheated oven and bake for 1 hour.

Chicken Mozzarella

Serves 6

3 whole chicken breasts,
  halved and boned
2 eggs
¾ cup bread crumbs
½ cup oil
2 cups tomato sauce

⅛ teaspoon garlic powder
¼ teaspoon basil
2 tablespoons butter
1 cup Parmesan cheese, grated
8 ounces mozzarella cheese

Pound chicken into ¼ inch thickness. Beat eggs slightly. Dip chicken in eggs and roll in bread crumbs. Fry in hot oil just until brown. Drain and place in shallow pan. Heat tomato sauce, garlic powder and basil until boiling; add butter and simmer 10 minutes. Pour over chicken. Sprinkle with Parmesan cheese, cover and bake at 350 °F for 30 minutes. Remove from oven, uncover, top with mozzarella cheese and bake 10 minutes.

Serve hot with rice.

Chicken Paprikash

Serves 6

1 medium onion, chopped
1 garlic clove, minced
¼ cup butter
3 whole chicken breasts,
  halved and boned (or 1
  chicken boned)

3 tablespoons paprika
½ teaspoon salt
2 cups chicken bouillon
2 tablespoons cornstarch
1 cup sour cream
¼ cup milk

Sauté onions and garlic in butter until onions are soft. Remove onions. In the same pan, sauté chicken until golden brown. Sprinkle chicken with paprika; cover and simmer 15 minutes. Add chicken bouillon and salt. Cover and simmer until tender, about 30 minutes. Remove chicken from pan. Add cornstarch to sour cream, mix well. Slowly add milk to sour cream and stir into chicken broth until gravy thickens. Add chicken and onions. Cover and slowly bring to a boil. Serve over noodles, rice or mashed potatoes.

Chicken Crêpes

Serves 4 to 6

Crêpe Batter:
1 cup flour, unsifted
3 eggs
4 tablespoons butter, melted
  and cooled (can use
  margarine or oil)

¼ teaspoon salt
1½ cups milk

Chicken Filling:
¼ cup butter or margarine
¾ pound mushrooms,
  chopped or 6 ounces
  canned mushrooms,
  drained
½ cup green onion,
  chopped

2½ cups chicken, cooked and
  chopped
½ cup sherry
Dash pepper
Dash salt

Sauce:
¼ cup flour, unsifted
⅔ cup sherry
10½ ounces chicken broth

2 cups light cream
½ teaspoon salt
⅛ teaspoon pepper

Topping:
½ cup Swiss cheese, grated

Make Crêpe Batter:
In medium bowl, combine flour, eggs, butter, salt and ½ cup milk. Beat with rotary beater until smooth. Beat in remaining milk until smooth. This can also be done in a food processor or blender. Refrigerate the batter, covered, several hours or overnight.

Prepare Filling:
Heat butter in large skillet. Add mushrooms and onions and sauté until golden brown, about 10 minutes. Add chicken, sherry, salt and pepper. Cook over high heat stirring frequently, until no liquid remains in skillet. Remove from heat and add half of sauce.

To Make Sauce:
In a medium saucepan, blend flour and sherry with a wire whisk. Stir in chicken broth, light cream, salt and pepper. Bring to a boil over medium heat, stirring constantly with a whisk. Reduce heat and simmer, stirring for 2 minutes. Add half of sauce to chicken filling (see above); stir until well blended. Set filling and rest of sauce aside.

Make Crêpes:
Slowly heat a 7-inch skillet until a drop of water sizzles and rolls off. Brush lightly with oil. Pour in enough batter to barely cover bottom of skillet. Rotate pan to make batter cover all parts.

Assemble:
Place about ½ cup filling on each crêpe, then roll up. Arrange seam side down in a single layer in a buttered, shallow baking dish. Pour rest of sauce over crêpes and sprinkle with grated Swiss cheese. Bake at 425°F for 15 minutes or until cheese is bubbly.

Chicken And Scampi   Serves 3 to 4

1 3 to 4 pound frying chicken, cut up and boned	1 clove garlic, crushed
	3 tablespoons parsley
1 tablespoon salt	½ cup port wine
½ teaspoon pepper	8 ounces canned tomato sauce
¼ cup butter	1 teaspoon dried basil
3 small onions, chopped	1 pound shrimp, raw

Sauté chicken in salt, pepper and butter until golden. Add onions, garlic, parsley, wine, tomato sauce and basil. Simmer, covered, for 35 minutes. Clean shrimp and add to simmering chicken. Cook, uncovered, 3 to 4 minutes, until shrimp are tender.

Chicken Tetrazzini

Serves 6 to 8

4 pound chicken
1 onion
1 bay leaf
Celery tops
Salt and pepper
1 bunch green onions,
    minced
¼ pound mushrooms,
    minced
¼ cup parsley, minced
½ cup celery, minced

1 clove garlic, pressed
½ cup butter
1 cup half-and-half
1 cup stock
1 tablespoon lemon juice
2 tablespoons white wine
2 tablespoons butter
2 tablespoons flour
1 (7 ounce) package vermicelli
¾ cup Parmesan cheese, grated

Boil chicken until tender with onion, bay leaf, celery, salt and pepper. Remove from heat; cool, strain stock and save. Cut up chicken in small pieces and set aside.

Sauté all vegetables and garlic in butter until soft. Add chicken, cream, stock, lemon juice and wine. Season to taste with salt and pepper and cook slowly over low heat until heated thoroughly. Make a paste of additional butter and flour. Blend into chicken mixture and stir until smooth and thickened.

Cook vermicelli in boiling stock. Drain and spread on bottom of a shallow buttered casserole. Pour chicken mixture over and sprinkle with Parmesan cheese. Bake 20 minutes at 350°F.

May be prepared ahead and refrigerated until serving time. Increase baking time by 10 to 15 minutes if this is done.

Ham And Chicken Tetrazzini   Serves 6

2 whole chicken breasts,
  medium size
1 small onion, quartered
1 carrot, cut
1 stalk celery, cut
Parsley
Bay leaf
Salt and pepper
½ pound fresh mushrooms,
  sliced
¾ cup butter
½ pound cooked ham, in
  julienne strips

8 ounces ½ to ¼ inch flat
  noodles
2 (10 ounce) packages frozen
  peas
2 cups heavy cream
1 cup imported Parmesan
  cheese, grated
1 cup chicken stock
Salt and white pepper
Minced parsley

Poach chicken breasts in water to cover with onion, carrot, celery, parsley, bay leaf, salt and pepper. Cool; remove skin and bones and cut chicken into strips. Strain stock and set aside. Melt ½ cup butter and sauté mushrooms lightly. Add ham and chicken and cook several minutes, stirring. Remove from heat.

In a heavy pan, bring unsalted water to a boil and add noodles gradually. Cook until noodles are firm but not soft. Drain and return to saucepan. Add ham mixture to noodles and mix well. Add butter and toss until each noodle is coated. Add frozen peas. Cook briefly to mix flavors. Add cream and simmer on low heat until sauce thickens and peas are cooked. Add cheese and mix well. Remove from heat. Sauce will be quite thick and can be thinned by adding stock; the finished results should be thick and creamy.

Season with salt and white pepper. Heat well, but do not boil. Pour tetrazzini into a heated dish and sprinkle with parsley.

Green noodles and sautéed shrimp may be substituted.

Chicken Curry

Serves 8

5 whole chicken breasts,
  halved and boned
Salt and pepper
Flour
6 tablespoons butter,
  divided
3 apples, finely chopped
3 medium onions, chopped
2 tablespoons curry powder
Dash ground ginger

4 cups beef broth
1 cup dry white wine
⅓ cup raisins, simmered in
  water for 5 minutes
5 ounces chutney, diced
1 cup heavy cream
Salt and white pepper
Banana slices
Flaked coconut

Salt, pepper and dust each breast with flour. Sauté chicken in 4 tablespoons butter until golden. In large skillet or pot, sauté apples and onions in 2 tablespoons butter until yellow and wilted. Add curry and ginger and cook for 5 minutes. Add broth and white wine. Place chicken in broth sauce and simmer for 1 hour. Remove chicken and add to the sauce drained raisins, chutney, cream, salt and white pepper.

Serve chicken in the sauce over buttered white rice. Garnish with banana slices and coconut.

Chicken Breasts Hollandaise

Serves 12

6 whole chicken breasts,
  halved and boned
Onion Salt, to taste
Pepper, to taste
Thyme, to taste

12 hearts of palm (split large
  ones in half)
1½ cups butter, melted
Hollandaise Sauce, see *Index*

Sprinkle inside of each breast with onion salt, pepper and thyme. Place one heart of palm in each breast; roll and toothpick together. Place breasts in large dish and pour melted butter over them. Cook 1 to 1½ hours at 325°F.

Make hollandaise sauce. When breasts are done, pour off some of the butter and pour hollandaise over chicken.

Chicken Fingers With Honey Sauce

Serves 4 to 6

3 whole chicken breasts,
  halved and boned
Salt
Pepper
2 egg whites

1 tablespoon water
Fresh cracker crumbs
Butter
Oil

Pound chicken breasts until thin. Season with salt and pepper. Cut into pieces about 2 x 2 inches. Beat egg whites slightly and add water; blend well. Have cracker crumbs ready. Dip chicken in egg mixture, then roll in crumbs to cover. Allow to rest on a rack 30 minutes or more before cooking. Sauté until golden brown in 1 part butter and 1 part oil (¼ inch deep).

Honey Sauce:
1 cup honey

½ cup horseradish

Blend honey and horseradish well. Serve with chicken fingers.

Sautéed Chicken Livers

Serves 4

½ pound chicken livers
1 cup flour
⅛ teaspoon pepper
1 small onion, finely
  chopped
4 tablespoons butter
1 cup fresh mushrooms,
  sliced

Juice of 1 lemon
¼ teaspoon salt
¼ cup red wine
Toast points
1 tablespoon fresh parsley,
  chopped

Roll chicken livers in peppered flour. Sauté livers with onion in butter (5 minutes maximum). Add mushrooms, lemon juice and salt. Stir in the wine and serve on toast points. Garnish each serving with chopped parsley.

Easy Lemon Chicken

Serves 6

3 whole chicken breasts
½ cup margarine
1 tablespoon flour
Salt and tarragon, to taste

½ cup chicken broth
2 lemons, sliced
Parsley

Bone chicken breasts, remove the skins. Cut each breast into strips. Melt butter over medium high heat and add chicken. Sprinkle with flour, add salt and tarragon. Cook 5 minues, stirring constantly. Add chicken broth and lemon slices. Cover and simmer for 15 minutes.

Serve with rice, sprinkle with parsley.

Chicken Divan Crêpes

Serves 6

¼ cup butter
¼ cup flour
2 cups chicken broth
2 teaspoons Worcestershire
   sauce
3 cups Cheddar cheese, grated

2 cups sour cream
2 (10 ounce) packages
   broccoli spears, cooked
2 cups chicken, cooked and
   chopped
12 crepes

Over medium heat, melt butter in small saucepan. Stir in flour and cook until bubbly. Add broth and Worcestershire sauce; cook, stirring until thickened. Add two cups of cheese. Empty sour cream into medium bowl; gradually add hot cheese sauce, stirring constantly. In large shallow baking dish, place cooked broccoli and cooked chicken on each crepe. Spoon one tablespoon sauce over each. Fold crepes and pour remaining sauce over all. Sprinkle with remaining cup of cheese. Cover and heat in 350°F oven for 20 to 30 minutes.

Tangy Lemon Chicken
Serves 4

2 cups margarine
1 (5 ounce) bottle horseradish
8 tablespoons cider vinegar
8 teaspoons salt
2 tablespoons Worcestershire
   sauce

3 teaspoons Tabasco
1 cup lemon juice
1 3-4 pound frying chicken,
   cut up

Combine all ingredients, except chicken, in saucepan over low heat. Let simmer for 30 minutes.

Dip chicken pieces into sauce to coat. Let sit in sauce 20 to 30 minutes. Cook on grill 45 to 60 minutes. (Can be baked in oven at 350°F for 1 hour.) After removing from heat, spoon a little sauce over chicken.

Cold Lemon Chicken
Serves 3 Allowing 2 Per Person

½ cup dry white wine
1 cup water
½ cup plus 2 teaspoons
   lemon juice
3 whole boneless chicken
   breasts, halved and
   skinned

¼ cup mayonnaise
4 teaspoons cucumber, peeled,
   seeded and finely chopped
2 teaspoons lemon rind, grated
¼ teaspoon salt
¼ teaspoon pepper
6 lemon slices

Combine wine, water and ½ cup lemon juice. Bring to a boil. Add chicken, cover, and cook over medium low heat for 20 minutes. Set aside to cool.

Mix mayonnaise, cucumber, lemon rind, 2 teaspoons lemon juice, salt and pepper. Spread in thin layers over drained chicken. Top each chicken breast with a lemon slice and wrap in foil. Chill thoroughly.

Chicken Filo

Serves 12

6-8 whole chicken breasts,
  boiled (reserve broth)
8 tablespoons butter
1 cup celery, chopped fine
1½ cups onion, chopped
  fine
1 cup chicken broth
½ cup fresh parsley,
  chopped fine

½ teaspoon nutmeg
½ teaspoon salt
⅛ teaspoon white pepper
3 eggs, beaten
1 pound Filo dough
8 tablespoons butter, melted

Boil chicken breasts until tender. Cool. Reserve all broth and chop the chicken. In a saucepan, melt butter and add celery and onions. Sauté until tender. Add chopped chicken and 1 cup broth. Cook until liquid is absorbed. Cool, then add parsley, nutmeg, salt and white pepper. Beat eggs until frothy, then fold them into the chicken mixture and mix gently. Divide chicken mixture into three equal bowls. Butter 8 sheets of filo individually and stack on top of each other. Spread chicken mixture from one bowl on top of the filo sheets leaving about 2 inches around the sides. Then roll like a jelly roll. This recipe makes three rolls and each roll serves 4.

When ready to bake, brush the top with butter. Bake at 350°F for 40 to 50 minutes or until the roll is brown and crispy.

Top with the following sauce before serving:

4 tablespoons butter
5 tablespoons flour
2½ cups chicken broth

3 egg yolks, beaten
¼ cup fresh lemon juice

Over low heat, melt butter; add flour, stirring constantly. Add hot chicken broth and cook until thickened, stirring constantly. Remove from heat. Beat egg yolks 3 minutes. Add lemon juice slowly. Add a little sauce to the yolks and lemon juice before adding them to sauce. Stir for 2 minutes so as not to curdle. Do not cook sauce. When reheating, do not let sauce come to a boil.

Chicken Jerusalem

Serves 4

¼ cup butter
1 cup fresh mushrooms,
  sliced
3 whole chicken breasts,
  halved
1 teaspoon monosodium
  glutamate
1 teaspoon salt

⅛ teaspoon pepper
14 ounces canned artichoke
  hearts
⅓ cup sherry
⅓ cup water
2 tablespoons flour
1 cup sour cream
¼ teaspoon paprika

Melt butter; add mushrooms and sauté. Remove mushrooms and reserve. Sprinkle chicken with monosodium glutamate, salt and pepper. Brown on both sides. Add artichokes, sherry and water. Cover and simmer 30 minutes. Add mushrooms the last 5 minutes of cooking time. Transfer to serving platter. Blend flour and sour cream into liquid remaining in skillet. Heat, but do not boil. Spoon over chicken.

Congealed Chicken (or Tuna) Mold

Serves 10

2 cups chicken or 2 (7
  ounce) cans tuna
2 tablespoons unflavored
  gelatin
½ cup cold water
½ cup boiling water
½ cup celery, diced
1 green pepper, diced
2 tablespoons cider vinegar
1 teaspoon salt (¼ teaspoon
  with tuna)

1 cup olives, sliced (½ cup with
  tuna)
1 teaspoon Worcestershire
  sauce
2 tablespoons lemon juice
1 tablespoon dry mustard
⅛ teaspoon Tabasco
1¾ cups mayonnaise or ½ cup
  mayonnaise and 1 cup sour
  cream

Soften gelatin in cold water. Add boiling water and all other ingredients. Fold in mayonnaise. Turn mixture into 1½ quart ring. Chill.

Marinated Chicken On The Grill

Yields Marinade
for 12 chicken pieces

1½ cups oil
¾ cup soy sauce
¼ cup Worcestershire sauce
2 tablespoons dry mustard
2½ teaspoons salt

1 tablespoon pepper
½ cup wine vinegar
1½ teaspoons parsley flakes
½ cup lemon juice
2 tablespoons sugar

Combine all ingredients and stir well. Pour over chicken pieces. Let stand in refrigerator overnight. Cook chicken on the grill in a pan for about 30 minutes, basting and turning frequently. Remove from pan and place chicken directly on grill for about 10 minutes.

Dyspeptic's Delight

(Dressing for Turkey or Other Fowl)

Yield Stuffing for
15 Pound Turkey

2 packages herb seasoned
  dressing
2 cups heavy cream
1 pound hot sausage
1 cup onion, chopped fine
1 cup celery, chopped fine
1 pound fresh mushrooms,
  sliced
1 tablespoon butter

1 tablespoon Worcestershire
  sauce
1 quart oysters
2 small bottles stuffed olives,
  chopped, or olive butter
Salt, pepper, and poultry
  seasoning, to taste

Soak dressing in cream while preparing other ingredients.

Cook sausage and break up. Sauté onions and celery lightly in small amount of sausage grease. Sauté mushrooms; add a little butter and Worcestershire sauce. Save liquid and add to dressing. Cook oysters until curly. Combine with other ingredients; season with salt, pepper and poultry seasoning and add olives. Mix well and stuff turkey.

Stuffed Cornish Hens With Orange Sauce
Serves 4

4 rock cornish game hens
1 (6 ounce) box long grain
   and wild rice

½ cup mushrooms, sliced
¼ to ½ cup almonds, sliced

Clean hens and set aside. Cook rice according to directions. Add mushrooms and almonds. Stuff mixture into hen cavity and secure legs. Lightly sprinkle birds with salt and pepper and dot with a small amount of butter. Bake 1½ hours at 325°F and serve with orange sauce.

Orange Sauce: *Yields 3 Cups*

1 cup light brown sugar,
   firmly packed
2 tablespoons cornstarch
½ teaspoon salt

½ cup water
4 tablespoons orange peel,
   grated
2 cups fresh orange juice

Combine sugar, cornstarch and salt. Stir in orange peel, juice and water. Cook over low heat, stirring constantly, until thickened and transparent.

Marinated Cornish Game Hens
Serves 4

¾ cup onion, chopped
¼ pound butter
1 clove garlic, minced
1 teaspoon salt
¼ teaspoon thyme
1 tablespoon parsley,
   chopped

1 bay leaf
1 cup beef bouillon
2 tablespoons dry sherry
2 hens, split and flattened
1 cup fresh mushrooms, sliced

Sauté onion in butter until soft. Add next 6 ingredients. Simmer, add sherry and correct seasonings. Rinse hens and dry inside and out; salt entire bird. Add hens to marinade and soak overnight, turning occasionally. Place hens, mushrooms and marinade in a baking pan and bake at 350°F for 1½ hours, basting occasionally. Serve with wild rice.

Loin Of Wild Boar

Serves 4

1 pound loin of boar
¼ cup butter
2 tablespoons flour
¼ teaspoon salt
⅛ teaspoon pepper
¼ pound mushrooms, sliced

2 tablespoons flour
1 cup milk
¼ teaspoon salt
Water
2 tablespoons white wine

Melt butter in saucepan, mix flour, salt and pepper; dredge loin with flour mixture. Sauté loin in butter until golden brown on all sides. Remove loin to oven proof dish. Sauté fresh mushrooms in remaining butter, then add flour, stirring constantly. Add milk and salt. When sauce thickens, add wine, stir and pour over loin in casserole dish.

Bake, covered, at 350°F for 45 minutes. Add a few tablespoons of water if sauce is too thick or if there is not enough to nearly cover loin.

Barbecued Duck Breasts

Serves 2

½ pound butter
½ cup catsup
1 tablespoon sugar
1½ tablespoons lemon juice
1 tablespoon Worcestershire
   sauce

1 teaspoon salt
¼ teaspoon ground pepper
1 clove garlic, pressed
1 small onion, chopped
½ teaspoon Tabasco
4 duck breasts halves

Combine all ingredients except duck breasts; cover and simmer 5 minutes. Place breasts on rack in flat pan and bake at 375°F for 1 hour, basting with barbecue sauce every 10 to 15 minutes.

Wild Duck With Orange Sauce   Serves 2

1 wild duck
Seasoned salt
Salt
Pepper
1 to 2 apples, quartered,
   depending on size of duck

3 tablespoons butter
1 cup white wine
Orange Sauce, see *Index*

Bring duck to room temperature covered with seasoned salt. Salt and pepper cavities and stuff with apples. Place duck breast side down in roaster. Put butter on bird and pour wine over. Cover and cook at 300°F for 1 to 1½ hours, depending on size. Serve with Orange Sauce.

Chafing Dish Doves   Serves 2 to 3

4 to 6 doves
Salt
1½ to 2 tablespoons butter
Steak or Worcestershire
   sauce, 1 teaspoon per
   bird

Red wine, 1 tablespoon per
   bird
Heavy cream, 1 tablespoon per
   bird
Tabasco, 2 drops per bird

Split doves down back and save liver and hearts. Stretch open so they lie flat. Salt well front and back. Put aside.

Heat chafing dish over alcohol flame. Melt butter in dish with top on. When butter is melted, put doves in, breast down. Put top on chafing dish and cook 3 to 4 minutes. Reverse doves, cover, and cook for 2 minutes. Add hearts and liver. Add Worcestershire or steak sauce, sprinkle lightly with Tabasco and add wine. Cover and simmer for 30 minutes.

Place on platter with hominy or wild rice. Pour heavy cream in dish and heat until cream mixes with other juices. Pour over birds and hominy or rice.

Dove or Quail Stroganoff

Serves 6 to 9

12 to 18 dove or quail
  breasts
1 medium onion, chopped
2 tablespoons butter, melted
2 tablespoons flour
1½ cups milk
½ cup mushrooms, lightly
  sautéed
½ cup celery, chopped fine

½ cup white wine
½ teaspoon oregano
½ teaspoon rosemary
¼ teaspoon pepper
½ teaspoon salt
1 teaspoon gravy browning
  sauce
1 cup sour cream

Arrange meat in dish. Sauté onions in butter, add flour and milk.
Make a sauce; add remaining ingredients except sour cream. Pour
mixture over birds. Cover dish lightly with foil. Bake at 350°F for 1
hour. Add sour cream to sauce and bake, uncovered, an additional
20 minutes. Spoon over wild rice.

Whole doves may be used. Flour lightly and brown in butter or
margarine first. Remove to baking dish; make sauce in pan doves
were browned in, using same proportions of flour and butter.

Dove Pilau

Serves 6

6 doves or 12 dove breasts
¼ pound bacon, cubed or
  ¼ cup bacon drippings
1 medium onion, chopped
5 cups chicken broth
Pinch of thyme

1 bay leaf
½ teaspoon salt
4 drops Tabasco
1 tablespoon parsley
1½ cups rice, uncooked
¼ pound button mushrooms

Fry bacon over low heat in a heavy dutch oven with a tight fitting
top until lightly browned. Add doves or dove breasts and brown.
Add onion and sauté until limp. Add the chicken broth and all the
seasonings. Bring to a boil and add the washed rice. Cover and
cook over very low heat about 25 minutes until the rice is tender
and the broth absorbed. Stir once with a fork. Add the mushrooms
and cook 5 minutes longer.

Quail St. Julian   Serves 4

10 quail, cleaned
Juice of 1 lemon
Salt, enough to sprinkle
   over all quail
Flour, to dredge in
4 tablespoons butter

2 medium onions, chopped
¾ cup water
2 tablespoons parsley, chopped
8 ounces fresh mushrooms,
   sliced
2 cups sour cream

Sprinkle lemon juice over quail and sprinkle with salt. Dredge in flour and brown in pan with 3 tablespoons melted butter. Remove and place in casserole with lid. Brown onion in butter remaining in pan and add water. Scrape up brown bits and pour over quail in casserole. Add parsley and cook for 45 minutes in 350°F oven.

Sauté mushrooms in 1 tablespoon butter and add to casserole. If serving immediately, add sour cream and cook 10 minutes longer, making sure sour cream is mixed with juice.

If doing quail ahead, heat in oven 15 to 30 minutes (depending on whether at room temperature or from refrigerator) and add sour cream last.

Glazed Dove Or Quail   Serves 4 to 6

12 dove or quail
Salt and pepper, to taste
Flour
½ cup butter

½ pound mushrooms, sliced
1 tablespoon lemon juice
1 cup orange juice
1 (10 ounce) jar currant jelly

Salt and pepper birds, dust with flour. Melt butter in saucepan. Brown birds in butter then remove to a baking dish. Sauté mushrooms in remaining butter. Mix lemon juice, orange juice and jelly in small saucepan, heating thoroughly. Pour mushrooms and butter and jelly mixture over birds. Bake 30 to 45 minutes at 325°F, turning birds occasionally.

Serve with wild rice.

Quail In Cream Sauce   Serves 4

8 quail
½ cup butter
2 scallions, chopped
2 cloves garlic, crushed
¾ cup celery, chopped
½ cup boiling water

1 cup vermouth (or dry white wine)
4 tablespoons flour
2 cups half-and-half
Salt and black pepper, to taste

In heavy skillet with tight fitting lid, melt ¼ cup butter. Add scallions, garlic and celery, then birds. Sauté birds on both sides until lightly brown. Add ½ cup boiling water and vermouth. Cover and simmer on low for ½ hour. Remove birds to platter, remove and reserve remaining liquid.

Add ¼ cup butter and flour. Stir and simmer for 5 minutes. Slowly add reserved liquid, then half-and-half, stirring constantly until thick. Season with salt and pepper. Return birds and simmer 10-15 minutes on low, turning once.

Serve on bed of wild rice, pouring sauce over all.

Quail And Creamed Celery   Serves 4

8 quail
Salt and pepper
4 tablespoons butter
1 to 2 tablespoons onion, minced
4 tablespoons flour

2 cups chicken stock
1 cup light cream
⅓ cup sherry
1 teaspoon parsley, chopped
2 cups celery, chopped

Salt and pepper quail. Brown slightly in butter; remove to casserole dish. Sauté onions until lightly browned. Add flour to butter and onions to make a roux. Combine stock with cream, sherry and parsley. Add to roux and allow to thicken (boil). Sprinkle celery over quail. Pour gravy over quail, cover casserole and bake in 350°F oven for 30 minutes.

Quail And Cherries
Serves 4

8 quail
Salt and pepper
5 tablespoons butter, melted
2 tablespoons brandy
¼ cup white wine
1 cup chicken stock

16 ounces canned black
  cherries, drained
¼ cup syrup from cherries
½ teaspoon lemon rind, grated
1 teaspoon lemon juice

Salt and pepper quail. Drizzle butter over birds and roast in oven until well browned. Add brandy, wine and stock, continue cooking 10 to 12 minutes, turning several times. Remove quail to hot plates.

Pour sauce in a small saucepan; add cherries, cherry syrup, lemon rind and lemon juice. Add a little more stock, if needed. Simmer until cherries are thoroughly warm. Spoon sauce over quail, place cherries around birds.

Quail With Grapes And Almonds
Serves 4

8 quail
Salt and pepper
Flour
5 tablespoons butter

¼ cup white wine
1 cup chicken stock
1 cup small white grapes
4 tablespoons sliced almonds

Salt and pepper quail and roll in flour. Sauté in butter until browned. Add wine and stock and simmer 15 minutes, turning several times. Add grapes and heat just until the grapes are warmed. Place quail on a hot plate, spoon sauce over them and arrange grapes around quail. Sprinkle with sliced almonds which have been lightly browned in butter.

Oyster Stuffing for Quail
Serves 6

4 to 5 oysters per quail
Salt and pepper
1 tablespoon Worcestershire
  sauce
1 cup saltines, crushed

Flour
12 quail
Butter, melted
Fresh parsley, chopped

Drain oysters thoroughly; lightly salt and pepper oysters. Place them in a bowl, pour Worcestershire sauce over them and mix so as to season each oyster. Dip each oyster into the cracker crumbs. Salt, pepper and lightly flour quail. Brown in butter. Place 4 to 5 oysters in each quail. Skewer quail closed with a toothpick. Brush with melted butter. Bake at 350°F for 45 minutes to 1 hour, basting occasionally.

Garnish with fresh chopped parsley.

Smothered Quail
Serves 4

½ cup cubed bacon
8 quail
¼ teaspoon salt
⅛ teaspoon pepper
6 tablespoons flour
2 scallions with tops, minced

1 tablespoon celery leaves,
  minced
3 cups chicken broth
Pinch thyme
½ bay leaf
1 tablespoon chopped parsley

Sauté bacon until brown; remove from skillet. Put lightly peppered and salted quail in drippings; when browned, add flour and onions and stir. Add all other ingredients and return bacon and quail to gravy. Cover, simmer 30 minutes, turning occasionally until done. Add more chicken broth, if necessary.

Venison ~ Aging, Preparing And Cooking

After the venison is skinned and dressed, it needs special care in the kitchen. As unsightly as the meat may seem, it is better not to wash it (certainly not all over). Scrape and trim away any unusable or wounded parts and age the meat in the bottom of your refrigerator for at least 5 days. Pour or wipe away any blood that may collect. This aging and draining is one of the secrets of tender meat.

After aging, cook or freeze the meat. Wipe it off with a damp cloth and, if freezing, check for sharp bones that may need filing to protect from puncturing the wrapping. Wrap first in plastic wrap and then in freezing paper.

Before cooking any cut of venison, marinate it. To prepare meat for the marinade, first cut away any fat (this gives a sharp taste if left) and then remove all membrane, muscles and tendons. Though it requires extra work, the tender meat is worth the extra trouble. Any meat that is pulled away by this process can be bound with butcher's twine.

Marinate the meat in wine with ¼ cup olive oil poured on top, or refer to recipe on page 173.

Venison Tenderloin On Grill

Serves 4

Venison tenderloin
3 cups red wine
Lard or bacon

2 tablespoons Worcestershire sauce

Marinate tenderloin 3 to 4 hours in red wine and wrap in lard or bacon. Put on preheated grill and cook 15 to 20 minutes, turning frequently. Should be pale pink inside. Serve immediately, keeping unused portion on warming tray covered with the bacon.

Venison Stew   Serves 6

½ cup bacon drippings
1 onion, chopped
1 pound fresh mushrooms,
    sliced
2 pounds boneless venison
    stew, cut into ¾ inch
    cubes
5 tablespoons flour

2 cups beef broth
1¾ cups red wine (Burgundy)
½ teaspoon garlic salt, optional
½ teaspoon salt
¼ teaspoon pepper
2 or 3 stalks celery, chopped
    fine, optional

Sauté onions and mushrooms in bacon drippings, remove and set aside. Brown venison in small portions in bacon drippings. Remove venison to a Dutch oven or large casserole dish. Stir in flour, add broth, wine and seasonings. Simmer 3 hours, then add sautéed onions and mushrooms; simmer one additional hour. Serve with rice or noodles.

Freezes well.

Venison Meat Loaf   Serves 6

1 pound venison, ground
½ pound fresh pork,
    ground
¼ teaspoon pepper
1 teaspoon salt
½ teaspoon oregano
½ teaspoon thyme
¼ teaspoon curry powder
½ cup onion, chopped
½ cup green pepper,
    chopped

1½ cups bread crumbs
2 eggs
⅓ cup milk
1 cup vegetable juice or tomato
    juice
1 tablespoon Worcestershire
    sauce
2 teaspoons prepared mustard
1 tablespoon parsley, chopped
Several strips bacon, uncooked

Mix all ingredients thoroughly. Cover with bacon and bake at 350°F for 1½ hours. Serve with Tomato Sauce (see Index).

Marinade For Leg Of Venison

2 cups wine or vinegar
2 sprigs or ½ teaspoon dry
  parsley
2 bay leaves
2 small carrots, sliced
2 small onions, sliced

10 peppercorns
2 cloves
Good pinch thyme
Pinch savory
¼ cup olive oil

The vinegar is much stronger than wine—left for 2 days, the meat will taste a bit like sauerbraten. When in a hurry, use dried soup vegetables instead of above recipe. (One-half bottle soup vegetables to 2 cups of wine or vinegar and ¼ cup olive oil.) Put meat in the smallest possible deep bowl or non-metallic container, or preferably a zip-lock bag, and cover with marinade. If you use a bowl, fill empty spaces around meat with apples or capped jars, as the spaces use up the wine. Refrigerate, and if in a bowl, turn meat frequently so that the marinade will penetrate evenly. Turn at least twice a day. Marinate a young, tender cut of venison at least 24 hours. Longer marinating makes the meat more tender. A large leg may be marinated up to 5 days.

Cook the meat according to your favorite recipe. For barbecuing, start salt and peppered meat in the oven with a meat thermometer, putting it on the grill for the last hour or two. Baste with half tart jelly, half butter.

Always check the hind quarter to make sure the hunters have removed the musk gland. Also, an old deer needs marinating longer than a yearling.

Venison Roast

Allow ¼ to ⅓ Pound per Person

Venison roast
½ cup oil
½ cup wine vinegar

3 tablespoons garlic salt
3 tablespoons lemon pepper
½ cup lemon juice

Combine oil, vinegar, garlic salt, lemon pepper and lemon juice; mix well. Marinate roast, covered, overnight in marinade.

Cook on grill or in oven, according to weight of roast, following time chart for beef. Venison is best medium rare to medium.

Venison Roast With Bacon

Allow ¼ to ⅓ Pound per Person

Venison roast
Salt and pepper

Bacon

Season roast lightly with salt and pepper. Cover roast completely with bacon. (Thick country style bacon is best.) Place roast on a rack in a roasting pan. Do not cover. Place in preheated 475°F oven. After about 10 minutes, reduce heat to 325°F. Roast 20 minutes per pound.

Use pan drippings to make gravy, to which beef bouillon, a bouillon cube, mushrooms, finely chopped onions or celery can be added.

Frog Legs Geechee

Allow 2 Per Person

Frog legs
Flour
Salt and pepper

Garlic powder or garlic salt
Butter
Lemon wedges

Roll frog legs in flour lightly seasoned with salt, pepper and garlic salt. Sauté in butter until golden brown, turning as needed. Cook about 10 minutes until meat separates easily from the bones. Serve with lemon wedges or sprinkle with lemon juice.

Duckling Savannah

Serves 6 to 8

2 ready-to-cook ducklings
(3½ to 4 pounds each)
Salt, to taste
Ground black pepper
3 medium carrots, diced
2 small onions, chopped
3 sprigs fresh thyme or ½
teaspoon dried thyme
3 stalks celery with tops,
diced

3 shallots, chopped
1 small bay leaf
2 clove cloves garlic, finely
chopped
2 tablespoons butter
½ cup peach brandy
6 peaches, peeled and pitted

Preheat oven to 400°F. Wash and dry ducks. Remove giblets and discard excess fat from body cavities. Sprinkle ¼ teaspoon salt and a dash of pepper in the body cavity of each duck. Rub ½ teaspoon salt and dash black pepper over skins.

Place ducklings, breastside up, on a rack in a large, shallow roasting pan. Roast, uncovered, until ducklings are brown, about 10 to 15 minutes. While ducks are roasting, mix carrots, onions, thyme, celery, shallots, bay leaf and garlic together and sauté in butter until soft, about 10 to 15 minutes. Remove the ducks from the roasting pan and place sautéed mixture *(mire poix)* in the bottom of the pan. Put the ducks back on top. Cover pan and return to oven. Reduce oven temperature to 325°F. Roast 1 hour or until ducks are tender. Remove ducks to a warmed platter and keep warm.

Strain the *mire poix* and pan drippings into a saucepan. Skim off and discard fat. Add brandy and bring the mixture to boiling point. Add peaches and heat only until they are hot. Add salt to taste. Remove hot peaches from sauce and place on warmed serving platter around ducks. Spoon the sauce over the peaches and the ducks after carving, or, if desired, carve at the table and pass the sauce in a sauceboat.

A FORMAL AFFAIR

A Formal Affair

Savannahians have always enjoyed dances and large formal affairs, but that was especially true in earlier days.

Tales abound of the debut parties and large balls and soirees given privately and by military units like the Georgia Hussars, the Savannah Volunteer Guards and the Chatham Artillery.

One account of the 1870's describes the yards of tarleton of all shades and colors that was pinked with a hot iron to create scalloped flounces and then fashioned into ball dresses. A bouquet of Parma violets fresh from the garden often would accompany such a dress and its owner to the party.

In those days most of Savannah lived in what today is called downtown. This made it convenient for couples to walk to parties, the young lady's escort carrying her slippers in a dainty bag. In inclement weather two young men might hire a carriage together to take them and their ladies to the ball.

According to one writer, a debut in that day was a most important adventure. "A few brave pioneers chose to go to college, but as a rule, there was little money to be expended on education of girls . . . So a girl stood or fell by her social talents from the time of her debut until she married."

While one set of debutantes in the 1890's made its bow to society at the first dance of the season given by the German Club, it was customary for young women to be introduced from home and never from a hotel or club.

A feature of those debut parties was what would seem today a fabulous supper. One writer recalled a menu of turkeys, ducks, venison, ham, salads, baked terrapin, cakes, charlottes, ice cream, champagne and coffee, but called that supper rather unexceptional.

Custom dictated that the ladies repair to the dining room to be served first and then retire to the parlors while the men took their turn.

Some of the most popular early social events were the dances given every two weeks by the German Club, a group of young society men of the day. The name had nothing to do with the West European country, but was a shortened reference to German cotillion, a complex dance with much changing of partners.

The Germans were quite formal occasions with dancing and then a grand march led by the chaperones to supper. After that the ladies would freshen up in the dressing rooms, while the men finished the champagne and smoked cigars.

Then the dancing would resume to the strains of the "orchestra," which consisted of a violin, violoncello with Natty Solomons at the piano. According to one local historian, so popular was Natty Solomons as a player of waltzes that no other orchestra ever furnished music for a party for one entire decade.

Broiled Beef Tenderloin With Mushroom Sauce
Serves 8

1 beef tenderloin (5 to 6 pounds)
⅓ cup butter
1 large clove garlic
½ pound fresh mushrooms, sliced
2 medium onions, sliced
Ground trimmings from meat or ¼ pound hamburger
2 tablespoons chili sauce

1 tablespoon Diable Sauce
Pinch dried marjoram
Pinch dried thyme
Pinch hickory smoked salt
4 drops Tabasco
2 dashes Worcestershire sauce
5 ounces dry red wine
2 ounces condensed beef bouillon
Salt and pepper
1 tablespoon flour

Sauce:

Melt the butter in a large skillet. Cut garlic lengthwise into slivers and sauté with the mushrooms and onions in hot butter until the onions are limp. Add the ground meat and break up with a fork while stirring constantly. After 4 or 5 minutes, add the remaining ingredients and stir well. Simmer until ready to pour over tenderloin when it is placed in a roaster.

To cook tenderloin:

Preheat the oven and broiling pan for 15 minutes at 550°F. Have the tenderloin at room temperature and place on a broiling pan not more than 2 inches from the heat. Cook for 8 minutes. Turn and cook for 7 minutes. Remove from the broiler and place in a roaster. Pour the sauce over the tenderloin and cook in a 350°F oven for about 10 minutes. Pour the sauce from the roaster over the meat and serve.

Beef Wellington

Serves 8 to 10

6 pound beef filet	Duxelles (Filling), recipe below
Salt and pepper	1 egg
Butter pastry, recipe below	1 tablespoon water

Roast beef seasoned with salt and pepper on a rack in shallow pan at 425°F for ½ hour. Cool for 2 hours, then trim fat.

Meanwhile, prepare butter pastry.

Butter Pastry:

3¾ cups flour	1 cup cold butter or margarine
1 teaspoon salt	¾ cup ice water
2 tablespoons shortening	

Combine flour and salt. Cut in shortening and cold butter until fine. Add water a tablespoon at a time for stiff dough. Make dough into a square and chill for 30 minutes.

Duxelles:

1 pound fresh mushrooms, finely chopped	1 cup white wine
	½ teaspoon salt
¼ cup butter or margarine	2 teaspoons flour
¼ cup green onions, chopped	¼ cup cooked ham, finely chopped
½ teaspoon marjoram	2 tablespoons parsley, chopped

Sauté mushrooms in butter with onions; cook until liquid evaporates. Add remaining ingredients except ham and parsley. Stir until thickened. Remove from heat, add ham and parsley. Cool.

Roll pastry into rectangle large enough to wrap around beef (about 3 inches longer than beef, 12 to 13 inches wide). Press cool duxelles into pastry, leaving one inch uncovered on all edges. Moisten pastry edges, enclose beef, pressing edges together. Trim off excess pastry from ends so single layer covers ends. Place roll seam side down in shallow baking pan. Cut decorations from pastry and place on top. Brush pastry with egg beaten with water. Bake at 400°F for 20 to 30 minutes until browned. Let stand 15 to 20 minutes before slicing.

Sliced Beef With Broccoli   Serves 4

1 pound top round or flank
  steak
4 tablespoons soy sauce
2 teaspoons sugar
¼ teaspoon garlic salt
4 teaspoons cornstarch

½ teaspoon ground ginger
  (optional)
6 tablespoons peanut oil
4 stalks fresh broccoli
4½ cups water

Cut meat into small, bite-sized pieces at an angle to the grain on the meat. Add soy sauce, cornstarch, sugar garlic salt, ginger and 2 tablespoons peanut oil. Cover and refrigerate at least 1 hour. Cut broccoli into small bite-sized pieces at a 45 degree angle to the vertical growth of the stalks. Put 2 tablespoons peanut oil in a wok on high heat (375 °F) and place marinated meat in it. Stir meat to brown quickly, about 2 minutes. Remove meat from wok and keep nearby in a warm container.

Put 2 tablespoons peanut oil in wok and heat to 375 °F (wok does not need to be washed between cooking meat and broccoli). Stir-fry broccoli about 3 minutes until it becomes dark green. Add water and cover for 3 minutes. Drain water. Add meat to wok and mix together. Serve over steamed rice.

Marinated Flank Steak   Serves 3 to 4

Flank steak (2 pounds or less)
¼ cup soy sauce
3 tablespoons honey
2 tablespoons cider vinegar

1½ teaspoons garlic salt
1½ teaspoons ground ginger
¾ cup oil
1 small onion, chopped fine

Prepare the meat by scoring about ¼ inch deep on each side and removing any fat or membrane. Combine the other ingredients and pour over the meat. Marinate meat overnight in refrigerator or on kitchen counter for at least 4 hours.

Remove meat from marinade and grill over charcoal for 10 minutes on each side. Slice thinly on the diagonal.

Alonzo's Flaming Tenderloin   Serves 4

6 tenderloin steaks, ¾ inch
  thick
Salt and pepper, to taste
¾ cup unsalted butter
3 shallots, chopped, or 6
  small spring onions,
  chopped (omit green
  stems)
½ clove garlic, crushed

3 tablespoons parsley, chopped
8 large fresh mushroom caps,
  chopped
Worcestershire sauce, to taste
1 tablespoon Dijon mustard
3 ounces Diable sauce
½ cup brandy, heated

Pound tenderloin steaks with wooden mallet to flatten "paper thin". Season with salt and pepper.

In a large skillet, melt ¼ cup butter and add shallots or onions, garlic and parsley. Cook 3 to 4 minutes and add another ¼ cup butter. When melted, add mushrooms and cook until tender, about 3 minutes. Push to side of skillet. Add remaining butter and when melted, add the meat. Season with Worcestershire sauce and brown meat, turning often. Add mustard and Diable sauce. Stir mushroom mixture into sauce with meat. (Meat cooking time should be 4 to 5 minutes.)

Heat ½ cup brandy, pour over tenderloin and ignite. Serve immediately.

Tenderloin Au Sherry   Serves 4

1 large pork tenderloin
Salt and pepper
1 tablespoon fat
½ cup water

1 pound fresh mushrooms,
  sliced
1 tablespoon butter
Sherry

Salt and pepper tenderloin and brown in hot fat. When well browned, add water. Cover with lid and simmer for about 1 hour, adding more water, if necessary. Sauté mushrooms in butter. When meat is done, add mushrooms to gravy which has been thickened. Add sherry to taste. Baste for a few minutes with gravy.

Piccadillo   Serves 8

2 medium onions, diced
2 large green peppers,
　diced
4 tablespoons olive oil
1½ pounds ground chuck
½ teaspoon monosodium
　glutamate
½ teaspoon celery salt
¼ teaspoon oregano
¼ teaspoon salt
¼ teaspoon pepper

¼ teaspoon garlic or onion
　powder
¼ teaspoon paprika
29 ounces canned tomato sauce
2 tablespoons Worcestershire
　sauce
1 (5 ounce) jar stuffed olives,
　reserve juice
1 (3 ounce) jar capers
1 cup seedless raisins
¼ cup juice from olives

Sauté onions and peppers in 2 tablespoons olive oil and set aside. Sauté meat in 2 tablespoons olive oil; stir in all seasonings. Add tomato and Worcestershire sauces and stir until well blended. Add remaining ingredients and cook 40 minutes on low heat, covered.

Serve over yellow or white rice.

Veal Habersham   Serves 6

6 cubed steaks or cutlets
Flour for dredging
3 to 4 tablespoons olive oil
Salt and pepper, to taste
½ cup mushrooms, sliced
　and drained

1 clove garlic, crushed
⅓ cup dry white wine
½ cup water
1 to 2 tablespoons flour
Parsley, chopped
Seasoned bread crumbs

Dredge veal cubed steaks or pounded cutlets in flour. Brown quickly in frying pan with olive oil. Salt and pepper generously. Transfer meat to baking dish. Add mushrooms, garlic and wine to pan and sauté. Add water and flour to make thin gravy. Sprinkle veal with parsley and bread crumbs. Pour gravy over veal. Bake, covered with foil approximately 30 minutes in 350°F oven.

Baked Stuffed Shoulder Of Veal   Serves 6 to 8

1 3-pound shoulder of veal
  (have butcher bone the
  shoulder and chop the
  bones)
6 cups water
1 large onion, quartered
2 carrots, chopped
1 stalk celery, chopped
1 tablespoon Bouquet garni
Salt and pepper, to taste
½ cup long grain rice,
  uncooked

Pinch of saffron
½ cup walnuts, finely chopped
Peel of 1 lemon, grated
4 slices bacon, cooked and
  chopped
4 tablespoons butter
1 egg, lightly beaten
½ to ¾ cup dry white wine
Watercress, to garnish

Put the bones and the cleaned and chopped vegetables in a saucepan with 6 cups of cold water. Add Bouquet garni and season well with salt and pepper. Cover and cook for 3 hours over low heat; strain and set stock aside. Stock can be made the day before.

Cook rice in 2 cups of reserved stock with a pinch of saffron for 12 to 16 minutes, uncovered, or until tender. Chop walnuts finely and grate the lemon rind. Cook bacon in butter until crisp. Remove bacon and chop coarsely.

Mix together with a spoon: cooked rice, bacon, walnuts, lemon rind, half the bacon fat from pan, salt, pepper and beaten egg.

With a sharp knife, open cavities of meat to make small pockets for stuffing. Spoon in stuffing. Close meat and tie with butcher's twine in several places. Brown veal in other half of the bacon grease. Place veal in roasting pan and pour ½ to ¾ cup wine over it. Roast veal in the center of a preheated oven at 350°F for 1½ hours. Baste frequently with the wine, adding stock when necessary.

When veal is done, remove twine and add ½ cup stock to pan drippings. Boil over high heat until liquid is reduced by half. Pour gravy into warmed sauceboat. Place veal on warmed serving dish, garnished with watercress.

Veal Piccata   Serves 6

Veal medallions, pounded
  as thinly as possible,
  allowing 8 ounces per
  serving, not more than ⅛
  inch thick
½ cup butter

½ cup lemon juice
Garlic powder
Paprika
Parmesan cheese, grated
Lemon, thinly sliced

In a large skillet, melt butter and add lemon juice. Sauté veal in lemon butter sauce until just bleached. Spread veal on a broiler rack. Sprinkle lightly with garlic powder and paprika. Cover generously with grated Parmesan cheese. Top each piece with a lemon slice. Spoon lemon and butter mixture over each scallopini. Broil until cheese begins to melt, about 5 to 6 minutes. Serve immediately.

Curried Leg Of Lamb   Serves 8

1 leg of lamb, about 5
  pounds
3 tablespoons lemon juice
1 tablespoon curry powder
2 cloves garlic, crushed

2 teaspoons salt
¼ teaspoon pepper
⅛ cup water
2 onions, finely chopped
½ cup dry vermouth

Preheat oven to 400°F. Sprinkle lamb with lemon juice. Mix garlic, curry, salt and pepper with water to make a paste. Spread the paste over the fatty side of the lamb and pat onions on top. Place in oven for 30 minutes. Remove lamb from oven and slowly pour vermouth over the top so as not to disturb onions. Reduce oven to 350°F. Return lamb and cook until meat thermometer reads 150°F for medium, or 15 minutes per pound.

Roast Leg Of Lamb
Serves 8

1 leg of lamb, about 7
  pounds
½ cup soy sauce
1 tablespoon oregano
1 tablespoon thyme
1 tablespoon rosemary

1 teaspoon dry mustard
½ teaspoon mace
2 cloves garlic, peeled
1 bay leaf
½ cup olive oil

Put soy sauce and the next 8 ingredients in a food processor. Use steel blade and add the olive oil slowly until ingredients form a smooth paste. Cover lamb entirely with the paste and refrigerate for 1 hour. Reserve some marinade for a sauce.

Preheat oven to 450°F and roast lamb for 15 minutes. Turn the oven down to 350°F and roast lamb for 10 to 12 minutes per pound for medium rare. If you are using a meat thermometer, cook until it registers 140°F.

Remove lamb from oven and let stand for 20 minutes before slicing.

Rack Of Lamb Madison
Serves 4

8-rib rack of lamb (not
  frenched)
Salt and pepper, to taste
3 tablespoons olive oil
3 tablespoons fine bread
  crumbs

1 tablespoon parsley, chopped
1 teaspoon oregano
1 teaspoon shallots, chopped
½ teaspoon garlic, put through
  press
Pinch anise seed

Season lamb with salt and pepper to taste and roast in preheated 400°F oven, uncovered, for 30 minutes. In a bowl combine remaining ingredients. Work mixture into a paste and spread over top of lamb. If this amount of paste does not sufficiently cover the lamb, make paste again. Roast lamb 20 to 30 minutes more, depending on degree of doneness desired.

For more than one rack of lamb, increase cooking time in each step 10 minutes per rack.

Gigot Christian Dior (Leg of Lamb)   Serves 8

1 leg of lamb
2 garlic cloves, optional
3 lemons
5 to 6 medium tomatoes,
  sliced
Lemon pepper spice
  marinade

Mixed *herbes de Provence*
  (rosemary, fennel, bay,
  oregano)
2 tablespoons red wine
Worcestershire sauce

Preheat oven to 400°F.

Cut as much fat as possible from lamb. Peel garlic cloves, cut into tiny slivers and place under lamb membranes and in crannies. Do not insert dircctly into meat as it will burn lamb. Grate all rind from lemons. Slice tomatoes thinly, leaving skin. Spray large roasting pan with non-stick vegetable spray and make a bed with tomato slices. Sprinkle liberally with lemon pepper spice marinade and with ⅓ of lemon rind. Squeeze juice of 1 lemon over tomatoes and 1 lemon over lamb. Pat remainder of lemon rind on lamb. Crush 2 pinches of herbs over lamb and place directly on tomato bed. Pour water over tomatoes, barely covering. Cook for 15 minutes per pound. Do not overcook. Baste once by squeezing juice of third lemon over lamb. If water has evaporated, replace. When lamb is 15 minutes from being done, remove from oven, place on a warm platter, cover with foil and return to 200°F oven.

Scrape all juice and tomatoes from pan into blender or food processor and puree. Pour liquid into frying pan or saucepan, add red wine and 2 to 3 dashes of Worcestershire sauce. Cook together until bubbly, then turn heat to low. Slice lamb. Serve with sauce and new potatoes. If you prefer a more refined sauce, strain to eliminate seeds.

Roast Crown Of Pork With Apple Stuffing

Serves 8

Crown of Pork Roast* (See
cutting instructions below)
¼ cup butter
½ cup onions, chopped
3 cups tart apples, cored
and chopped
2 tablespoons sugar

¼ teaspoon thyme
¼ teaspoon sage
1 teaspoon salt
⅛ teaspoon pepper
4 cups bread cubes
¼ cup parsley, chopped
2 tablespoons apple cider

*Have the butcher prepare a crown roast allowing 2 ribs per person. Be sure that the backbone is removed so that it can be carved.

Heat the oven to 325°F. Place roast in a shallow open roasting pan with no water. Cover the rib ends with aluminum foil and insert the meat thermometer in the meatiest part of the chop. Roasting will take 3½ to 4 hours or 35-40 minutes per pound. Place heatproof bowl in the center of the roast so that it will keep its shape.

Stuffing: Sauté the onion in butter until soft and add apples, sugar, thyme, sage, salt and pepper. Cover and cook over low heat until the apples are soft. Toss the bread cubes, apple mixture, parsley and cider in a large bowl.

One hour before the roast is done, remove the bowl from the center and spoon the stuffing in the center of the roast. Cook until the roast registers 185°F on the meat thermometer.

Barbecue

Serves 6 to 8

Boil fresh pork or ham. Let simmer 6 to 7 hours with the following:

28 ounces canned tomatoes
5 ounces soy sauce
4 or 5 large onions,
chopped
4 or 5 garlic buds, chopped

½ cup brown sugar
½ cup cider vinegar
Worcestershire sauce and
Tabasco, to taste
Salt and pepper, to taste

Cool; remove fat and skim off fat juice. Cut meat into small pieces or mash with fork. Use leftover sauce for meat.

Sherry Pork Chops And Apples
Serves 6

2 tablespoons oil or fat
6 thick pork chops
3 medium hard apples,
  unpared, cored and sliced
¼ cup brown sugar

½ teaspoon cinnamon
2 tablespoons butter
Salt and pepper, to taste
½ cup sherry

Brown chops in oil or fat in a heavy skillet. Arrange apple slices in a greased 9 x 13-inch baking dish. Mix sugar and cinnamon and sprinkle mixture over apples. Dot apples with butter and place pork chops on the apple slices. Sprinkle with salt and pepper and pour sherry over all.

Cover and bake at 350°F for 1 to 1½ hours.

Pickled Knockwurst
Serves 4 to 6

2½ cups water
1¾ cups white vinegar
2 tablespoons sugar
1½ teaspoons salt
20 peppercorns

16 whole allspice
1½ pounds knockwurst, sliced
  on angle into ½ inch slices
1 medium Bermuda onion,
  sliced into rings

In a saucepan combine water, vinegar, sugar, salt, peppercorns and allspice. Bring mixture to a boil. Reduce heat and simmer 10 minutes. Let the marinade cool until it is lukewarm. Slice knockwurst and onions and arrange them in a 2-quart jar, alternating layers. Pour marinade over knockwurst, cover jar and refrigerate 3 days.

Will keep in refrigerator for several weeks.

Stuffed Pork Chops   Serves 4

4 double-thick pork chops,
   about ¾ inch thick (have
   butcher cut pocket in side
   ½ to ¾ inches long)
⅓ cup water
3 tablespoons butter
1 cup herb stuffing mix
¼ cup celery, chopped fine

½ cup flour, or enough to coat
   chops
¼ cup corn oil
Pepper, to taste
Water
½ cup mushrooms, sliced
2 tablespoons butter
Parsley

Pork chops should be at room temperature. Trim off excess fat.

Prepare stuffing according to package directions. Add finely chopped celery. Stuffing should be light and crumbly. If not, slowly add more stuffing mix until the mixture is drier. Spoon stuffing into the chop cavities until as full as possible. Close openings with toothpicks, about 3 per chop.

Put flour in a paper bag and shake each chop (or dust on plate) until well coated, being careful not to dislodge toothpicks. Heat oil on medium high heat in a skillet (with lid), preferably an iron one. When a drop of water spits in oil, put chops in, sprinkle with pepper and brown one side, uncovered. Sear stuffed edge, holding with fork if necessary. Brown second side. Pepper lightly. Remove chops to plate. Tilt pan so grease remains on top and browned bits remain in bottom of pan. Pour off grease, keeping browned bits.

Return pan to medium heat. When bits are hot and browning, add cold water, a little at a time, until bottom of pan is covered about ¼ up the side. Put chops back in pan. Add enough water to reach opening of stuffed cavity. Cover. Simmer for 1½ hours. Add water if needed to keep water at level of cavity.

Slice and sauté ½ cup mushrooms in butter until limp. Test chops with fork for tenderness. There should be plenty of liquid to make a large amount of gravy.

Arrange chops on platter and garnish with mushrooms and parsley.

Georgia Country Ham

Serves 12

1 Georgia country ham (10
  to 12 pounds)
1 cup brown sugar

1 cup bourbon or sherry
1 cup water

Have the hock cut off ham so that it will fit into a roaster. Soak ham overnight in cold water and scrub the ham with a stiff brush. Change water a couple of times to get rid of the excess salt.

Mix sugar, bourbon and water; press into the fat of ham. Cover tightly with foil in roaster and bake at 200°F for 8 hours.

Ham Stroganoff

Serves 5 to 6

½ pound ham, cut in strips
  or pieces
2 tablespoons butter
½ cup onion, chopped

6 ounces mushrooms, sliced
2 teaspoons flour
1½ cups sour cream
Rice

Sauté ham pieces, onion and mushrooms in butter until onion is tender. Sprinkle flour over it; stir over low heat. Stir in sour cream until thickened. Serve over rice.

Ham Loaf

Serves 8

1½ pounds lean pork,
  cooked and ground
1½ pounds ham, cooked
  and ground
½ bell pepper, chopped
½ medium onion, chopped

1½ cups milk
2 eggs
1 cup cracker crumbs
Pepper
2½ cups tomato sauce

Combine ham, pork, bell pepper, onion, milk, eggs, crumbs, pepper and 1½ cups tomato sauce and put in loaf pan. Pour remaining cup of tomato sauce on top and bake at 350°F for 1½ hours.

Serve with spicy mustard.

PICNICKING;
A FAVORITE
PASTIME

Picnicking: A Favorite Pastime

Savannahians love a picnic. Today they pack up a cooler and head for the beach or perhaps open up a hamper in Colonial Cemetery. Others board a boat for a nearby island, but seldom with the style that accompanied the famous Daufuskie Picnic, an annual event during the late nineteenth century.

At that time Daufuskie Island, in the mouth of the Savannah River, was owned by the Stoddard brothers, John, Harry and Albert.

Each spring Harry Stoddard would offer his place, called Bloody Point, to the German Club for its annual outing that ended the social season.

Apparently, it was a gala affair to which everyone wore his or her best and at which the music never stopped.

The tide and moon played a vital part in setting the date since the chartered riverboat had to catch the high tide on arriving in the morning and departing at nightfall.

When the appointed date arrived, between 100 and 300 persons met at the wharf at the end of Abercorn Street around 9:30 a.m., the heads of families carrying big baskets filled with food, a full table service and wine, usually champagne, for a dozen people.

Also on the boat went the piano for Natty Solomons' orchestra which set up in the two-story house or out under the trees for the dancing that went on all day. When the orchestra took a break, the brass band outside would start up.

Lunch was served outside on white tablecloths with plenty of champagne that had been cooled in small hand pails.

Around 6:30 the band would strike up a march, signaling everyone to head for the beach some two or three hundred yards from the house. There young and old alike would dance a Virginia Reel before boarding the boat for Savannah. On the way home the younger set often would entertain everyone with college songs, popular tunes of the day and selections from the operas of Gilbert and Sullivan, much in vogue at the time.

According to early participants, the famous picnic was known throughout the Southern coastal states, but apparently was never quite duplicated outside Savannah.

Buttermilk Biscuits

Yields 1 Dozen

2 cups flour
2 teaspoons baking powder
1 teaspoon salt
½ teaspoon soda

2 teaspoons sugar
⅓ cup shortening
⅔ cup buttermilk

Preheat oven to 450°F.

Sift dry ingredients together. Cut in shortening; add buttermilk and mix until dough is pliable.

Knead dough on a lightly floured board for 30 seconds (25 times). Roll ½ inch thick, cut with biscuit cutter and place close together on an ungreased cookie sheet. Bake 10 to 12 minutes.

Whole Wheat Honey Bread

Yields 2 Loaves

2 packages yeast
1 tablespoon brown sugar
¼ cup hot water
1 cup milk
1 cup hot water

1 tablespoon salt
¼ cup dark molasses
3 tablespoons bacon fat, melted
½ cup honey
6 cups whole wheat flour

Dissolve and soak yeast and brown sugar in ¼ cup water for 10 minutes. Combine other ingredients except flour with yeast mixture. Add flour and knead for 10 minutes. Place in a greased bowl and let rise until doubled in bulk (about 1 hour). Punch down and knead for 5 minutes. Let rise again. Punch down and let rest for 10 minutes. Place dough in 2 greased and floured loaf pans. Let rise until almost doubled. Bake for 45 minutes at 350°F.

Brittlebread ®
Serves 10 to 12

2¾ cups flour, unsifted
¼ cup sugar
½ teaspoon salt

½ teaspoon soda
½ cup butter
8 ounces plain yogurt

Blend flour, sugar, salt and soda. Cut butter into the dry mixture. Add yogurt and mix to a soft dough. Break off marble size pieces of the dough and roll very thin on a floured board. Sprinkle with salt or sugar. Bake at 400°F for 5 to 8 minutes on ungreased cookie sheet. Turn off heat and allow to crisp in oven.

Can be mixed in food processor.

Buttermilk Bran Muffins
Yields 8 Dozen

6 cups All Bran
2 cups boiling water
1 cup butter or margarine,
    melted
3 cups sugar

4 eggs, unbeaten
1 quart buttermilk
5 cups flour, unsifted
5 teaspoons soda
5 teaspoons salt

Put 2 cups bran in bowl; pour boiling water over it. Let stand while assembling other ingredients. Mix in melted butter.

Mix rest of bran with sugar, eggs, and buttermilk. Sift flour, soda and salt together. Combine all ingredients. Cover and store overnight in refrigerator. When ready to use, pour into greased muffin tins and bake at 400°F for 20 to 25 minutes.

Use as needed. Will keep about 6 weeks in refrigerator.

Yummy Muffins
Yields 6 Muffins

1 cup self-rising flour
½ cup milk

¼ cup mayonnaise

Mix all ingredients well and fill muffin tins. Bake in 350°F oven for 20 minutes.

Lemon Muffins

Yields 2 Dozen

1 cup butter
1 cup sugar
4 eggs, separated
½ teaspoon lemon extract
2 cups flour

2 teaspoons baking powder
1 teaspoon salt
½ cup lemon juice
2 teaspoons lemon peel, grated

Cream butter and sugar until smooth. Beat egg yolks and add to butter/sugar mixture; beat until light and fluffy. Add lemon extract. Sift dry ingredients and add alternately with lemon juice, mixing thoroughly after each addition. Fold in stiffly beaten egg whites and lemon peel. Blend thoroughly. Fill buttered muffin tins ¾ full and bake at 375°F for 20 minutes.

Pecan Popovers

Yields 6 to 8 Popovers

½ cup pecans
2 eggs
1 cup milk

1 cup flour, sifted
¼ teaspoon salt

Chop pecans in blender container; empty blender and set nuts aside. Put eggs and milk in blender container; cover and blend 2 seconds. Add flour and salt; cover and blend 10 seconds. Stir in pecans and blend again.

Fill well-greased custard cups ½ full. Place cups on baking sheet and bake at 475°F for 15 minutes. Reduce heat to 350°F and bake 25 to 30 minutes longer or until brown and firm. A few minutes before removing from oven, prick each popover with a fork to let steam escape. If you prefer popovers dry and crisp, turn oven off and leave in oven 30 minutes with door ajar. Serve hot.

Sally Lunn

Serves 12

1 package dry yeast
2 cups warm milk
2 eggs
2 tablespoons sugar

2 teaspoons salt
5 cups flour
2 tablespoons butter, melted

Soften yeast in warm milk in a large, warm mixing bowl. With an electric mixer, add eggs and sugar to yeast mixture. Add salt and about 3 cups of flour. Remove from mixer and beat in the remaining flour. Add butter and beat again. Batter will be thin. Let rise in mixing bowl until doubled in bulk, about 1 hour.

Beat down and pour into a well-greased tube pan or bundt pan. Let rise again until doubled, about 1 hour. Bake at 350°F for 1 hour, covering with foil after the first half hour.

Homemade Dinner Rolls

Yields 3 to 4 Dozen

2 cups milk
⅔ cup solid shortening
2 packages dry yeast
1 tablespoon sugar

2 eggs, beaten
4 teaspoons salt
¾ cup sugar
7 to 8 cups flour

Scald 2 cups milk in pan. Let the shortening melt into the milk and cool until lukewarm. Dissolve yeast in lukewarm mixture. Add sugar and eggs. Add salt and ¾ cup sugar. Add 4 cups of flour gradually until thick like pancake batter. Stir in 3 to 4 more cups flour until it is in dough-like consistency. Let sit on counter for 10 minutes. Knead (as little as possible) until in consistency of ball. Put in greased bowl and refrigerate (covered) for 10 hours or overnight.

Roll into 3 quarter-size balls per greased muffin cup. Cover and let rise in a warm place for 2½ hours. Bake at 400°F for 10 to 12 minutes.

Angel Flake Rolls
Yields 5 Dozen

2 packages dry yeast
⅓ cup water, lukewarm
3 teaspoons sugar
1 cup oil

2 cups buttermilk
5 cups self-rising flour,
   unsifted
Butter, melted

Dissolve yeast in lukewarm (not hot) water with sugar. Be sure yeast and sugar are completely dissolved before adding oil and buttermilk which have been mixed together. Add flour, unsifted, and stir until blended. Place on pastry board and flour both sides. Pat out to about ¼ inch and cut with biscuit cutter. Dip or brush both sides with melted butter, fold in half and place on ungreased baking pan. Place in refrigerator until ready to bake. Remove from refrigerator and let stand at room temperature for at least 15 minutes before baking.

Bake at 425°F for 12 to 15 minutes or until browned.

English Muffin Bread
Yields 1 Loaf

2½ to 3 cups flour
1 package yeast
1¼ cups water

1 tablespoon sugar
¾ teaspoon salt
Cornmeal or grits

In a large mixing bowl, combine 1 cup of flour and yeast, set aside. In a small saucepan, heat water, sugar, and salt until sugar is dissolved. Add to dry ingredients and beat at low speed of electric mixer ½ minute. Scrape sides of bowl; beat 3 minutes at high speed. By hand, stir in enough of the remaining flour to make a soft dough. Shape into a ball. Place in a lightly-greased bowl. Turn once to grease surface. Cover, let rise 1 hour or until doubled. Punch down, cover, and let rest 10 minutes.

Grease a 1½ or 2 quart round casserole and sprinkle with cornmeal or grits. Place dough in bowl. Cover, let rise 45 minutes to 1 hour or until doubled. Bake at 400°F for 40 to 45 minutes. Cover loosely with foil if top browns too quickly.

Bread is best hot or toasted with butter.

Charlotte's Fluffy Light Bread

Yields 2 Loaves

6 cups flour, sifted
1 teaspoon salt
½ cup sugar
1 package dry yeast

5⅓ ounces evaporated milk
1 cup margarine
1 cup potatoes, mashed
2 eggs, room temperature

Mix 2 cups flour, yeast, salt, sugar in mixing bowl. Add to this ½ cup evaporated milk mixed with ½ cup water. Beat slowly with electric mixer. Heat 1 cup margarine with ¼ cup water over *low* heat. Add this to mixture in mixing bowl and beat. Add ¼ cup flour and 2 eggs and mix on high speed for 2 minutes. Add 1 cup mashed potatoes and remainder of flour. Pat a little oil on top and let rise until double in bulk. (It is best to place bowl in cold oven, placing a pan of hot water underneath and let rise an hour or more.) Cut bread dough down and cover with a towel and refrigerate overnight.

The next day, put dough on a floured board and knead for 3 minutes. Let rest 5 minutes, then knead for 3 more minutes. Cut in half and place in 2 loaf pans. Let rise in cold oven following same procedure as before. This takes about 2 hours.

Place in cold oven on middle rack and bake at 350°F for 30 minutes. Cut oven off and leave bread in for 5 minutes. Remove from oven and cool on racks.

Easy Beer Bread

Yields 1 Loaf

2 cups self-rising flour
3 tablespoons sugar

12 ounces canned beer, warm
1 tablespoon butter, melted

Combine flour, sugar and beer; stir just until all ingredients are moistened. Pour into a greased loaf pan. Bake at 375°F for 30 to 35 minutes. Brush with melted butter. Remove bread from pan and cool.

Cheese Bread
Yields 2 Loaves

3 tablespoons sugar
1 tablespoon salt
2 packages active dry yeast
4½ to 5½ cups flour
1½ cups milk
½ cup water
2 tablespoons butter or
  margarine

1½ cups sharp Cheddar cheese,
  coarsely grated
1 egg
Sesame seeds
White of 1 egg

In large bowl, combine sugar, salt, yeast and 1¾ cups flour. In saucepan, heat milk, water and butter or margarine until very warm (105°F to 115°F). Gradually add liquids to dry ingredients; beat at medium speed of electric mixer for 2 minutes. Add cheese, egg and enough remaining flour to make a thick batter, mixing to blend well. Beat at medium speed for an additional 3 minutes. By hand, gradually stir in remaining flour, enough to make a stiff batter which leaves the sides of the bowl. Cover loosely with a light towel and let rise in warm place until doubled in bulk (about 1 hour).

Preheat oven to 375°F. Stir batter down and beat vigorously for 30 seconds. Turn batter into 2 deep, well-greased loaf pans. Combine white of one egg with splash of cold water; brush mixture over each loaf. Sprinkle generously with sesame seeds. Bake 40 to 50 minutes or until done.

Memmie's Spoon Bread   Serves 4-6

1 cup corn meal, sifted
1½ cups boiling water
1 cup milk
2 teaspoons baking powder

1 teaspoon salt
2 eggs, slightly beaten
2 tablespoons butter

Pour boiling water over corn meal slowly, stirring until smooth. Stir in butter and salt. Let cool slightly. Add milk and beaten eggs. Mix well and *lastly* fold in baking powder. Pour into lightly-greased baking dish and bake at 375-400°F for 40 minutes or until brown.

Spoon out and serve immediately with butter or gravy.

Hard Corn Pone   Serves 6

1 cup boiling water
1 cup white corn meal
1 teaspoon salt

1 tablespoon bacon drippings
1½ teaspoons sugar

Pour boiling water over dry ingredients. Beat until blended. Drop batter from a spoon or pat into a pone onto a hot, greased black iron griddle. Bake at 400°F for 20 to 30 minutes.

Charles' Cornbread   Yields 9 Pieces

1 cup corn meal
½ cup corn oil
3 teaspoons baking powder
2 eggs

1½ teaspoons salt
1 cup cream style corn, or fresh
  if available
1 cup sour cream

Preheat oven to 400°F. Mix ingredients until blended. Pour into a greased 8 x 8 x 2-inch dish and bake for 30 minutes.

Monkey Bread

Serves 8 to 10

5 cups flour
  (approximately)
3 packages active dry yeast
2 tablespoons sugar
1 teaspoon salt

1½ cups milk
⅓ cup butter or margarine
1 egg
¾ to 1 cup butter or
  margarine, melted

In large bowl of mixer stir together 1½ cups flour, yeast, sugar and salt; set aside. Heat milk and the ⅓ cup butter until very warm (120° to 130°) and pour over flour-yeast mixture. Add egg and beat 3 minutes at medium speed, scraping bowl occasionally. Add 1 cup flour and beat 3 minutes longer. Stir in remaining 2½ cups flour and mix with wooden spoon until thoroughly blended.

Grease top of dough. Cover and let rise in warm, draft-free place until doubled in bulk, about 30 minutes. Turn out on lightly floured surface and knead lightly until smooth. Divide dough in half. Roll out each half in 18 x 12 inch rectangle. Cut in ¾ inch strips, then crosswise in 3 inch pieces. Dip each piece in melted butter, then toss helter-skelter into 10-inch tube pan. Cover and let rise until doubled in bulk, about 1½ hours.

Bake on bottom rack in preheated 425°F oven about 30 minutes or until golden brown and done. Turn out on rack to cool slightly before serving.

Zucchini Bread

Yields 2 Loaves

3 eggs
2 cups sugar
1 cup oil
2½ cups flour, sifted
1 teaspoon salt
¼ teaspoon baking powder

2 teaspoons baking soda
1 tablespoon cinnamon
2 cups zucchini, grated (do not
  pare)
1 cup pecans, chopped
2 teaspoons vanilla

Mix thoroughly the eggs, sugar and oil. Stir in flour, salt, baking powder, baking soda and cinnamon. Add zucchini and pecans. Flavor with vanilla.

Pour batter into 2 greased and floured loaf pans or 1 large bundt pan. Bake at 350°F for 50 to 60 minutes, depending on size of pan.

Oatmeal Bread

Yields 2 Loaves

2 cups boiling water
1 cup oatmeal, uncooked
2 packages yeast
1/3 cup lukewarm water
1 tablespoon salt
1/2 cup honey

2 tablespoons butter, melted
2 1/2 to 3 cups flour
1 1/2 to 2 cups whole wheat flour
1 egg yolk
Sesame seeds

Pour boiling water over oats. Let stand until thoroughly softened. Soak yeast in lukewarm water (not hot). Add salt, honey and butter (cooled to lukewarm) to oats. Making sure oats are just lukewarm, add yeast and mix well.

Gradually add flours and knead with hands until dough is smooth and elastic. This should take approximately 10 minutes. Put into a light-oiled bowl, turning to coat dough on all sides. Cover with a cloth and let rise for 1 hour or until doubled in bulk. Oil 2 bread tins.

Punch down the risen bread dough and cut in half. Knead each half briefly and shape into loaves. Place them in bread tins. Cover and let rise until pans are full. Preheat oven to 350°F.

Beat egg yolk lightly with 1 teaspoon of water. Brush surface of each loaf with egg mixture and sprinkle with sesame seeds. Bake 35 to 40 minutes.
Freezes well.

Banana Nut Bread

Yields 1 Loaf

2 cups flour
1 teaspoon soda
1/4 to 1/2 teaspoon salt
1/2 cup butter or margarine
1 cup sugar

2 eggs
1 teaspoon vanilla
3 ripe bananas, mashed
1 cup nuts, chopped (optional)

Mix flour, soda and salt. Set aside. Cream butter and sugar. Add eggs and vanilla. Mix well. Add bananas and mix well. Fold in dry ingredients and nuts. Place in a well-greased 9 x 5 x 2-inch loaf pan and bake at 350°F for 55 to 60 minutes.

Dill Bread

Yields 1 Loaf

2 tablespoons onion, chopped
1 tablespoon butter
1 package active dry yeast
¼ cup warm water
1 cup large curd cream style cottage cheese, heated lukewarm

2 tablespoons sugar
2 teaspoons dill seed
1 teaspoon salt
¼ teaspoon soda
1 egg
2½ cups flour, sifted

Cook onion in butter until tender. Soften yeast in water. Combine in mixing bowl cottage cheese, sugar, onions, dill seed, salt, soda, egg and softened yeast. Mix well. Add flour to make a stiff dough, beating well. Cover, let rise until doubled (about 1¼ hours).

Stir down and turn into well-greased 9 x 5 x 2 inch loaf pan. Let rise until light, about 40 minutes. Bake at 350°F for 50 to 55 minutes. Cover with foil last 15 minutes. Brush with butter. Sprinkle with salt, if desired.

Apricot Bread

Yields 2 Loaves

1 cup dried apricots
½ cup hot water
1 cup sugar
1 cup brown sugar
3 cups flour
½ teaspoon soda

2 teaspoons baking powder
½ teaspoon salt
3 eggs, beaten
1 cup sour cream
1 cup pecans, chopped

Cut apricots in pieces and put in hot water to soak. Sift dry ingredients and add eggs. Stir in sour cream and pecans; then add soaked apricots, undrained. Put in 2 greased loaf pans. Bake in preheated 350°F oven for 1 hour. Check for doneness in 45 minutes.

Lemon Bread

Yields 1 Loaf

½ cup margarine
1 cup sugar
2 eggs, slightly beaten
1⅔ cups flour, sifted
1 teaspoon baking powder

¼ teaspoon salt
½ cup milk
½ cup pecans, chopped fine
Grated peel of 1 lemon

Cream margarine with sugar; add eggs. Sift flour, measure and sift again with baking powder and salt. Alternately add flour mixture and milk to shortening mixture, stirring constantly. Mix in nuts and grated lemon peel. Bake in greased 5 x 9 inch loaf pan in 350°F oven for 1 hour.

Topping:
¼ cup confectioner's sugar   Juice of 1 lemon

Combine sugar with lemon juice and pour over top of loaf as soon as it comes from oven. Cool before slicing.

Pumpkin Bread

Yields 3 Loaves

4 cups flour
⅔ teaspoon baking powder
2¼ teaspoons baking soda
1½ teaspoons salt
1 teaspoon cinnamon
1 teaspoon cloves
½ teaspoon ginger

½ teaspoon allspice
5 eggs
3½ cups sugar
3 cups pumpkin
1⅓ cups oil
¾ cup cold water

Grease and line bottom of 3 loaf pans with brown paper overlapping ends so loaf can be lifted out when done.

Sift dry ingredients; beat eggs very well, add sugar and beat well. Add pumpkin, oil and water and beat well. Add dry ingredients and mix well. Fill pans about ⅔ full. Bake at 325°F for 1 hour, until nicely browned and toothpick comes out clean.

Sticky Buns

Yields 5 Dozen

2 cups water
½ cup sugar
2 teaspoons salt
2 eggs, well beaten
2 envelopes yeast
½ cup warm water
1 teaspoon sugar

½ cup shortening, softened
½ cup butter or margarine,
   softened
9 to 10 cups flour
   (approximately)
2 teaspoons cinnamon
1 cup sugar

Mix water, sugar, salt and eggs. Soften yeast in ½ cup warm water and 1 teaspoon sugar. Add yeast mixture to egg mixture. Add shortening and butter; mix well. Add flour, 1 cup at a time. Beat well; knead in the last 3 to 4 cups flour. Cover and let rise until doubled in bulk, about 2 hours.

Punch down, roll out dough on floured board. This is a very large piece of dough. It should be rolled into a rectangle. Sprinkle with a mixture of cinnamon and sugar. Roll in jelly roll fashion making a very long, thin roll. Cut into about 5 dozen ½ inch thick pin-wheel rolls.

Topping:
1 cup butter or margarine,
   melted
1 cup white corn syrup

2 cups brown sugar
2½ cups pecans or walnuts,
   chopped (approximately)

Combine butter, corn syrup and brown sugar; mix well. Put about 1 tablespoon of topping in the bottom of 5 dozen muffin cups, then sprinkle about 1 teaspoon of chopped nuts on top of topping. Place 1 pin-wheel slice of dough on top of the topping and nut mixture. Let rise about 2 hours or until doubled and rising out of the pan.

Bake at 350°F for 12 to 15 minutes. Remove pans and cool for 5 to 10 minutes; turn pans upside down so the topping can coat the bottom of the roll. Remove the rolls before the muffins have time to stick to the pan.

Cinnamon Raisin Bread   Yields 2 Loaves

1½ cups milk
½ cup butter
¼ cup sugar
3 teaspoons salt
2 envelopes dry yeast
½ cup very warm water

2 eggs, room temperature
6¾ cups flour, approximately
2 cups raisins
½ cup sugar
½ teaspoon cinnamon

Combine milk, butter, sugar and salt in a small saucepan. Heat until butter is melted; cool to lukewarm. Dissolve yeast in warm water in a *large,* warm bowl. Beat in eggs and cooled milk mixture. With an electric mixer, beat in about 4 cups flour. Remove from mixer, stir in raisins and some of the remaining flour until like a heavy batter which sticks to side of bowl. Knead in the remaining flour on a floured board. Knead 5 to 10 minutes. Place in a greased bowl, coat dough with oil, cover and let rise in a warm place until doubled in bulk, about 1 hour. Punch down, divide dough in half.

Roll out, sprinkle with cinnamon and sugar mixture. Roll up in jelly roll fashion. Place in loaf pans. Cover and let rise in warm place until doubled. Bake at 350°F for about 55 minutes.

Country Biscuits   Yields 5 Dozen

8 heaping tablespoons solid
  shortening

2 cups milk
4½ cups self-rising flour,
  sifted

In bowl, combine shortening and milk. Add flour so that dough does not stick to hands (add more flour if necessary). Mix with fork and hands. Roll out ⅓ portion at a time on a floured board and cut into small round circles (size of silver dollar). Bake at 400°F until light brown, about 10 to 12 minutes.

These freeze well.

AT HOME

At Home

A hundred years ago a young Savannah woman might consent to promenade with a beau up the east side of Bull Street to Forsyth Park (never to the "Bay" or to "Factor's Walk," where the men conducted their business), but "dates," of course, were unknown. What took their place was an elaborate system of calling.

Ladies called on each other in the mornings, usually on foot, and sometimes making as many as twenty calls a day. Young men made their calls in the evenings or on Sundays, alone or with friends.

One popular Savannah custom for a number of years was the practice of making New Year's calls. A hostess who did not wish to receive callers tied to her doorbell a small basket in which callers could leave their cards. Otherwise, families often received guests from noon to midnight.

Sometimes a group of two or more girls would gather at a friend's house for the evening, where a chaperone was always nearby. Dressed elegantly in dinner gowns, the young women would receive young men in evening dress with top hat and white kid gloves.

No one sat during a call, but stood and chatted and perhaps sampled a bit of sherry or Madeira and cake. Calls were very short and when another coterie of visitors arrived, the first group bowed themselves out.

By the 1890's, the custom of New Year's calls had ended, but young women still carried on their friendships with young men through evening calls at home. A couple on the verge of engagement to be married might go to church together or to call on their prospective families, but even those actions signaled an imminent announcement.

Cakes and Cookies

Moravian Sugar Cake

Serves 12 Breakfast Squares
or 24 Squares for Tea

2 envelopes dry yeast
1 cup warm water
2 tablespoons dry skim milk
2 tablespoons dehydrated
  potato
¾ teaspoon salt

2¾ cups flour
2 eggs
⅓ cup butter, melted and
  cooled
⅓ cup plus ½ teaspoon sugar

Topping:
⅔ cup brown sugar
1 teaspoon cinnamon

½ cup butter, melted and
  cooled

Sprinkle dry yeast and ½ teaspoon sugar into 1 cup warm water; stir to dissolve. When yeast begins to foam, add dry skim milk, dehydrated potato, ⅓ cup sugar, salt and ¾ cup unsifted flour. Beat 2 minutes on medium speed of mixer. Add eggs, ⅓ cup melted and cooled butter and 1 cup flour. Beat 2 minutes on high speed of mixer. Add 1 cup of flour. Mix by hand with a wooden spoon. This will make a very soft dough. Cover and put in a warm place to rise until doubled in bulk, about 1 hour. Beat down and let rise again for half an hour. Stir down and spread in a greased shallow pan, about 17 x 12 inches and 1 inch deep. Let rise until doubled.

Spread brown sugar evenly over the top of mixture and sprinkle cinnamon over sugar. Make indentations in dough with fingertips and drizzle butter over dough. Bake for 15 minutes at 375°F or until brown.

Holiday Apple Cake

Serves 12 to 16

2 cups sugar
1½ cups oil
2 eggs
2 teaspoons vanilla
1½ tablespoons lemon juice
2 cups flour
1½ teaspoons soda

1 teaspoon salt
¼ teaspoon nutmeg
½ teaspoon cinnamon
3 cups apples, peeled and diced
1 cup nuts, chopped
1 cup dates, chopped

Mix first 5 ingredients, beat well. Sift flour, soda, salt and spices; add to first mixture. Beat. Add apples, nuts and dates; mix well.

Bake at 325°F for 1½ hours in tube pan. Wrap in foil or liner and store in refrigerator for 2 to 3 weeks before serving.

Chopped Apple Cake

Serves 10 to 12

1 cup sugar
¼ cup butter
1 egg
1 cup flour
1 teaspoon soda
1 teaspoon cinnamon

¼ teaspoon nutmeg
¼ teaspoon salt
2 cups apples, chopped, cored, unpeeled
¼ cup raisins or chopped dates
1 cup nuts, broken

Cream shortening and sugar. Add beaten egg. Sift dry ingredients. Add fruits and nuts; mix well. Pour into 9 x 9 inch greased pan. Bake 45 minutes in 350°F oven.

This is especially tasty if served warm with whipped cream.

Special Apple Cake

Serves 12 to 15

2 eggs
1 cup light brown sugar
1 cup sugar
1¼ cups oil
3 cups flour
½ teaspoon salt

1 teaspoon baking soda
1 teaspoon cinnamon
2 teaspoons vanilla
3 cups apples, peeled and diced
1 cup nuts, chopped (optional)

Preheat oven to 350°F. Beat eggs; add sugar and oil. Beat this mixture 3 minutes and add dry, sifted ingredients. Mix well. Add apples, nuts and vanilla. Grease and flour tube or Bundt pan. Bake for 1 hour.

Fig Cake

Serves 16

3 eggs
1 cup buttermilk
1 cup oil
1½ cups sugar
2 cups flour
1 teaspoon soda
1 teaspoon salt

1 teaspoon vanilla
1 teaspoon cinnamon
1 teaspoon allspice
1 cup nuts, ground
1½ cups canned figs, drained
    and coarsely chopped

Preheat oven to 350°F. Mix eggs, buttermilk, oil and sugar; add flour, soda, salt, vanilla, cinnamon and allspice. Mix well. Add nuts and figs. Pour into a greased and floured tube pan or 4 small loaf pans and bake 50 to 55 minutes.

While still hot, pour sauce over cake and return to oven until bubbly and slightly brown.

Sauce:
½ cup buttermilk
1 cup sugar

¾ cup butter
½ teaspoon soda

Cook in large saucepan until sauce reaches the soft ball stage.

Pumpkin Cake   Serves 16

4 eggs, beaten
2 cups sugar
1 cup oil
2 cups flour
2 teaspoons baking soda

2 teaspoons pumpkin pie spice
½ teaspoon salt
2 cups pumpkin
½ to 1 cup nuts, chopped

Mix eggs, sugar and oil; add flour, soda, pumpkin pie spice and salt. Beat well and add pumpkin and chopped nuts. Bake at 350°F for 55 minutes in well-greased and floured pan. Dust with powdered sugar when cool.

Carrot Cake With Rum Sauce   Serves 16

2 cups flour
2 cups sugar
1 teaspoon salt

2 teaspoons baking powder
2 teaspoons soda
2 teaspoons cinnamon

Mix all dry ingredients together and add:

1½ cups oil
4 eggs

2 cups carrots, grated
¾ cup nuts, chopped

Mix well. Pour into greased and floured tube pan and bake at 325°F to 350°F for 1 hour and 15 minutes. Cool and remove from pan.

Rum Sauce:
6 tablespoons butter   1 cup light brown sugar

Combine together and cook for 1 minute. Remove from heat and add:

¼ cup milk
2 tablespoons dark rum

Enough confectioner's sugar
to thicken (about 1 cup)

Spread on cooled cake.

Carrie's Carrot Cake

Serves 16

2 cups sugar
1½ cups oil
4 eggs
2 teaspoons salt
2 teaspoons cinnamon

2 teaspoons soda
2 cups flour
3 cups carrots, grated
1 teaspoon vanilla

Preheat oven to 350°F. Mix sugar and oil, then add eggs. Mix well; add salt, cinnamon, soda and flour which have been sifted together to the sugar mixture. Add carrots and vanilla.

Cut wax paper to fit 4 8-inch cake pans. Thoroughly grease pans then put in wax paper. Grease and flour these. Pour mixture into pans and bake for 20 to 25 minutes. Cool before icing.

Icing:

8 ounces cream cheese
½ cup butter
4 cups confectioner's sugar

1 tablespoon vanilla
1¼ cup nuts, chopped

Cream first 4 ingredients together, then add nuts. Use as filling for layers and ice like a torte.

Kentucky Pound Cake

Serves 12 to 15

1½ cups oil
4 eggs
2 cups sugar
2½ teaspoons cinnamon

1 cup pecans, chopped
2½ cups self-rising flour
8¼ ounces canned crushed
    pineapple and juice

Preheat oven to 300°F. Cream oil, eggs and sugar. Add remaining ingredients; blend together well. Grease and flour tube pan. Bake 1 hour and 20 minutes. Add topping when cake is cool.

Topping:

½ cup margarine
¾ cup milk

1 cup brown sugar
1 teaspoon vanilla

Mix all ingredients in saucepan. Boil over medium heat until thickened. (Recipe may be cut in half.)

Cold Oven Pound Cake   Serves 10 to 12

½ pound butter
3 cups sugar
3 cups flour
6 large eggs

1 cup heavy cream
1 teaspoon vanilla or almond
    extract

Cream together butter and sugar. Alternately add flour and eggs. Add heavy cream. Pour into greased and floured tube or Bundt pan. Start in cold oven at 350°F for 1 hour and 15 minutes. Turn pan around and bake 10 minutes longer.

Caramel Nut Pound Cake   Serves 12 to 15

1 cup butter
½ cup solid shortening
1 pound box light brown
    sugar
1 cup sugar
5 large eggs
½ teaspoon baking powder

½ teaspoon salt
3 cups flour
1 cup milk
2 teaspoons vanilla
½ teaspoon coconut flavoring
1 cup pecans, chopped

Cream butter and shortening. Add brown sugar a little at a time. Beat well. Add white sugar and beat until light and fluffy. Add eggs. Sift baking powder and salt with flour. Add to mixture, alternately with milk. Add vanilla, coconut flavoring and nuts. Bake in tube pan for 1½ hours at 325°F. Cake may be frosted.

Frosting:
1 cup nuts, chopped and
    toasted in butter
¼ cup margarine
2 cups confectioner's sugar

1 teaspoon vanilla
Milk to make spreading
    consistency

Mix all ingredients well and spread on warm cake.

Cake is better second or third day.

Fresh Coconut Cake   Serves 12 to 15

1 cup butter	3 teaspoons baking powder
2 cups sugar	½ teaspoon salt
4 eggs	1 cup milk
3 cups flour, sifted	1 teaspoon almond flavoring

Cream butter and sugar until light; add eggs one at a time, beating each in thoroughly. Sift and add dry ingredients alternately with milk and flavoring. Bake in 3 greased and floured 9-inch cake layer pans in a 350°F oven for 20 to 25 minutes. When layers are cold, brush fresh coconut juice (small amount) on top of each to make layers moist.

Filling:

2 small or 1 large fresh coconut, grated	1 teaspoon vanilla
	1 teaspoon lemon juice
Coconut water plus enough tap water to make 2½ cups	¼ teaspoon salt
	2 heaping tablespoons cornstarch
2 cups sugar	¼ cup water

Bring coconut water and sugar to a rapid boil. Boil for 5 minutes. Add ⅔ of the coconut to water and sugar mixture and cook 5 to 8 minutes. Add vanilla, lemon juice and salt. Mix cornstarch in ¼ cup water, pour into filling, stirring. Let boil for 2 minutes. Cool in refrigerator until cold and stiff. Spread between and on top of cake layers.

After cake has settled, sprinkle the remaining coconut on top and sides of cake. Keep cake refrigerated.

Lemon Cheese Cake
Serves 16

Crust:

¾ cup butter, softened
1 egg
1¼ cups flour

⅓ cup plus 1 teaspoon sugar
Peel of 1 small lemon, grated
4 drops lemon extract

In a small bowl and at low speed of mixer, mix butter, egg, flour, ⅓ cup sugar, lemon peel and lemon extract. Shape the dough into a ball. Wrap in waxed paper and chill 1 hour. Preheat oven to 400°F. Press one-third of the dough into the bottom of a spring form pan. Sprinkle with remaining 1 teaspoon sugar. Bake for 8 minutes. Cool. Reset oven temperature to 475°F.

Filling:

5 (8-ounce) packages cream
    cheese, room temperature
¼ cup milk
1¾ cups sugar

3 tablespoons flour
4 eggs
Peel of 1 small lemon, grated

In a large bowl and at medium speed of mixer, beat cream cheese with milk until smooth and fluffy. Slowly beat in sugar. With mixer on low speed, beat in flour and remaining ingredients. Beat at medium speed for 5 minutes.

Press remaining dough around sides of pan to within 1 inch of the top. Do not bake. Pour cream cheese mixture into pan. Bake for 12 minutes. Turn oven to 300°F and bake 35 additional minutes. Leave cheese cake in oven at least 30 minutes to cool, then cool on a wire rack. Chill overnight if possible, remove from spring form pan and serve.

If cake appears to be too soft in the center after the 35 minutes at 300°F, extend the time 10 to 20 minutes.

Mississippi Mud Cakes   Yields 58 Squares

1 cup margarine
½ cup cocoa
4 eggs, well beaten
1½ cups flour, unsifted
2 cups sugar

Dash salt
1½ cups pecans, chopped
1 (6¼ ounce) bag miniature
    marshmallows

Melt margarine, add cocoa and well-beaten eggs. Add flour, sugar, salt and pecans. Mix well. Grease and flour a 9 x 13 x 2 inch pan; spread mixture into pan and bake at 350°F for 30 to 35 minutes. Cake is done when sides pull away from pan. Remove from oven and while still hot, pour over top 1 package miniature marshmallows. Cover all with the following mixture:

½ cup margarine, melted
1 pound confectioner's
    sugar

½ cup cocoa
½ cup milk
½ teaspoon vanilla

Combine all ingredients and mix well. Spread over cake. Allow to cool completely. Cut into 2 inch squares.

Black Forest Cherry Cake   Yields 2 9-inch Layers

2 squares chocolate,
    unsweetened
¼ cup water
⅔ cup butter, softened
1½ cups sugar

3 large eggs
1 teaspoon vanilla
2 cups cake flour, sifted
½ teaspoon baking soda
1 cup sour cream

Melt chocolate squares in water; set aside to cool. Grease 2 9-inch cake pans, dust with flour and line bottoms with wax paper. Cream softened butter and sugar in mixer. Add eggs, cooled chocolate and vanilla. Alternately add flour, sifted with baking soda, and sour cream. Pour batter into prepared cake pans and bake in a preheated 350°F oven for 18 to 20 minutes or until a cake tester inserted in center comes out clean.

Cool layers in pans on racks for 10 minutes, remove from pans and cool completely before frosting.

Black Forest Cherry Cake Icing   Serves 8 to 10

2 or 3 9-inch chocolate cake
  layers (recipe precedes)
3 cups heavy cream, chilled
½ cup confectioner's sugar
¼ cup kirsch
1 cup maraschino cherries,
  chopped or 1 cup dark
  sweet cherries, drained

Semi-sweet baking chocolate for
  curls, optional
6 to 12 maraschino cherries
  with stems, optional

Syrup
½ cup sugar
¾ cup cold water

⅓ to ½ cup Kirsch

Make syrup by combining sugar and cold water; bring to a boil and boil for 5 minutes. Remove and allow to cool to lukewarm. Stir in kirsch.

Transfer cake layers to waxed paper; pierce with a fork and drizzle syrup over them. Let stand overnight. Next day, whip cream until slightly thickened. Sift confectioner's sugar over cream and continue beating until stiff peaks form. Pour in kirsch and beat until liqueur is absorbed. Spread ½ inch layer of cream on cake layer and sprinkle with half the cherries. Repeat with second layer of cake. Coat cake sides and top with remaining cream. Make curls with carrot peeler and arrange 6 to 12 cherries with stems on top. Refrigerate.

Chocolate Rum Icing
(For Sponge Cake)   Yields Frosting for 6 Sponge Layers

1 pound sweet, unsalted
  butter (do not melt)
4 egg yolks
12 ounces chocolate chips,
  melted and cooled slightly

¾ cup dark rum
2 layers of sponge cake,
  each split into 3 layers

Cream first 4 ingredients. Spread on tops and sides of the six sponge cake layers, stacking them as you go. If desired, sprinkle the top and sides of the icing with finely chopped pecans.

Banana Black Cake
Serves 16

1 cup butter
2 cups sugar
4 eggs, beaten
2 cups blackberry jam
¾ cup strawberry preserves
2 bananas, mashed
2 teaspoons soda
5 tablespoons buttermilk
2 teaspoons cinnamon

1 teaspoon allspice
½ teaspoon cloves
1 teaspoon nutmeg
3 heaping cups flour
4 ounces dates, chopped
1 cup raisins
½ cup candied cherries, chopped
1 cup nuts, chopped

Cream sugar and butter; add beaten eggs, jam, preserves and bananas. Dissolve soda in buttermilk. Sift spices with flour. Add flour and buttermilk alternately into batter. Stir in dates, raisins, cherries and nuts. Bake in tube pan in 300°F oven for 3 hours. Set pan of water under cake and place a foil tent over cake. Remove tent during last 45 minutes of baking time.

Best if made several days in advance.

Moist Chocolate Cake
Serves 10

2 squares unsweetened chocolate
1 cup milk
1¾ cups sugar
4 eggs, separated
1 cup flour

1 teaspoon baking powder
2 cups heavy cream
4 tablespoons confectioner's sugar
1 teaspoon vanilla

In top of double boiler, melt chocolate in milk. Cook 5 minutes, stirring constantly. Remove from heat and allow to cool. Beat egg yolks, then add sugar. Stir until smooth. Add chocolate mixture and stir. Add to this, flour and baking powder. Beat egg whites until stiff. Fold into chocolate mixture. Pour into three 8-inch cake pans, greased and floured. Bake in preheated oven 350°F for 20 minutes.

When cake is cool, whip cream. Add confectioner's sugar and vanilla. Ice layers with whipped cream and refrigerate.

Cake is better made a day ahead.

Chocolate Fudge Cake

Serves 16 to 18

½ cup butter
2 cups sugar
4 squares bitter chocolate
2 eggs
2 cups flour

2 teaspoons baking powder
1½ cups milk
2 teaspoons vanilla
1 cup pecans, chopped

Cream butter and sugar. Melt chocolate and allow it to cool. Beat eggs slightly and add to butter and sugar; stir in cooled chocolate. Sift dry ingredients together and add to butter mixture alternately with milk. Blend in vanilla and chopped pecans.

Bake in 2 greased and floured 9-inch cake pans for 30 minutes at 350°F. After cake has cooled, frost with your favorite frosting.

Chocolate Charlotte Rousse Cake

Serves 12

4 squares unsweetened
  chocolate
¾ cup sugar
⅓ cup milk
6 eggs, separated
1½ cups unsalted butter or
  margarine

1½ cups confectioner's sugar
⅛ teaspoon salt
1½ teaspoons vanilla
3 dozen lady fingers, split
1 cup heavy cream, whipped
Unsweetened chocolate, shaved

In a large saucepan, melt chocolate squares over low heat. In a bowl, mix sugar, milk and egg yolks. Add sugar and egg mixture to melted chocolate. Cook until smooth and thickened, stirring constantly. Cool. In a large bowl, cream butter well, add ¾ cup confectioner's sugar and cream again. Add chocolate mixture to butter and sugar and beat well. Beat egg whites with salt until stiff. Gradually add the remaining ¾ cup confectioner's sugar. Fold into chocolate mixture then add vanilla.

Line a spring form pan with lady fingers. Alternate layers of lady fingers and chocolate mixture in one thirds. Chill overnight. Garnish with whipped cream and shaved chocolate.

Italian Cream Cake

Serves 16 to 18

½ cup butter
½ cup solid shortening
2 cups sugar
5 eggs, separated
2 cups flour

1 teaspoon soda
1 cup buttermilk
1 teaspoon vanilla
3½ ounces canned coconut
1 cup nuts, chopped

Cream butter, shortening and sugar until light and fluffy. Add egg yolks. Mix well. Sift flour and soda together. Add to creamed mixture alternately with buttermilk beginning and ending with dry ingredients. Add vanilla, coconut and nuts. Fold in stiffly beaten egg whites. Pour into three 9-inch greased and floured cake pans. Bake at 350°F for 30 to 35 minutes or until done.

Icing:

¼ cup butter, softened
8 ounces cream cheese,
   softened

1 pound box confectioner's
   sugar
1 teaspoon vanilla

Cream butter and cream cheese together. Add sugar and vanilla. Mix well. If too stiff, add milk, 1 teaspoon at a time until spreading consistency. If desired, garnish with pecans, tinted coconut or candied fruits.

Cake cuts better if prepared a day ahead.

Italian Meringue Cake

Serves 10 to 12

4 egg whites, at room
  temperature
¼ teaspoon cream of tartar
Pinch salt

1 cup sugar
¾ teaspoon almond extract
½ cup pecans, chopped

Filling:

8 ounces semi-sweet
  chocolate pieces
4 tablespoons water

3 cups heavy cream
½ cup sugar
1½ pints fresh strawberries

Beat egg whites until stiff after adding cream of tartar and pinch of salt. Gradually beat in sugar about 1 tablespoon at a time. Continue beating until meringue is stiff and glossy. Fold in almond extract and pecans.

Line baking sheets with wax paper and draw 3 circles, each 8 inches in diameter. Spread meringue evenly over the circles, about ¼ inch thick. Bake in 250°F preheated oven for approximately 50 to 60 minutes or until meringue is pale gold but still pliable. Remove from oven and carefully remove wax paper. Place on cake racks to dry.

Filling:

Melt semi-sweet chocolate pieces and water over hot water in double boiler. Whip cream until slightly stiff. Gradually add sugar and beat until very stiff.

Place meringue layer on cake plate and spread with a thin coating of melted chocolate. Spread with whipped cream about ½ to ¾ inch thick. Top with a layer of sliced strawberries. Repeat with second layer; add third layer and top with whipped cream and drizzle chocolate in any design over top.

Decorate edges of cake with whole strawberries or place whole strawberries over top. Refrigerate for 2 hours before serving.

Do not make on a humid day.

Orange Chiffon Cake

Serves 16

Separate eggs while cold and let reach room temperature
before starting cake.

2 cups flour, unsifted
1½ cups sugar
3 teaspoons baking powder
1 teaspoon salt
½ cup oil

7 egg yolks
2 tablespoons orange rind,
   grated
1 cup egg whites (7 or 8)
½ teaspoon cream of tartar

In large bowl, stir together first 4 ingredients. Make a well in
center and add in order, oil, egg yolks, ¾ cup cold water and
orange rind. Stir until smooth.

Put egg whites and cream of tartar in large mixing bowl. Beat
with mixer until very stiff peaks are formed. Gradually pour egg
yolk mixture over beaten whites, folding gently just until blended.
Pour into ungreased tube pan. Bake in 325°F oven 65 to 75 minutes, or until cake springs back when touched lightly with fingertip.

Invert pan on funnel and let hang until cake is completely cool.
Remove from pan by loosening cake around inner and outer edges
then hitting pan against counter top. Leave cake bottom side up.

Frost cake with the following:

Beige 7-Minute Frosting:
1 cup sugar
½ cup brown sugar, firmly
   packed
⅓ cup water

1 tablespoon light corn syrup
⅛ teaspoon salt
2 egg whites, unbeaten
1 teaspoon vanilla

Combine all ingredients except vanilla in top of double boiler
and mix well. Place over boiling water and immediately beat with
electric mixer 7 to 10 minutes or until mixture holds stiff peaks.
Remove from heat and immediately beat in vanilla.

Top icing with toasted coconut. Toast 3½ ounces canned coconut in moderate oven on baking sheet and watch carefully as it
burns quickly.

Orange Cheesecake

Serves 12 to 18

1 cup flour, sifted
¼ cup sugar
1 tablespoon orange rind,
   grated
½ cup butter

1 egg yolk
½ teaspoon vanilla
Orange sections, for garnish
Mint sprigs, for garnish

Combine flour, sugar and rind. Cut in butter until mixture resembles coarse meal. Add egg yolk and vanilla and blend well. Pat ⅓ of the dough onto the bottom of a 9-inch springform pan. Bake in a hot oven at 400°F for 5 minutes or until golden brown. Remove and cool. Pat remaining dough evenly around sides of pan to ½ inch from top.

Pour orange cheese filling (see below) into pan. Place aluminum foil under pan on oven rack and bake in hot oven at 400°F for 8 to 10 minutes until the crust browns slightly. Reduce heat to 225°F and bake 1 hour and 20 minutes longer. Remove and cool slowly, then refrigerate. Serve garnished with orange segments and mint sprigs.

Orange Cheese Filling:

5 (8 ounce) packages cream
   cheese, room temperature
1¾ cups sugar
3 tablespoons flour
1 tablespoon orange rind,
   grated
¼ teaspoon salt

¼ teaspoon vanilla
5 eggs
2 egg yolks
¼ cup frozen orange juice
   concentrate, thawed and
   undiluted

Combine cheese, sugar, flour, orange rind, salt and vanilla in a large bowl. Beat at low speed until smooth. Add eggs and egg yolks, one at a time, beating well after each addition. Stir in orange juice. Pour mixture into prepared pan.

Rich Sherry Cream Cake   Serves 14

5 egg yolks
¾ cup sherry
½ cup sugar
1 envelope unflavored
  gelatin
½ cup water

2 cups heavy cream
¼ cup sugar
1 large angel food cake
Whipping cream and toasted
  almonds for garnish

Beat egg yolks well. Cook egg yolks, sherry and ½ cup sugar in top of a double boiler until it is a thick custard. Soak gelatin in ½ cup water. Fold gelatin mixture into warm custard. Whip the cream with ¼ cup sugar. When custard mixture is cool, fold in whipped cream. Break angel food cake into chunks about the size of a small egg. Alternate cake and custard in tube pan. Congeal in refrigerator. Unmold. Ice with whipped cream and garnish with almonds.

Apple Caramel Squares   Serves 12

2½ cups sugar
3 eggs
1½ cups oil
3 cups flour
1 teaspoon salt

1 teaspoon soda
2½ cups apples, peeled and
  diced
1 cup pecans, chopped
1 teaspoon vanilla

Glaze:
½ cup butter
1 cup light brown sugar

¼ cup milk

Combine sugar, eggs and oil. Mix well and add flour, salt and soda. Fold in thinly sliced apples and pecans. Add vanilla. Pour into 13 x 9-inch pan and bake at 300°F for 1 hour.

For the glaze, combine the margarine, brown sugar and milk in small saucepan. Bring to boil, stirring constantly for 3 minutes. Pour over hot cake.

White Chocolate Cake   Serves 16 to 18

¼ pound white chocolate
½ cup boiling water
2 cups sugar
1 cup butter
4 eggs
1 teaspoon vanilla

2½ cups cake flour
1 teaspoon baking powder
1 cup buttermilk
1 cup angel flake coconut
1 cup nuts, chopped

Melt chocolate in boiling water and let cool. Cream butter and sugar. Beat in eggs one at a time. Add chocolate and vanilla. Add flour and baking powder mixture alternately with milk. Stir in coconut and nuts. Pour into three 9-inch greased and floured cake pans. Bake at 350°F for 20 to 25 minutes.

Icing:
½ cup water
¼ cup white corn syrup
3 cups sugar
4 egg whites

½ teaspoon cream of tartar
1 teaspoon vanilla
1 cup confectioner's sugar

Cook first 3 ingredients until syrup spins first thread stage. Beat egg whites with cream of tartar until very stiff. Pour hot syrup into egg whites. Add vanilla and confectioner's sugar; stir until well blended. Spread on layers and on top.

Seven Minute frosting will not hold up on this cake.

White Clouds   Yields Approximately 3 Dozen

2 egg whites
½ cup sugar
½ teaspoon vanilla

¼ teaspoon salt
½ cup pecans, chopped

Beat egg whites until stiff. Add remaining ingredients. Drop by spoonfuls onto cookie sheet covered with oiled parchment paper. Bake in a 275°F oven for 40 to 60 minutes.

Cola Cake
Serves 12

2 cups sugar	2 eggs
2 cups flour	½ cup buttermilk
1 cup cola	1 teaspoon soda
½ cup butter or margarine	1 teaspoon vanilla
½ cup solid shortening	1½ cups small marshmallows
3 heaping tablespoons cocoa	

Sift sugar and flour; set aside. Bring to a boil 1 cup cola, butter, shortening and cocoa. Remove from heat and add to flour mixture; add eggs, beat; add buttermilk, soda, vanilla and marshmallows. Mix well. Bake in greased 13 x 9 inch pan at 350°F for 40 minutes.

Cola Frosting:

½ cup butter	1 cup pecans, chopped
⅓ cup cola	1 pound box confectioner's
3 tablespoons cocoa	sugar
1 cup small marshmallows	

Bring to a boil the butter, cola and cocoa. Remove from heat, add marshmallows, pecans and confectioner's sugar. Mix well and spread on warm cake. If frosting is too thick, add more cola.

Whiskey Ice Box Cake
Serves 10

2 envelopes unflavored gelatin	8 tablespoons bourbon
½ cup cold water	1 cup sugar
½ cup boiling water	1 teaspoon lemon juice
6 large eggs, separated	2 cups heavy cream
	3 packages lady fingers, split

Soak gelatin in cold water, add boiling water and dissolve; set aside. In a large bowl, beat egg yolks until thick, add bourbon very slowly, beating. Beat in sugar, lemon juice and cool gelatin. Chill about 15 to 20 minutes. Whip cream and fold into the gelatin mixture. Beat egg whites and fold into whipped cream and gelatin mixture. Line a spring form pan, bottom and sides, with lady fingers. Pour mixture in slowly. When half full, add a layer of lady fingers and finish filling pan with custard mixture. Chill overnight.

Supreme Cheese Cake

Serves 12 to 14

2 cups graham cracker
    crumbs
1 teaspoon cinnamon
¼ cup sugar
½ cup butter, melted
36 ounces cream cheese,
    softened

1 tablespoon lemon juice
1¼ cups sugar
4 eggs
2 cups sour cream
4 tablespoons sugar
1 teaspoon vanilla

Grease a 10-inch spring form pan with margarine. Mix the graham cracker crumbs, cinnamon, ¼ cup sugar and melted butter well. Press into the sides and bottom of spring form pan. Set aside.

Using electric mixer, blend softened cream cheese with lemon juice. Add 1¼ cups sugar and eggs, one at a time, beating well after each addition. Pour into spring form pan and bake in a preheated 375°F oven for 25 minutes. Remove cake and set oven temperature to 450°F.

While cake is baking, blend the remaining ingredients and pour over baked cream cheese mixture after it is removed from the oven. Immediately return to oven and continue baking for approximately 12 to 15 minutes. Remove from oven; cool. Remove spring form and refrigerate for 12 hours.

Holiday Rum Balls

Yields 4½ Dozen

3½ cups vanilla wafer
    crumbs
1½ cups confectioner's
    sugar, divided

1 cup pecans, finely chopped
¼ cup unsweetened cocoa
⅓ cup light or dark rum
⅓ cup light corn syrup

Mix crumbs with 1 cup of confectioner's sugar, pecans and cocoa. Stir in rum and corn syrup. Shape into 1-inch balls, roll in remaining sugar. Store in tightly covered container.

Cheesecake Bars

Yields 16 Bars

5 tablespoons butter
⅓ cup light brown sugar
1 cup flour, sifted
¼ cup pecans or walnuts,
   chopped
½ cup sugar

8 ounces cream cheese,
   softened
1 egg
2 tablespoons milk
1 tablespoon lemon juice, fresh
½ teaspoon vanilla

Preheat oven to 350°F.

In mixing bowl, cream butter and brown sugar. Add flour and nuts; mix well. Set aside 1 cup of this mixture for topping. Press remainder of mixture in bottom of 8 x 8 inch pan. Bake 12 to 15 minutes.

Blend sugar and cream cheese until smooth. Add egg, milk, lemon juice and vanilla. Beat well with electric mixer. Spread over bottom crust. Sprinkle with reserved cup of topping and return to oven and bake 25 minutes longer. Allow to cool, then chill.

Kentucky Colonels

Yields 4 Dozen

¾ cup pecans, finely
   chopped
½ cup Kentucky bourbon
   (do not use blended
   whiskey)
½ cup butter

1 pound confectioner's sugar
8 ounces unsweetened
   chocolate
1 tablespoon paraffin,
   approximately

Soak pecans in ¼ cup of the bourbon for 4 hours. Cream butter and sugar and add remaining bourbon. Combine well with the soaked pecans. Put in refrigerator and allow to become cold enough to roll into small balls the size of a quarter.

Meanwhile, melt chocolate and paraffin in top of double boiler over hot, but not boiling water. Once candy is formed into balls, put onto waxed paper-lined cookie sheet and return to refrigerator to allow balls to become cold and firm. Using a candy dipper or toothpick, dip into melted chocolate. Chill and when set, store in tin cans in refrigerator. Several weeks aging improves the flavor.

Brandy Snaps

Yields 12 to 16

5 tablespoons sugar
2 tablespoons butter
2 tablespoons dark corn
  syrup

¼ cup flour
½ to ¾ teaspoon ground
  ginger

Filling:
2 teaspoons sugar
1½ to 2 tablespoons brandy

1 cup heavy cream, whipped
  and sweetened

Cream sugar, butter and syrup; stir in sifted flour and ginger. Make into 12 to 16 balls and place well apart on greased baking sheets. These cookies spread so do not put more than 5 or 6 on a baking sheet. Bake in a 300°F oven until a rich brown color, about 10 to 15 minutes. Allow to cool slightly; remove from sheet with a spatula and while soft, roll around the oiled handle of a wooden spoon. Remove when set.

Fill snaps with sweetened and flavored whipped cream just before serving.

Snaps cool very quickly; if last 2 or 3 on cookie sheet get too brittle to roll, return to oven for a minute to re-soften.

Nutty Fingers

Yields 4 Dozen

½ cup plus 2 tablespoons
  butter
4 tablespoons confectioner's
  sugar, sifted

1 tablespoon ice water
1 tablespoon vanilla
2 cups flour, sifted
1 cup pecans, finely chopped

Cream butter and sifted sugar; add water. Add vanilla, flour and nuts, mixing well. Roll into finger shapes. Place on greased cookie sheet and bake in 350°F oven for 15 to 20 minutes.

When cool, roll in confectioner's sugar.

Chocolate Crinkles
Yields 4 Dozen

½ cup butter or margarine
1⅔ cups sugar
2 teaspoons vanilla
2 eggs
2 1-ounce squares
  unsweetened chocolate,
  melted

2 cups flour
2 teaspoons baking powder
½ teaspoon salt
⅓ cup milk
½ cup nuts, chopped
Confectioner's sugar, sifted

Cream butter, sugar and vanilla; beat in eggs, then chocolate. Sift together dry ingredients; blend in alternately with milk. Add nuts. Chill for 3 hours.

Form 1-inch balls, place on cookie sheet 2 to 3 inches apart. Bake at 350°F for 15 minutes. Dust with confectioner's sugar.

Choco Chewey Scotch Bars
Yields Approximately 48 Bars

12 ounces chocolate chips
15 ounces canned,
  sweetened condensed
  milk
2 tablespoons butter or
  margarine
1 cup butter or margarine,
  melted

1 pound box dark brown sugar,
  firmly packed
2 eggs
2 cups flour
1 teaspoon salt
1 teaspoon vanilla
1 cup pecans, chopped
½ cup flaked coconut

In top of double boiler, melt chocolate pieces with milk and 2 tablespoons butter. Blend until smooth. Set aside.

In large bowl, combine melted butter, brown sugar and eggs. Add flour and salt and blend well. Stir in vanilla, pecans and coconut; mix well. Spread two-thirds of dough in greased jelly-roll pan. Spread chocolate mixture over dough. Dot top of chocolate mixture with remaining brown sugar dough. Swirl slightly with top of knife.

Bake at 350°F for 30 to 35 minutes or until dough is golden brown. Cool and cut into bars.

Crème de Menthe Brownies Yields Approximately 5 Dozen

4 ounces unsweetened baking chocolate	2 cups sugar
	½ teaspoon salt
1 cup margarine	1 teaspoon vanilla
4 eggs	1 cup flour, sifted

In double boiler, melt chocolate and margarine over water; cool slightly. In mixing bowl, beat eggs until light and fluffy. Beat in sugar gradually. Add remaining ingredients including chocolate mixture. Beat 1 minute. Pour into greased 13 x 9-inch pan. Bake at 350°F for 25 minutes. Do not overbake. Cool. Base will be fudge.

Filling:

½ cup margarine	¼ cup whipping cream
4 cups confectioner's sugar, sifted	¼ cup crème de menthe

Beat together margarine and sugar while gradually adding milk and crème de menthe. Mixture will be light and fluffy. Spread over base and chill 1½ hours.

Topping:

6 ounces chocolate chips	3 tablespoons water
4 tablespoons margarine	

Melt chocolate chips and margarine over water. Mix and spread over filling. Chill. Store in refrigerator.

Freezes well.

Grandpa's Oatmeal Cookies   Yields 4 Dozen

1 cup light brown sugar,
  packed
½ cup sugar
¾ cup margarine
1 egg
¼ cup evaporated milk

1 teaspoon vanilla
1 cup flour
1 teaspoon salt
½ teaspoon soda
3 cups oats, uncooked
½ cup pecans, chopped

Preheat oven to 350°F. Cream sugars and margarine. Add egg, evaporated milk and vanilla. Beat until creamy. Sift flour, salt and soda and add to creamed mixture. Stir in oats and pecans.

Drop by teaspoonfuls onto greased cookie sheet. Bake for 10 to 12 minutes.

Irish Lace Cookies   Yields Approximately 9 Dozen

½ cup sweet butter
1 cup sugar
1 egg
1 teaspoon vanilla

2 tablespoons flour
⅓ teaspoon salt
1 cup quick cooking oatmeal

Cream butter and sugar. Add egg and vanilla; mix well. Add flour, salt and oatmeal. Line cookie sheet with aluminum foil and drop dough by ½ teaspoonfuls onto foil. Bake 5 to 8 minutes in 350°F oven or until lightly browned. Let cool before removing from foil.

Butter can be melted and put in food processor with remaining ingredients.

Scotch Shortbread
Yields 16 Wedges

2 cups flour   ½ cup butter (no substitute)
¼ cup sugar

Put flour and sugar in a mound on a pastry board. Gradually knead the sugared flour into butter with hands until a firm dough is formed. Roll into a round shape about 1 inch thick; put into a shortbread mold or bake in a 9-inch pie pan. Decorate edges by marking with a fork. Bake at 325°F for about 1 hour or until pale fawn in color. Dredge with sugar when done. Cut into small wedges while still warm.

French Butter Cookies
Yields 2½ Dozen

1 cup flour, sifted   ½ cup butter (no substitute),
½ cup sugar   softened, or if done in food
                                 processor, cut into 6 slices

Combine the above thoroughly, then add:
1 egg yolk   1 teaspoon vanilla or 1
                                 tablespoon rum or brandy

Mix together until dough can be shaped into a ball. Roll into log 2 inches in diameter. Chill 2 hours. Cut in half lengthwise. Slice into ⅛ inch slices and bake at 350°F on ungreased baking sheet ¾ inch apart for 8 minutes.

Can be mixed in food processor using steel blade.

CHILDREN
AT PLAY

Children at Play

Savannah can be a veritable paradise for children. At the riverfront there are ships to watch as they glide into port from foreign lands. On the water there are fiddler crabs to catch, and downtown there are shady squares to play in.

Sarah Josephine Hathaway described those squares in the early 1800's when she wrote, "These manifold grassy parks, or lungs of the city as I have heard them called, are very picturesque and inviting, and highly suggestive of health and comfort. They are alive and musical with the glee of the groups of happy children and the loud laughter and merry shouts of their nurses, who swarm in them every day. One would think life was all sunshine."

Annie Schley Haines Carpenter's reminiscences of her childhood in Savannah during the latter part of the century picture juvenile newswriters, budding actresses and gamesmen of all sorts.

"Time never seemed to hang heavy on our hands," observed Carpenter, recalling pulling candy, playing store, picking wildflowers in Laurel Grove Cemetery and the challenge of a banana-eating contest in the earthen-floored basement. (Her friend Frieda Rauers ate five bananas non-stop.)

At the least her group could undertake an expedition to what is now Oglethorpe Avenue to watch the fire department perform its 4 p.m. drill.

Once a trio of young entrepreneurs started its own newspaper after befriending the neighborhood gossip and engaging a grandmother to write the news longhand on foolscap. The subscription price, five pins, was soon changed to five pennies, and one editorialist warned, "All who do not pay their subscription promptly will be abashed and slandered."

On another occasion the threesome's older sisters staged a play for the benefit of Christ Church, erecting a platform with a curtain in the parlor of one of the homes. Chairs were brought from all over the house and, charging admission of ten cents, the theatrical company collected ten dollars which they sent off to the Rev. Robert White with a letter.

On rainy days there were indoor pastimes like jackstraws; books, authors and quotations, card games, Parcheesi and tiddly-winks. On nice days one could use a carbon stick discarded from a street light to draw off the squares for hopscotch or take wickets, balls and mallets to Orleans Square for a game of croquet.

Once while skating on the sidewalks at St. John's Episcopal Church, a group of youngsters was invited up to the bell tower to try ringing the bells.

A more rowdy amusement than skating or croquet, however, was hunter-hunt-the-hare-o. It involved two teams, each with a captain who laid the strategy through which the players pursued the bearer of a talisman. According to Carpenter, the game was played in Chippewa Square, but the limits encompassed the city, with daring young players heard to chant:

> East Broad to West Broad
> Anderson to Bay,
> If you don't like the limits
> You don't have to play.

Peach Cobbler
Serves 8

2 cups peaches, sliced
½ cup sugar
½ cup margarine
¾ cup flour

2 teaspoons baking powder
1 cup sugar
¼ teaspoon salt
¾ cup milk

Mix peaches with ½ cup sugar and set aside. Preheat oven to 350°F. Put margarine in bottom of deep baking dish and set in oven to melt.

Make a batter of remaining ingredients and pour over melted butter—*do not stir*. Put peaches on top of batter; again, *do not stir*. Bake until crust is light brown and puffy, approximately 35 to 45 minutes.

Blueberries may be used instead of peaches, if desired. If fresh fruit is not available, use only frozen.

Fresh Peach Crisp
Serves 6

1 cup flour
½ cup sugar
½ cup light brown sugar,
  firmly packed
¼ teaspoon salt
½ teaspoon ground
  cinnamon

½ cup margarine
4 cups fresh peaches, sliced
1 tablespoon lemon juice
2 tablespoons water

Combine flour, sugar, salt and cinnamon; cut in margarine with 2 knives or pastry blender until mixture resembles coarse corn meal.

Combine peaches, lemon juice and water; spoon into a greased 9 x 9 x 1¾-inch baking dish. Sprinkle flour mixture over peaches. Bake covered at 350°F for 15 minutes. Remove cover and bake 35 to 45 minutes longer.

Fresh Peach Cream Pie   Serves 8

⅓ cup sugar (may need more)
1 cup sour cream
2 eggs, beaten

3 cups fresh peaches, sliced and peeled
1 9-inch graham cracker crust

Mix sugar and sour cream. Blend into the beaten eggs. Add 2 cups peaches. Line a 9-inch pie plate with graham cracker crust and pour in the cream-peach mixture. Place remaining peaches on top. Bake at 350°F for 1 hour.

Caramel Banana Pie   Serves 8

14 ounces canned sweetened condensed milk
2 or 3 bananas
1 9-inch graham cracker crust

1 cup heavy cream
¼ cup confectioner's sugar
1 or 2 (1⅛ ounce each) English toffee candy bars, crumbled

Pour condensed milk into an 8-inch glass pie plate. Cover with foil. Pour ¼ inch hot water into a shallow 2-quart casserole and place covered pie plate into the casserole. Bake at 425°F for 1 hour and 20 minutes, or until the condensed milk is thick and caramel colored. (Add hot water to casserole as needed.) Remove foil when done and set aside.

Cut bananas crosswise into ⅛ inch slices and place in the bottom of graham cracker crust. Spread caramelized milk over banana layer. Cool for at least 30 minutes. Combine heavy cream and confectioner's sugar in a small mixing bowl; whip until stiff. Spread over caramel layer. Sprinkle with crumbled candy. Chill at least 3 hours or overnight before serving.

Fresh Blueberry Pie   Serves 6

1½ cups graham cracker crumbs
¼ cup confectioner's sugar
6 tablespoons butter, melted

1 pint fresh blueberries
1 (8 ounce) jar red currant jelly
1 cup sour cream

Combine first three ingredients to make crust. Pat firmly on bottom and around sides of 8-inch pie pan. Bake in 350°F oven about 15 minutes or until light brown. Cool on wire rack.

Rinse and drain blueberries well. Heat jelly over low heat, stirring frequently until melted. Pour jelly over berries and pour into pie shell. Let cool. Cover with a generous layer of sour cream and chill for several hours.

Sour Cream Apple Pie   Serves 8

2 cups apples, sliced (Rome variety)
¾ cup sugar
4 tablespoons flour
1 egg, beaten

1 cup sour cream
½ teaspoon vanilla
1/8 teaspoon salt
1 9-inch pie shell

Arrange sliced apples into unbaked pie shell. Mix the remaining 6 ingredients together and pour over the apples. Bake at 350°F for 1 hour.

Topping:
⅓ cup sugar
⅓ cup flour

¼ cup butter
1 teaspoon cinnamon

Blend the above ingredients together and crumble this topping over the top of the baked pie. Bake for 15 minutes longer. Serve warm.

Harvest Table Apple Pie
Serves 8

1 9-inch double crust pastry	¼ teaspoon salt
6 to 8 medium cooking apples	3 tablespoons sugar
	3 tablespoons butter
1 tablespoon cornstarch	⅓ cup dark corn syrup
1 teaspoon cinnamon	

Prepare pastry and roll out half for bottom crust. Peel and slice apples; arrange in crust (apples will be piled high). Combine cornstarch, cinnamon, salt, sugar, butter and syrup. Pour over apples. Roll out top crust, cut slits and place over apples (can make lattice crust). Place on cookie sheet and bake at 425°F for 45 minutes or until crust is brown and apples are tender. Spread with the following topping:

¼ cup brown sugar	2 tablespoons butter
2 tablespoons flour	¼ cup nuts, chopped
3 tablespoons dark corn syrup	

Mix all ingredients together and spread on pie. Return pie to oven for 10 minutes or until the topping is bubbly.

Lemon Chess Pie
Serves 8

2 cups sugar	¼ cup milk
1 tablespoon flour	¼ cup lemon juice
1 tablespoon corn meal	1 lemon rind, grated
4 eggs, unbeaten	1 9-inch pie shell, unbaked
¼ cup margarine, melted	

Toss sugar, flour and corn meal with a fork. Combine remaining ingredients, mixing well. Pour into unbaked shell and bake at 450°F for 10 minutes, reduce heat to 350°F and bake for 25 additional minutes.

Lemon Angel Pie

Serves 8

4 eggs, separated
1½ cups sugar
¼ teaspoon cream of tartar
3 tablespoons lemon juice

1 tablespoon lemon rind, grated
¼ teaspoon salt
2 cups heavy cream

Crust:

Beat the egg whites until foamy. Gradually add one cup of sugar and the cream of tartar. Beat until stiff but not dry. Spread on bottom and sides of a buttered 9-inch pie pan. Bake at 300°F for 1 hour. Cool.

Filling:

Beat egg yolks slightly. Stir in the remaining ½ cup sugar, lemon juice, lemon rind and salt. Cook over hot water until thickened. Cool. Whip the cream until stiff. Fold half the whipped cream into lemon mixture and pour mixture into meringue shell. Top with remaining whipped cream. Chill for 24 hours.

Rhubarb Crisp

Serves 6

4 cups rhubarb, cut in 1 inch strips
¾ cup sugar
2 tablespoons quick-cooking tapioca

½ teaspoon salt
11 ounces canned mandarin oranges, drained

Topping:
1 cup oats
⅓ cup brown sugar

¼ cup flour
¼ cup margarine

Combine all base ingredients except oranges and let stand 30 minutes. Add oranges and put in 8-inch square ungreased pan. Combine oats, brown sugar and flour and sprinkle over rhubarb mixture. Dot with butter. Bake 45 minutes at 350°F.

Pumpkin Cream Cheese Pie
Serves 8

12 ounces cream cheese,
  softened
¾ cup sugar
1½ tablespoons flour
¾ teaspoon lemon peel,
  grated
¾ teaspoon orange peel,
  grated

¼ teaspoon vanilla
2 eggs
2 egg yolks
1 cup pumpkin, cooked and
  pureed
1 9-inch graham cracker crust
Crystalized ginger for garnish
  (optional)

Topping:
1½ cups sour cream
2 tablespoons sugar

½ teaspoon vanilla

Combine cheese, sugar, flour, peels, vanilla, eggs, egg yolks and pumpkin. Beat at medium speed until smooth. Pour into crust. Bake at 350°F for 35 to 40 minutes, or until center of pie is firm when gently shaken.

Combine sour cream with sugar and vanilla. Mix well. Spread top of pie evenly with topping, bake 10 minutes longer. Let pie cool completely on wire rack, about 1 hour. Refrigerate at least 4 hours before serving. Garnish with crystalized ginger, if desired.

Pumpkin Pecan Pie
Serves 8

1 pie crust, 9-inch deep dish
3 eggs, beaten
1 cup pumpkin
1 cup sugar
½ cup dark corn syrup

1 teaspoon vanilla
½ teaspoon cinnamon
¼ teaspoon salt
1 cup pecans, chopped

Mix all ingredients thoroughly and pour into unbaked pie crust. Preheat oven to 350°F and bake about 40 minutes.

Pumpkin Chiffon Pie

Yields 2 9-inch Pies

1 envelope unflavored
gelatin
¾ cup dark brown sugar,
firmly packed
½ teaspoon salt
½ teaspoon nutmeg
½ teaspoon cloves
1 teaspoon cinnamon

½ cup milk
¼ cup water
3 eggs, separated
2 cups pumpkin, cooked and
well-blended
¼ cup sugar
2 9-inch pie shells, baked
Whipped cream, for garnish

In a large sauce saucepan, mix first six ingredients. Stir in milk, water, egg yolks and pumpkin and mix well. Cook over medium heat, stirring constantly until gelatin is dissolved and mixture heated thoroughly; about 10 minutes. Remove from heat. Chill, stirring occasionally, until mixture mounds slightly when dropped from a spoon. Beat egg whites until stiff. Gradually beat in sugar. Fold gelatin mixture into stiffly beaten egg whites. Turn into pie shells and chill until firm. Top with whipped cream.

Nut Meringue Pie

Serves 6 to 8

3 egg whites
1 teaspoon vanilla
1 cup sugar
¾ cup saltine crumbs
¾ cup nuts, chopped

1 teaspoon baking powder
1 cup heavy cream
1 tablespoon confectioner's
sugar

Preheat oven to 350°F. Beat the egg whites and vanilla until stiff; slowly add 1 cup sugar. Mix together cracker crumbs, nuts and baking powder. Fold crumb mixture into egg white mixture. Spread mixture into greased 9-inch pie pan and heat 25 minutes. Remove and let cool completely.

Whip heavy cream and add confectioner's sugar. Spread on top of cooled meringue. Cover and refrigerate several hours.

This should not be made on a humid day.

Strawberry Meringue Tarts

Yields
Approximately 40

3 egg whites, at room
  temperature
½ teaspoon almond extract
½ teaspoon cream of tartar
Dash salt

1 cup confectioner's sugar,
  sifted
1 cup sour cream
Whole strawberries (about 40)

Combine egg whites, almond extract, cream of tartar and salt; beat until frothy. Add sugar, 1 tablespoon at a time, beating until glossy and stiff peaks form. Drop meringue by tablespoonfuls onto cookie sheet covered with heavy brown paper. Using back of small spoon, make small depression in top of each meringue. Bake 45 minutes at 250°F. Turn oven off, leave in oven with door closed for 1 hour. Cool away from drafts. Place 1 teaspoon sour cream in each meringue, top each with a strawberry.

These should not be made on a humid day.

Brandy Coffee Pie

Serves 8

1½ cups macaroon wafer
  crumbs
¼ cup butter, softened
1 teaspoon almond extract
2 egg whites
¼ cup sugar

2 cups heavy cream, whipped
1 teaspoon instant coffee
1 teaspoon boiling water
3 to 4 tablespoons brandy, or to
  taste
Toasted almonds, ground fine

Mix crumbs with butter. Use just enough butter to hold crumbs together. Add almond extract. Press into 9-inch pie plate. Chill until firm.

Beat egg whites until stiff. Add sugar and incorporate well. Fold egg whites into whipped cream. Dissolve coffee in boiling water and let cool. Add to cream mixture with brandy. Turn into crumb shell. Cover top with ground almonds. Freeze and serve frozen.

Shoo-Fly Pie

Serves 8

Filling:

½ teaspoon soda, dissolved
   in ¾ cup boiling water

½ cup molasses
1 egg yolk, beaten well

Combine ingredients and mix well. Set aside.

Crumbs:

¾ cup flour
½ teaspoon cinnamon
⅛ teaspoon each: nutmeg,
   ginger, cloves
½ cup brown sugar

½ teaspoon salt
2 tablespoons shortening
1 9-inch pie shell, unbaked
Whipped cream, to garnish

Combine dry ingredients with shortening, using hands to work into crumbs.

Line a 9-inch pie plate with pastry. Pour in filling and top with crumbs.

Bake in a hot oven at 400°F until crust starts to brown (about 10 minutes). Reduce heat to 325°F and bake until firm, about 10 to 15 minutes. Garnish with whipped cream to serve.

Hoosier Pie

Serves 6 to 8

¼ cup butter
1 cup sugar
3 eggs, beaten
¾ cup light corn syrup
1 teaspoon vanilla
¼ teaspoon salt

½ cup chocolate chips
½ cup pecans, chopped
2 tablespoons bourbon
1 10-inch pie shell, unbaked
1 cup heavy cream, whipped

Preheat oven to 375°F. Cream butter; beat in sugar slowly. Add eggs, corn syrup, vanilla and salt. Blend well. Stir in chocolate chips, pecans and bourbon. Pour filling into pie shell and bake 40-45 minutes. Serve topped with whipped cream.

Fudge Pie

Serves 8

2 squares bitter chocolate
½ cup margarine or butter
¼ cup flour, sifted

1 cup sugar
2 eggs

Melt chocolate and butter in double boiler. Mix flour and sugar. Beat eggs and combine with flour and sugar. Add chocolate and butter. Put in well-greased 9-inch pie pan and bake at 350°F for 30 to 45 minutes.

Serve with topping of whipped cream or vanilla ice cream. Better when served hot.

Sherry Pie

Serves 8

4 eggs, separated
1 cup sugar
¾ cup sherry
Pinch salt
1 envelope gelatin, unflavored

¼ cup cold water
1 (3 ounce) package unfilled lady fingers
1 cup heavy cream
Unsweetened chocolate, grated

Separate eggs. Beat egg yolks with ½ cup sugar in top of double boiler. Add sherry and pinch of salt. Stir constantly until thick and custard-like. Add gelatin that has been dissolved in ¼ cup cold water. Beat egg whites until stiff with remaining ½ cup sugar. Fold into sherry mixture. Butter and line a pie plate with lady fingers and pour sherry mixture on top. Whip cream and spread on top. Sprinkle with grated chocolate. Place in refrigerator for several hours before serving.

This can also be put into a buttered cut-glass bowl and layered alternately with lady fingers and sherry mixture, topping all with whipped cream and chocolate.

Calypso Pie   Serves 8

Crust:
1½ cups chocolate wafer   4 tablespoons butter, melted
  crumbs

Sauce:
4½ ounces bitter chocolate   Pinch salt
  squares   1½ teaspoons vanilla
6 tablespoons butter   ¾ cup slivered almonds,
1 cup sugar   toasted
1 cup evaporated milk

Filling:
½ gallon coffee ice cream,   ¼ cup Kahlua
  softened

Topping:
½ pint heavy cream,   8 maraschino cherries
  whipped

Crust: Mix cookie crumbs and butter and press into a greased 9-inch pie plate. Refrigerate.

Sauce: Put chocolate, butter, sugar, milk and salt in the top of a double boiler. Cook, stirring continuously for 4 minutes, or until the sauce thickens a little. Add vanilla and chill.

Filling: Put ice cream mixture into pie shell and drizzle with Kahlua. Spread sauce over ice cream mixture and sprinkle with almonds. Put into freezer.

To serve, top each slice with whipped cream and garnish with cherries.

Rum Pecan Pie

Serves 8

½ cup butter or margarine,
  softened
½ cup sugar
¾ cup light corn syrup
¼ cup maple flavored syrup

3 eggs, lightly beaten
3 tablespoons light rum
¾ cup pecans, coarsely,
  chopped
Brandied Butter Pastry
  (recipe below)
¾ cup pecan halves, for topping

Cream butter and sugar until light and fluffy. Add corn syrup, maple syrup, eggs and rum; beat well. Stir in chopped pecans.

Line a 9-inch pie pan with Brandied Butter Pastry.

Pour filling into pastry and top with pecan halves. Bake at 350°F for 55 minutes.

Brandied Butter Pastry:
1 cup flour
¼ teaspoon salt

6 tablespoons cold butter
3 tablespoons cold brandy

Combine flour and salt; cut in butter until mixture resembles coarse meal. Sprinkle brandy over mixture and stir until particles cling together when pressed gently. Shape dough into a ball and chill 20 minutes before rolling out.

For a baked crust, prick pastry with a fork; bake at 425°F for 12 minutes or until golden.

Luscious Ice Cream Pie

Serves 8

Crust:

½ cup butter, melted
7 ounces flaked coconut

2 tablespoons flour
½ cup pecans, chopped

Combine all of the above ingredients; mix well and press on bottom and sides of a 10-inch pie pan. Bake at 375°F for 10 to 12 minutes, or until lightly browned; cool.

Filling:

½ gallon chocolate ice
  cream softened
1 cup heavy cream

¼ cup confectioner's sugar
Sweet chocolate curls
½ to ⅔ cup Amaretto liqueur

Spoon softened ice cream into pie shell and freeze until firm. Beat heavy cream until foamy; gradually add confectioner's sugar, beating until soft peaks form. Spread over pie; top with chocolate curls. Pour 1 tablespoon Amaretto over each serving.

Coffee ice cream may be substituted for chocolate ice cream and Kahlua liqueur may be substituted for the Amaretto.

Cream Pie Marilyn

Serves 8

1 cup graham crackers,
  finely crushed
6 tablespoons butter
1 package unflavored
  gelatin
¼ cup cold water

3 egg yolks
½ cup sugar
¼ teaspoon salt
1 cup heavy cream, whipped
1½ tablespoons instant coffee
¼ cup Irish whiskey

Combine graham cracker crumbs with butter which has been melted. Press on the bottom and sides of a 9-inch pie plate and bake at 375°F for 8 minutes. Cool. In a small bowl, sprinkle gelatin over water to soften. Let stand 10 minutes. Stand the bowl in a pan of simmering water and stir gelatin until completely dissolved. Let gelatin cool until it is very syrupy.

In another bowl, beat egg yolks with sugar and salt until lemon colored and thick. Stir in the gelatin. Fold in 1 cup heavy cream, whipped, and coffee dissolved in Irish whiskey. Chill mixture until it is slightly thickened and pour into pie shell. Chill 4 hours. Garnish with lightly sweetened whipped cream, if desired.

Chocolate Meringue Pie

Serves 6 to 8

Shell:

3 egg whites
⅛ teaspoon cream of tartar
Pinch salt
¾ cup confectioner's sugar,
    sifted

¾ cup pecans, chopped
1 teaspoon vanilla

Beat egg whites until foamy and add cream of tartar and salt. Continue beating until they stand in soft peaks. Gradually add sugar, one tablespoon at a time beating after each addition. Continue beating until meringue is very stiff. Fold in nuts and vanilla. Pour meringue into buttered 9-inch pie plate and build up sides with a spoon ½ inch above edge of plate. Bake at 300°F for 50-55 minutes. Cool.

Filling:

4 ounces sweet chocolate
3 tablespoons black coffee

1 teaspoon vanilla extract
1 cup heavy cream, whipped

Combine chocolate and coffee in saucepan over low heat. Stir until smooth. Cool mixture and stir in vanilla extract. Fold whipped cream into chocolate and turn into meringue shell. Chill 2 hours.

Chocolate Chess Pie

Serves 8

1 cup sugar
2 eggs
½ cup margarine
1 square unsweetened
    chocolate

Dash salt
1 teaspoon vanilla
1 9-inch pie crust, unbaked

Combine sugar and eggs; beat well. Melt margarine and chocolate in saucepan. Add chocolate to sugar and eggs. Add salt and vanilla, mixing well. Pour into 9-inch pie crust and bake at 325°F for 30 to 35 minutes.

Serve warm topped with whipped cream.

Cold Strawberry Soufflé
Serves 4

1 pint fresh strawberries
1 envelope unflavored
  gelatin
½ cup sugar
¼ cup water

¾ teaspoon lemon juice
1 tablespoon kirsch
2 egg whites
½ cup heavy cream

Prepare collar for soufflé dish by cutting 4-inch strip of waxed, brown paper or foil long enough to fit around ½-quart dish. Brush inside with oil. Fasten strip around dish with tape, enough to rise 2 inches above dish and set aside. Four individual ramekins can be used.

Hull strawberries, leaving 8 aside for garnish, and puree remainder in blender or food processor. Mix gelatin with half the sugar in saucepan, add water and cook over low heat, stirring until gelatin dissolves. Stir this mixture into strawberries, add lemon juice and kirsch. Refrigerate, stirring occasionally, until mixture thickens slightly (about ½ hour).

Beat egg whites until frothy, gradually beat in remaining sugar and beat until stiff. Fold egg whites into strawberry mixture; whip cream until stiff and fold into mixture. Gently pour into soufflé dish and refrigerate 4 hours. Garnish with whole strawberries.

Lemon Soufflé
Serves 6

8 eggs, separated
1 cup sugar
⅓ cup flour
1 cup milk

2 tablespoons butter, melted
Juice and grated rind of 1
  lemon
½ teaspoon cream of tartar

In small mixer bowl, beat egg yolks, sugar and flour. To this mixture add milk, butter, lemon juice and rind; beat just until thoroughly mixed. Wash beaters. In large mixer bowl, beat egg whites and cream of tartar until stiff. Fold lemon mixture into egg whites. Pour into a buttered 3-quart casserole. Bake at 325 °F in pan of hot water for 30 to 40 minutes.

Cold Lemon Soufflé

Serves 8 to 10

1 envelope unflavored
  gelatin
¼ cup cold water
6 egg yolks
1 cup sugar

1½ tablespoons lemon rind,
  grated
¾ cup lemon juice
6 egg whites
1½ cups heavy cream

Put waxed paper collar around 1-quart soufflé dish. Mix gelatin in water and set aside. Add sugar to egg yolks and beat. Add lemon rind and juice to egg yolk mixture. Cook over low heat until thickened. Remove from heat and stir in gelatin mixture. Cool 20 minutes. Beat egg whites and fold into egg yolk mixture. Beat cream and fold into egg mixture. Refrigerate overnight.

Serve with whipped cream.

Nutmeg Mousse

Serves 8 to 10

6 eggs
1½ cups sugar
2 envelopes gelatin
½ cup cold water
1 tablespoon nutmeg,
  freshly grated

1 teaspoon vanilla
2 cups heavy cream
Lady fingers

Beat eggs until frothy; add sugar and beat until creamy. Sprinkle gelatin over water in a pan and put the pan over low heat until gelatin is dissolved. Stir gelatin mixture into egg/sugar mixture and add nutmeg and vanilla. Beat cream until it holds definite shape and fold into egg mixture. Line a 2½-quart mold or bowl with split lady fingers and pour in the mousse. Refrigerate until firm, about 2 hours.

Mocha Mousse
With Tia Maria Sauce   Serves 4

Mousse:

3 egg yolks
⅜ cup sugar
¾ cup strong coffee (if
    using instant, use 1½
    teaspoons)

1 envelope gelatin
¼ cup cold water
1½ cups heavy cream

Sauce:

1½ cups strong coffee
¾ cup sugar
1 tablespoon arrowroot

⅛ cup cold water
1 ounce Tia Maria

Mousse:

In top of double boiler, beat yolks slightly and add sugar, still stirring. Stir in coffee slowly and place over hot water, not letting water touch bottom of pan. Stir until thickened. Dissolve gelatin in cold water, melt gelatin and add to coffee mixture. Stir and remove from heat; let cool. Whip cream and fold into coffee mixture. Pour into 1-quart mold and chill 2 hours. Unmold and pour sauce over before serving.

Sauce:

Heat coffee with sugar. Stir arrowroot into water and add to coffee. Simmer and stir until thickened. Add Tia Maria and chill.

Oranges Stuffed With Ice Cream   Serves 6

6 Jerusalem oranges
    (oranges with thick skins)
1 quart orange sherbet
¾ quart vanilla ice cream

3 ounces Cointreau
Small amount pulp and juice of
    orange
Mint, for garnish

Cut tops off oranges, scoop out pulp with grapefruit spoon and reserve small amount of pulp and juice. Mix sherbet with softened ice cream; add Cointreau, pulp and juice. Stuff into orange shells and freeze 2 hours. Garnish with sprig of mint.

Lemon Charlotte

Serves 12

5 eggs, separated
1 cup sugar
Juice and rind of 3 large
  lemons
1 tablespoon unflavored
  gelatin

2 teaspoons vanilla extract
3 cups heavy cream
2 packages lady fingers

Beat 5 egg yolks until light and fluffy. Add sugar, beating until thick and pale. Add grated lemon rind. Soften gelatin in juice of lemons for 5 minutes. Heat mixture in small pan on stove until gelatin dissolves (2 or 3 minutes). Add lemon juice mixture to eggs. Beat egg whites until stiff. Whip cream and add vanilla. Fold all ingredients together. Line bottom and sides of a very large spring form pan with the lady fingers. Pour mixture into pan and refrigerate until firm. Unmold on serving platter.

Baked Fruit

Serves 8

20 ounces canned cling
  peach halves, drained
20 ounces canned pineapple
  chunks, drained
17 ounces canned dark
  sweet pitted cherries,
  drained

17 ounces canned unpeeled
  apricots
1 cup brown sugar
1⅓ cups light rum
2 cups sour cream

Preheat oven to 350 °F. Combine fruits and apricot liquid in a shallow 3-quart baking dish. Sprinkle fruit with brown sugar and pour 1 cup rum over fruit. Bake 1½ hours, uncovered, stirring once.

Pour remaining ⅓ cup rum over fruit. Serve warm with generous spoonful of sour cream on each serving.

Hot Fruit Compote

Serves 6

16 ounces canned peaches
16 ounces canned pears
16 ounces canned dark
   pitted cherries
16 ounces canned crushed
   pineapple
2 bananas, sliced

2 dozen almond macaroons,
   crushed
¼ cup sherry
Brown sugar
Butter
Whipped cream or ice cream,
   for garnish

Drain all fruit on a paper towel. Cut into chunks and layer with macaroons in a greased casserole dish, beginning and ending with macaroons on top. Sprinkle with brown sugar and butter. Pour sherry on top. Bake at 350°F for 30 minutes.

Garnish with whipped cream or ice cream.

Sauterne-Poached Pears With Cream

Serves 6

6 whole pears, any variety
1½ cups sauterne
1 cup light brown sugar, or
   more to taste
12 to 15 thin strips of
   lemon peel

1 teaspoon lemon juice
3 teaspoons butter
½ cup light rum, warmed
1 cup heavy cream, whipped
   and sweetened with vanilla
   extract

Peel, halve and core pears. Put pears, wine, sugar, lemon peel and juice and butter in a shallow enamelware pan. Cover pan and poach pears over low heat until tender, 45 minutes to an hour. When pears are tender, remove to chafing dish. Cook liquid until syrupy, approximately 10 minutes; pour over pears.

This can be prepared early in the day. At serving time, heat pears in syrup in chafing dish. Have warmed rum ready. Pour rum over fruit and ignite. When flames die out serve pears with cold, whipped cream.

Cantaloupe Supreme

Serves 4

2 cantaloupes
1½ pints strawberries
1 pint vanilla ice cream

2 egg whites
½ cup sugar
Dash kirsch

Cut bottoms off melons so they sit easily on a cookie sheet. Cut in half and remove seeds. Using a grapefruit knife, loosen fruit from rind. Cut fruit into fairly small pieces and put back in rind. Cut strawberries in half and add just enough sugar to sweeten. Add these to the melons and put a dash of kirsch over all.

Make a meringue from egg whites and add sugar slowly. Turn on broiler and put rack on the second level. Put 1 scoop of ice cream on each melon and cover well with meringue. Put in oven to brown lightly.

Blueberries can be used in place of strawberries and amount of meringue can be doubled.

Zabaglione

Serves 4

4 egg yolks
⅓ cup sugar
Dash salt
½ cup blended Marsala
   wine *See note

Fresh strawberries or
   raspberries, optional

In top of double boiler, combine egg yolks, sugar, salt and Marsala. Blend well. Cook over simmering water. Water should not touch top of double boiler. While cooking, beat with electric mixer until mixture stands in stiff peaks when beater is raised, about 5 minutes.

Serve warm over vanilla ice cream or cold with fruit.

*Note: Blend ¼ cup Cream Marsala with 2 tablespoons sherry and 2 tablespoons Almond Marsala and mix well. If not available, use Cream Marsala.

Eggnog Pudding

Serves 8

1 tablespoon gelatin
2 tablespoons cold water
¼ cup milk
2 eggs, separated
½ cup sugar

¼ cup bourbon
2 cups heavy cream, whipped
12 lady fingers, split, or pound
    cake, thinly sliced
Pecans, chopped

Soak gelatin in cold water. Boil milk and pour over softened gelatin. Beat egg whites until very stiff. Beat egg yolks, add sugar and bourbon; beat to blend. Add softened gelatin and egg whites. Fold in half the whipped cream. Pour the pudding into a bowl with 6 of the lady fingers or half of the cake. Top with remaining lady fingers or cake. Chill until set. Turn out onto serving plate, ice with remaining whipped cream and sprinkle with pecans.

Floating Island

Serves 8

8 eggs
1 cup sugar
1 tablespoon vanilla

2 tablespoons sherry
2½ cups milk
4 tablespoons sugar

Separate eggs and cream yolks with 1 cup sugar. Add vanilla and sherry and mix well. Slowly add milk and turn heat on. Mix well, stirring constantly. Bring custard to a boil and take off heat. Put through colander and place in oven proof dish. Whip egg whites until stiff and add 4 tablespoons sugar. Place over custard and put under broiler until whites are brown. Chill thoroughly and serve in glass bowls.

Floating Island may be poured over fresh strawberries, if desired.

Strawberries Over Ice Cream   Serves 6

6 tablespoons butter
¾ cup sugar
½ pint fresh strawberries, washed, hulled and halved

1½ ounces strawberry liqueur
1½ ounces brandy
Vanilla ice cream

Melt butter, add sugar and stir. Add strawberries and cook until slightly softened. Add strawberry liqueur. Heat brandy. Place strawberry mixture over ice cream, pour brandy over and ignite.

Winter Strawberries   Yields Approximately 120 Strawberries

1½ cups walnuts, finely grated
1½ cups coconut, finely grated
3 (3 ounce) packages strawberry gelatin

14 ounces canned sweetened condensed milk
1 teaspoon vanilla
⅓ cup red-colored sugar
Green spearmint leaves

Combine walnuts, coconut, gelatin, condensed milk and vanilla in medium bowl. Work until smoothly mixed. Form into ball and chill for at least one hour.

Shape chilled mixture into strawberries, using about one teaspoon of mixture for each strawberry. Chill again.

Roll strawberries in red sugar. Cut stems from spearmint leaves; insert stem in each strawberry. Refrigerate in air-tight container until ready to serve.

Crème Brûlée   Serves 8 to 10

1 quart heavy cream	8 egg yolks
1 vanilla bean	Salt
4 tablespoons sugar	¾ to 1 cup light brown sugar

Preheat oven to 350°F. In a large saucepan, scald cream with vanilla bean. Add sugar and stir until completely dissolved.

In a large bowl, beat egg yolks until light lemon color, then stir hot cream mixture carefully into egg yolks with a pinch of salt. Strain mixture into a 10-inch shallow baking dish or eight 4-ounce ramekins. Place dish in a pan of hot water and bake 50 to 60 minutes; bake ramekins 35 to 40 minutes. Custard is done when knife inserted in center comes out clean. Refrigerate until chilled.

Push brown sugar through a sieve. Spread on top of custard, making a layer ¼ inch thick. It must be as smooth as possible. Broil about 4 to 6 inches from broiler until sugar has caramelized, turning dish as necessary so it caramelizes evenly. Cool before serving.

To serve, crack caramelized crust with spoon.

Banana Ice   Yields 8 scoops

2 bananas	2 eggs
Juice of 2 oranges	1 cup sugar
Juice of 2 lemons	2 cups water

In a blender (preferably) or large bowl, combine the bananas, orange juice, lemon juice, eggs, sugar and water. Blend well. Pour into ice cube trays or any low, flat pan and freeze partially. Take out and beat again until frothy. Freeze until solid.

To serve, place a scoop in a sherbet dish and garnish with fresh strawberries.

Chocolate Roll

Serves 10

5 eggs, separated
1 cup sugar
6 ounces semi-sweet
   chocolate
3 tablespoons cold water

½ cup pecans, finely chopped
1½ cups heavy cream,whipped
Vanilla or brandy
Grated chocolate

Beat egg yolks in electric mixer with sugar until it becomes very thick. Melt chocolate in cold water over gentle heat. Fold chocolate and pecans into egg mixture. Beat egg whites until stiff and fold into mixture.

Line a jelly roll pan with oiled waxed paper (oiled on both sides). Spread chocolate mixture evenly and bake at 350°F for 15 minutes, or until mixture springs back when lightly pressed with fingertip and toothpick comes out clean. Remove from oven and cool slightly. Cover with a *slightly damp cloth*. Chill 12 hours in refrigerator. Remove cloth and dust chocolate mixture heavily with grated chocolate. Cover with a sheet of waxed paper and invert the cake onto a board or serving dish. Lift off the jelly roll pan and remove waxed paper on which the roll was baked.

Spread with whipped cream flavored with vanilla or brandy. Roll up in jelly roll fashion. Sprinkle generously with confectioner's sugar and decorate with whipped cream roses and candied violets.

Pirates' House Trifle

Serves 8

1 pint heavy cream
Sugar, to taste
¾ cup sherry

1 quart boiled custard (see
   recipe below)
1 pound angel food cake

Whip cream and sweeten to taste. Add ¼ cup sherry. Add balance of sherry to egg custard. Cut cake into thin layers. Use a 2-quart casserole and place a layer of cake in bottom; add custard, then whipped cream. Alternate layers ending with whipped cream.

Let set in refrigerator at least 1 hour before serving.

Pirates' House Boiled Custard:

2 tablespoons cornstarch
1 quart milk
3 eggs

6 tablespoons sugar
2 teaspoons vanilla

Mix cornstarch with small amount of milk. Add beaten eggs and sugar to balance of milk, then add cornstarch mixture. Cook in double boiler until custard coats spoon, about 15 minutes. Add vanilla and remaining ½ cup sherry.

A specialty of The Pirates' House restaurant.

Bourbon On A Cloud

Serves 8

¾ cup sugar, divided
1 envelope unflavored
  gelatin
3 eggs, separated

¾ cup bourbon
1 cup heavy cream, whipped
Lady fingers

Blend ½ cup sugar and gelatin in top of double boiler, stir in slightly beaten egg yolks. Slowly blend in bourbon, a small amount at a time. Place mixture over simmering (not boiling) water; cook, stirring constantly, about 10 minutes or until mixture thickens slightly. Beat egg whites until foamy. Add remaining sugar and continue beating until soft peaks form. Gradually fold bourbon mixture into egg whites. Chill. Fold in whipped cream. Cut lady fingers in half. Line a 4-cup mold with lady fingers, placing cut sides to the outside. Pour bourbon mixture into mold. Chill 6 hours or overnight.

Chocolate Steamed Pudding   Serves 6

2 squares baking chocolate   1½ teaspoons baking powder
2 tablespoons butter   Dash salt
1 egg   1 cup heavy cream
½ cup sugar   1 tablespoon sugar
½ cup milk   1 teaspoon vanilla
1 cup flour

Grease top of deep double boiler and set aside.

Melt chocolate in butter in small pan. In a medium size bowl, mix ingredients in order given, sifting in flour, baking powder and salt. Cook 1 hour or more in double boiler top, covered, over boiling water. Serve hot with 1 cup heavy cream, whipped, sweetened with 1 tablespoon sugar and 1 teaspoon vanilla.

The trick is to get it out of the pan and onto the serving plate with the same side up as in the pan. It will be cake-like at the bottom and moist at the top.

This pudding can be made in the morning for dinner, reheating during dinner. If this is done, cool with top off so that moisture will not condense and drip on pudding.

Coffee Jelly   Serves 8

2 envelopes unflavored   ¾ cup sugar
  gelatin   Pinch salt
½ cup coffee liqueur   1 cup heavy cream, whipped
3 cups hot coffee

In bowl, sprinkle gelatin over coffee liqueur to soften. Add coffee, sugar and salt. Stir mixture until it is clear. Pour liquid into 8 individual molds and chill until firm. When ready to serve, add a touch of whipped cream.

May be prepared the day before serving.

Crème Glacée Au Caramel

Serves 6 to 8

6 egg yolks
1 cup sugar
1 cup water
2½ cups heavy cream,
  whipped (whip ½ cup
  separately for topping)

1 teaspoon vanilla
Kahlua, for garnishing, if
  desired

Beat egg yolks until thick and pale. Place sugar and ½ cup water in a small, heavy saucepan. Stir over low heat until sugar dissolves. Turn heat up and boil steadily until a golden brown caramel. Do not stir. If sugar begins browning too qucikly, place in a pan of cold water to stop the cooking. Add the remaining ½ cup water. It will splatter for a while. Stir, over heat until caramel is melted and liquid is boiling. Beat the caramel a little at a time into the egg yolks. Whisk well until creamy. Set over a bowl of ice and continue whipping until mixture thickens and cools.

Combine vanilla with two cups of whipped cream and chill thoroughly. Fold cream with vanilla into caramel mixture with rubber spatula. Spoon into individual dessert bowls. Freeze 2½ hours.

Top with whipped cream and drizzle with Kahlua, if desired. Serve immediately.

Wine Jelly

Serves 8

2 envelopes unflavored
  gelatin
¼ cup cold water
1 cup boiling water
⅔ cup sugar

Pinch of salt
¼ cup lemon juice
¼ cup orange juice
2 cups sweet sherry

Soak gelatin in cold water about 10 minutes. Add boiling water; stir well and cool partially. Add sugar, salt, lemon juice, orange juice and sherry. Place in mold to congeal.

Garnish each serving with a dollop of sour cream or sweetened whipped cream.

CHRISTMAS IN SAVANNAH

Christmas in Savannah

Savannah's is not a white Christmas, but a joyous one just the same with long-held family traditions that set that special time apart from all other seasons of the year.

In the late nineteenth century, the holiday season featured something for nearly everyone. For the culturally bent, there was almost always a Christmas Day performance at the Savannah Theatre. For the sports-minded, there were horse races at Thunderbolt at Christmas and on New Year's Day. It was then also that the Savannah Rifle Association held its annual shooting contest for turkeys. An advance notice for that event in 1896 read: "There will be an oyster roast with accompaniments. It is presumed all the members of the Association know what that means."

On Christmas Day the adults often ventured from one Open House to another, tasting at each a spiked and spicy eggnog made from a well-kept family recipe. The children, however, anticipated a more special enter-tainment—the shooting of fireworks in Forsyth Park Extension. As one Savannahian remarked, "How the small boy looked forward to the week of weeks when he could give full vent to his natural instinct for which he was made: to make a noise!"

Some of the most evocative Yuletide accounts, however, are those of Christmas at the spacious Gordon home on East Oglethorpe Avenue. Now it is open to the public as the birthplace of Girl Scout founder Juliette Gordon Low, but earlier it was known to the family as "The Old House" and Juliette Low simply as "Daisy."

The noted author Arthur Gordon described a few years ago his memories of arriving home for Christmas after a two-day ride from boarding school: "I don't remember those journeys, particularly, but I certainly remember the arrivals: the stampede up the steep steps of the old white-columned house, the wreaths in the windows, the smilax en-twined around the tall mirrors and the old portraits, the coal fires sputter-ing in their grates under the black-marble mantels, the indescrib-able blended smells of good food and old leather and coal smoke and furniture polish, the wonderful soaring knowledge that it was almost Christmas and we were home."

To read the description of Juliette Low's niece, Daisy Gordon Law-rence, Christmas dinner at the Gordons was an event to live for all the other days of the year.

It took place at two o'clock in the afternoon, the adults sitting at the big damask-covered dining table and the children and their nurses at a side table nearby.

After a simple grace came the oyster stew served by Mrs. Gordon from a silver grape-encrusted tureen. Then it was time for the stuffed turkey that had been fattened for weeks at Belmont, the family farm near Louisville. Served with the turkey were ham, rice, gravy, candied yams, pickled peaches and a variety of vegetables.

All the children then joined the adults at the big table in time for dessert, a flaming plum pudding and a cylinder of homemade ice cream. As it was served, the butler passed around the champagne. There was even a tiny bit for the little ones so that they could join in the traditional toast, "To absent friends."

At nightfall the children walked down Bull Street to the fireworks show at Forsyth Park, but their grandfather thoughtfully had the carriage brought to take the tired ones home again. After a cup of hot cocoa, they tumbled into bed with one thought uppermost in their minds. "Christmas was only 364 days off."

The Telfair Academy of Arts and Sciences, Inc. is the oldest public art museum in the Southeast. Designed in 1818 by William Jay as a home for the Telfair family, the mansion and its furnishings were bequeathed by Miss Mary Telfair to become a museum, which was officially opened in 1886.

Savannahians love to entertain and the Telfair family was no exception. In later years the Telfair mansion was the scene of many dancing parties and balls: in the 1960's, a ball with a French theme; in the 1970's, a masked ball, a disco party, and a ball with dance cards and fancy-titled dances.

The Telfair Ball, as we know it today, began in 1981 as a major fundraiser for the Museum. The Ball is a white-tie, sophisticated evening, beginning with pre-ball parties held in private homes, then on to the Telfair mansion for live and silent auctions, dancing to a "big-name" orchestra, and a midnight supper.

The pre-ball parties are either cocktail buffets or seated dinners. All Ball guests are invited to one of these parties . . . a perfect way to begin a gala evening.

Foggy Marsh Punch
Caviar Egg Mold* p. 27
Artichokes Stuffed with Crab* p. 35
Fresh Mushroom Soup* p. 49
Marinated Pork Tenderloin
Steamed Julienne Vegetables with Lemon Butter Sauce* p. 285
Chatham Salad with Creamy Herb Dressing
Almond Curry Rice* p. 116   Angel Flake Rolls* p. 198
Fresh Fruit with Grand Marnier Sauce
After Dinner Coffee
Miss Evelyn's Toffee* p. 284

Foggy Marsh Punch

Serves 15 to 18

1 (750 ML.) bottle
  champagne, chilled
10 ounces frozen raspberries
  or strawberries, softened
  slightly

2 liters of any carbonated
  clear soft drink, chilled
1½ pounds of dry ice, broken
  into 5-inch pieces

Mix first three ingredients in a large punch bowl. Just as guests arrive, add a piece of dry ice for an enchanted, foggy look! Dry ice evaporates at the rate of one pound per hour unless stored in a very airtight container! It may be purchased at commercial ice houses.

Chatham Salad with Creamy Herb Dressing

2 cups romaine lettuce, torn
  into bite-size pieces
1 cup iceberg lettuce, torn
  into bite-size pieces
1 cup bib lettuce, torn into
  bite-size pieces
14 ounces canned hearts of
  palm, drained and sliced

14 ounces canned artichoke
  hearts, drained and
  quartered
½ cup carrot, grated
2 tablespoons parsley, minced
2 tomatoes, diced

Creamy Herb Dressing:
6 tablespoons vegetable oil
6 tablespoons tarragon
  vinegar
½ teaspoon ground pepper
¼ teaspooon garlic salt

2 teaspoons Dijon mustard
½ cup mayonnaise
¼ teaspoon dill
1 teaspoon sugar

Mix dressing ingredients altogether and refrigerate. Place the salad in a large bowl and just before serving toss well with the dressing.

Marinated Pork Tenderloin

¼ cup soy sauce
2 tablespoons dry red wine
1 tablespoon honey
1 tablespoon brown sugar

1 clove garlic, minced
½ teaspoon cinnamon powder
1 green onion, minced
2 lean pork tenderloins

Mix together the first seven ingredients. Pour into a large plastic bag or airtight container. Add tenderloins and marinate for 2 to 24 hours. (The longer the better!) Remove tenderloins and tie them together if they are small, to prevent the ends from drying out.

Cook on the grill for 40 to 60 minutes depending on the size of your tenderloins. Baste every 15 minutes with the marinade. Tenderloins may be baked in the oven for 40 minutes at 375°F if preferred. Again, baste them every 15 minutes. Slice into thin medallions to serve. (Pork loins may be used instead of tenderloins if the marinade is doubled.)

Fresh Fruit Salad with Grand Marnier Sauce

4 egg yolks
1½ teaspoons cornstarch
½ cup sugar
1 cup milk, scalded
¼ cup Grand Marnier

1 teaspoon vanilla extract
1 teaspoon orange rind,
  grated
½ cup heavy cream, whipped
Fresh fruits

Combine egg yolks, cornstarch, and sugar. Beat until it is pale yellow. Pour into a double boiler and add the scalded milk. Set over simmering water, stirring constantly until thickened and will coat a spoon. Watch carefully as this stage curdles easily. Remove from heat. Stir in Grand Marnier, vanilla, and orange rind. Cool completely and refrigerate (covered) for 2 to 3 hours. Just before serving, fold the whipped cream into the sauce with a spoon. (Left over sauce freezes well.)

Serve over a combination of fresh fruits: oranges, strawberries, kiwi, bananas, green seedless grapes, apples, and peaches. DO NOT use watery fruits such as watermelons.

When the first sign of chill bites the air, Savannahians' thoughts turn to oysters. There are many ways to enjoy this luscious bivalve — in soups and stews, fried and served with hush puppies, in a casserole or on the half shell. But the finest rendition, by far, is the roasted oyster.

Oyster roasts are among the most popular forms of entertainment in the Low Country. Savannahians have been known to roast oysters in a fireplace or on a grill in the backyard, but they taste best cooked over a pit on a riverbank under a spreading canopy of oaks.

The condition of the oysters is of the utmost importance. Pick them up the day of the party and keep them cool, but not on ice — which tends to pop them open prematurely. It's convenient to get them from your seafood dealer already cleaned, but if you plan to do it yourself, just put them in a basket and hose them off well.

Build a fire in a shallow pit, around four by six feet, depending on the number of oysters you plan to cook. Let the fire die down a bit and top it with a similar-sized sheet of metal supported by concrete blocks. When the metal is hot, lay the oysters on top in a single layer and cover with a wet burlap sack. This creates the steam that does the cooking. Check the oysters every few minutes until they barely pop open — that's when they're juicy and best and ready for shucking. With a flat shovel move them over to plank tables covered with newspaper that have been out-fitted with oyster knives for each guest, cocktail sauce, saltine crackers, melted butter, and perhaps some lemon wedges. While your guests are enjoying themselves, start the next batch on the fire.

How many oysters can an oyster lover eat? Plan on a bushel for 6 or so people. Some guests will consider the oysters their dinner and eat accordingly. Others will view them as an hors d'oeuvre and will be ready to dive into whatever else you may be serving. It's customary to follow up with something simple like sliced ham, Savannah red rice, and a green salad.

OYSTER ROAST

Twelve Bushels of Oysters (to serve fifty)
Cocktail Sauce, Melted Butter, Saltine Crackers
Georgia Country Ham* p. 191
Buttermilk Biscuits* p. 194
Savannah Red Rice* p. 115
Tossed Green Salad
Chocolate Caramel Bars* p. 283
Pralines
Plenty of Cold Beer and Soft Drinks

Cocktail Sauce   Serves 6 to 8

1 cup catsup
2 tablespoons Worcestershire
  sauce
2 tablespoons lemon juice
2 tablespoons prepared
  horseradish

Salt to taste
A few drops of Tabasco if not
  hot enough!

Mix all ingredients. Keep in the refrigerator at least one hour before serving.

Pralines   Makes 2 dozen

½ cup brown sugar, firmly
  packed
1 cup granulated sugar
1½ tablespoons light corn
  syrup
⅛ teaspoon salt

½ cup evaporated milk
3 tablespoons butter
1 teaspoon vanilla extract
1 cup pecans, halves and
  pieces, toasted

Butter a heavy bottomed 2 quart saucepan. Combine sugars, corn syrup, salt, milk, and butter in saucepan and stir until blended. Cook over medium heat until mixture reaches 240°F, stirring often. Add pecans and continue heating until the temperature reaches 246°F. Remove from heat.

Let candy cool for 2 minutes. Add vanilla and beat with a spoon until creamy. Quickly drop by spoonfuls onto wax paper to make 2 inch circles. If candy hardens too quickly, add a few drops of milk and heat gently, stirring until creamy. Candy should drop smoothly from the spoon. Store in an airtight container, separating layers with wax paper.

It is said that "Everyone is Irish in Savannah" on Saint Patrick's Day. The largest parade south of New York City's follows a route through the downtown squares. Many "Irishmen" that live in the beautiful, old homes on these squares host St. Patrick's Day Buffets. Partygoers can enjoy the parade from the porches as well as the best Irish fare.

Irish Coffee* p. 284
Zucchini Squares* p. 282
Hot Ham and Cheese Rolls* p. 282
Molded Corned Beef Salad on Cabbage Bed
Bacon/Broccoli Toss
Tomato Aspic with Artichoke Hearts* p. 61
Mock Potato Salad
Crème de Menthe Brownies* p. 233
Irish Lace Cookies* p. 234

Bacon Broccoli Toss

Serves 10 to 12

6 to 8 cups raw broccoli flowerets (approximately 2 bunches)
½ cup raisins (white and/or dark)
10 slices of bacon, browned, drained and crumbled

1 small purple onion, finely chopped (any small onion will do but the purple one adds great color)

Sauce:
¼ cup vinegar
¼ cup sugar
1 tablespoon dry mustard

3 tablespoons flour
½ cup water
¾ cup mayonnaise

Mix first five ingredients of sauce and cook slowly over medium heat until thickened. Let cool. Add mayonnaise. Combine broccoli, raisins, bacon, and onion and mix with sauce. Refrigerate. Toss just before serving.

Molded Corned Beef Salad   Serves 8 to 10

1 envelope unflavored
  gelatin
½ cup cold water
¼ cup onion, chopped
3 tablespoons lemon juice
1 teaspoon salt
1 cup mayonnaise

1½ cups cabbage, finely
  shredded
1 cup celery, chopped
½ cup sweet pickle relish
1½ cups corned beef, cooked
  and shredded

In a small saucepan, sprinkle gelatin over cold water, place over low heat, and stir constantly for 3 to 5 minutes until dissolved. Remove from heat. Stir in onion, lemon juice and salt. Gradually stir gelatin mixture into mayonnaise. Add cabbage, celery, pickle, and corned beef. Stir until thoroughly combined. Turn into ½ quart mold, and refrigerate for at least two hours or until firm. Unmold and serve on a bed of cabbage.

Mock Potato Salad   Serves 8

3 pounds potatoes, peeled
1 large onion, thinly sliced
1 package creamy Italian salad
  dressing mix, prepared as
  directed to make 16 ounces

1 teaspoon dill weed
Salt and pepper as desired

Slice the potatoes in ¼-inch widths. Boil in salted water until just tender (approximately 8 minutes) and drain. Layer potatoes, onion slices, salt, pepper, dressing and dill. Repeat, covering well with dressing. Top with a little dill. Cover and chill several hours before serving.

Ah, summer in Savannah! The carefree days under a fan on the large old porches of Tybee Island after a day on the beaches or in a boat. Dining must be simple, yet grand, with fresh seafood the order of the day.

Zucchini Soup
Glorified Vidalia Onions
Shrimp Remoulade
Marinated Tomatoes with Avocado Wedges
Assorted Fresh Fruits
Brittlebread* p. 195
Lemon Cream

Zucchini Soup   Serves 6

2 large zucchini, sliced
1 green pepper, cut in wedges
½ large onion, diced
3 cups chicken stock

1½ cups sour cream
1 tablespoon fresh parsley
¼ teaspoon dried dill
Salt and pepper to taste

Simmer zucchini, green pepper, and onion in chicken stock for 25 minutes. Pour ¼ of this mixture into a blender and blend until smooth. Repeat this process adding sour cream, parsley, and dill to the last ¼ of the stock mixture. Blend, then add salt and pepper to taste.

Serve warm or cold garnished with a small bit of sour cream sprinkled with dill weed.

Glorified Vidalia Onions

Serves 12

5 to 6 medium Vidalia sweet
  onions, sliced and finely
  chopped
½ cup apple cider vinegar

1 cup sugar
2 cups water
½ cup mayonnaise
1 teaspoon celery salt

Soak onions in water, sugar, and vinegar for 2 to 4 hours in the refrigerator. Drain well for 45 minutes in a colander. Pat dry. Mix onions with mayonnaise and celery salt. Serve with club crackers.

Shrimp Remoulade

Serves 6

Shrimp Salad:
1½ pounds shrimp, cooked,
  peeled, and deveined
¾ cup celery, chopped

1 cup mayonnaise
Juice of ½ lemon
Salt to taste

Stir all ingredients together lightly.

Remoulade Sauce:
1 large egg, hard cooked and
  chopped
2 shallots, finely chopped
4 cloves garlic, finely chopped
¼ cup fresh spinach, cooked,
  chopped, and well drained
2 cups mayonnaise

1 tablespoon Worcestershire
  sauce
1 tablespoon creole mustard
1 tablespoon fresh lemon juice
1½ ounces anchovy paste
Dash of liquid hot pepper
  sauce

Fold ingredients together to blend well. Serve the shrimp salad on a bed of lettuce with the Remoulade Sauce to the side for guests to spoon on top.

Marinated Tomatoes

Serves 12

6 to 8 medium tomatoes,
  quartered
3 tablespoons sugar
3 tablespoons fresh parsley,
  snipped
1½ teaspoons garlic salt
1 teaspoon seasoned salt

¾ teaspoon oregano
½ teaspoon freshly ground
  pepper
¾ cup vegetable oil
½ cup red wine vinegar
Avocado wedges, optional

Mix oil and wine vinegar together. Shake well and refrigerate. Sprinkle dry ingredients over the quartered tomatoes. Pour oil and vinegar mixture over all and refrigerate for 12 to 24 hours in a covered container. Turn occasionally to blend marinade.

Drain well before serving. Arrange on a bed of lettuce with avocado wedges as a garnish.

Lemon Cream

Serves 8 to 10

½ gallon vanilla ice cream,
  softened slightly
Juice of ½ lemon
Rind of 2 lemons, finely
  grated
6 ounce can of lemonade,
  thawed

Sautéed pecans (Recipe on
  Page 281)
Lemon slice
Sprig of mint

Allow ice cream to soften 5 to 10 minutes out of the freezer. Combine with lemon juice, rind, and lemonade. Refreeze immediately. Serve in individual dishes sprinkled with pecans and garnished with a slice of lemon and a sprig of mint.

The next few pages are devoted to that hard-to-find, just right appetizer. Whether it be the most casual of get-togethers or the most formal affair, here are some novel suggestions for your enjoyment.

Chutney Nut Spread

Serves 12

8 ounces cream cheese, softened
½ teaspoon dry mustard
1 teaspoon curry powder
9 ounces of chutney
5 green onions, chopped using green tops too

½ cup dry roasted peanuts, chopped
½ cup flaked coconut
Red or green maraschino cherries

Mix first three ingredients with ¼ of the chutney. Spread in an 8 inch circle on a serving platter. Spread the rest of the chutney over the top. Then layer green onions and peanuts and top with coconut. Garnish with cherry "flowers" on top of the coconut. Serve immediately or refrigerate up to three hours. Serve with crackers.

Crepes Fromage

Makes 12 crepes

4 ounces Swiss cheese, grated
4 ounces sharp Cheddar cheese, grated
4 tablespoons fresh Parmesan cheese, grated
2 tablespoons fresh parsley, minced

1 tablespoon chives, chopped
1 tablespoon Worcestershire sauce
⅛ teaspoon freshly ground pepper
12 (6-inch in diameter) crepes - *See basic crepe batter recipe on page 152*

Mix cheeses and seasonings well. Place full tablespoon of cheese mixture on each crepe and roll up tight. Place in buttered baking dish and bake at 400°F for 10 minutes. Remove and serve while still warm.

Spicy Ham Roll-ups with Mustard Sauce

Serves 8

Four 10 inch flour tortillas
16 ounces cream cheese,
  softened
1 pound ham, diced finely
  (May use food processor)

7 ounces green chilies,
  drained and chopped
8 ounces black olives, drained
  and chopped

Mix cream cheese, ham, chilies, and olives together and spread on tortillas. Roll up and place on a cookie sheet. Cover with a damp cloth and refrigerate for 4 hours or overnight. Cut into ¾ to 1 inch slices. Serve with salsa or the spicy mustard sauce that follows.

Mustard Sauce:
2 ounce can dry mustard
1 cup malt vinegar
1 cup sugar

3 eggs
½ cup mayonnaise (or more)

Mix the above ingredients together. Heat in a double boiler over medium heat until thickened. Refrigerate. Serve in a bowl beside the ham roll-ups for dipping.

Almond Cheese Delight

Serves 8

2 cups sharp Cheddar
  cheese, grated
1 green onion, chopped
4 slices bacon, cooked and
  crumbled
1 cup mayonnaise

2½ ounce package sliced
  almonds
¼ teaspoon salt (Add only if
  you are serving
  immediately)

Mix all of the above ingredients together. Shape into a half sphere and decorate with curled green onion tops. Best when made a day ahead.

Sauteed Pecans

1 pound pecan halves, shelled   Salt to taste
½ cup butter

Preheat oven to 300°F. Place butter and salt in a shallow baking pan to melt. Remove from oven and add pecans. Stir to coat all pecans well with butter and salt. Bake at 300°F for one hour stirring every 15 minutes to coat pecans well. After one hour, sprinkle pecans lightly with more salt and stir well. Cool and serve.

Boiled Peanuts   Serves 6 to 8

4 pounds green peanuts, in   6 quarts water
   their shell   6 to 10 tablespoons salt

Wash green peanuts and place in a large pot with water and salt. Cover and bring to a boil. Boil slowly for 1½ to 2 hours. Water should be briny. More water and salt may be added if necessary while cooking. Test for doneness after 1½ hours. Peanuts should be soft, but not mushy inside. Rinse in plain (unsalted) water. Drain well.

Note: Green peanuts are available from June until September. After cooling, they may be frozen in plastic bags. When ready to serve, simply reheat to a boil, and drain.

Spiced Pecans   Makes 3½ cups

1 cup sugar   1 teaspoon ground cinnamon
1 tablespoon butter   3 cups shelled pecan halves
¼ cup water

Bring sugar, butter, water and cinnamon to a boil. Stir constantly at a slow boil for 2 minutes — no longer. Mix pecans into mixture. Cool. Turn out on wax paper.

Zucchini Squares

Serves 8 to 10

4 cups zucchini, thinly sliced
1 cup onion, chopped
½ cup butter
2 tablespoons parsley, chopped
½ teaspoon salt
½ teaspoon black pepper
¼ teaspoon sweet basil
¼ teaspoon garlic powder
¼ teaspoon oregano
2 eggs, well beaten
8 ounces mozzarella cheese, grated
2 teaspoons Dijon mustard
1½ (8 ounce size cans) refrigerated dinner rolls

In a large skillet, cook zucchini and onion until tender. Stir in parsley and seasonings. In a large bowl, blend eggs and cheese. Stir into vegetable mixture.

Separate dough into rectangles and press over the bottom and up the sides of an ungreased 9 x 13 inch glass pan. Spread this "crust" with mustard. Pour vegetable mixture evenly over the dough.

Bake at 375°F for 20 to 23 minutes. Let sit in dish for 10 to 15 minutes before cutting into bite size squares.

Hot Ham and Cheese Rolls

Serves 15 to 20

1 cup butter or margarine, softened
3 tablespoons dry mustard
3 tablespoons poppy seeds
1 medium onion, diced finely
1 teaspoon Worcestershire sauce
4 packages party rolls
12 ounces Swiss cheese, sliced thinly
12 ounces ham, sliced thinly

Mix first five ingredients well. Spread on rolls. Cut ham and cheese to fit rolls. Place one slice of each on each roll. Wrap in foil. Heat at 400°F for 10 minutes. (These freeze well before being cooked. Heat for 20 minutes if they are frozen.)

Apple Caramel Dip

Serves 25 to 30

½ cup butter, melted
2 cups dark brown sugar
1 cup light corn syrup
2 tablespoons water
14 ounces sweetened
condensed milk

1 teaspooon vanilla
10 apples, seeded and cut into
8 wedges each

Cook butter, sugar, water, and milk until all the sugar is dissolved over medium heat, stirring constantly. Remove from heat and add vanilla. Cut unpeeled apples into wedges, and then in half again. Dip into salted water for about 1 minute to prevent them from turning brown. (Apples should be done as close to serving time as possible.) Seal apples in an airtight container until use. To serve, heat caramel sauce and pour into chafing dish. Place apples in a bowl beside the caramel with toothpicks for dipping.

The caramel sauce will keep in the refrigerator for 4 to 6 weeks. It is divine served warm over ice cream or pound cake.

Chocolate Caramel Bars

Serves 15 to 20

14 ounce bag of caramels
½ cup evaporated milk
1 package German Chocolate
Cake mix

¾ cup butter, melted
⅓ cup evaporated milk
1 cup pecans, chopped
1 cup chocolate chips

In the top of a double boiler, combine caramels and ½ cup evaporated milk. Cook over low heat until caramels are melted. Remove from heat. Grease and flour a 9 x 13 inch baking pan. Mix cake mix, butter, ⅓ cup evaporated milk, and pecans in a bowl. Press half of this mixture into floured pan and bake it at 350°F for 8 minutes. Remove from oven and sprinkle chocolate chips evenly over it. Pour caramel mixture over the top of the chocolate chips. Flatten the remaining cake mixture in your palms and place over the top of the caramels. Return to the oven at 350°F for 18 to 20 minutes. Let cool, then refrigerate. Cut into small bars.

Miss Evelyn's Toffee

Serves 12

¾ cup butter
1 cup light brown sugar,
firmly packed
2 (2½ ounce) packages sliced
almond, toasted slightly

4 ounces semi-sweet chocolate
chips

Melt butter and sugar in an iron skillet. Set timer for 9 minutes and turn heat to medium-medium low. Cook these two ingredients, stirring constantly. Watch carefully as this burns easily, but the sugar must totally dissolve. Mixture should boil slightly, thicken and lighten in color at this stage. Immediately after 9 minutes, remove from heat. Reduce heat to low and place back on burner for 3 minutes. Add almonds while still on burner and stir quickly to coat. Once almonds are coated, quickly spread mixture in an 8 x 10 inch glass pan. Mixture will begin to harden immediately. Sprinkle chocolate chips over top and wait 3 minutes for them to melt slightly. Spread them evenly with a spatula for a thin chocolate glaze. Refrigerate. Cut into small 1-inch pieces for an elegant "sweet" for your buffet table. These freeze beautifully and can be made weeks in advance.

Hot Irish Coffee

Serves 1

1½ ounces Irish whiskey
Black coffee, hot and strong

Sugar
Whipped cream

Pour Irish whiskey into a stemmed glass or mug. Fill to within ½ inch of the brim with black coffee. Add sugar to taste and stir well. Top with whipped cream. DO NOT STIR. The flavor is obtained by drinking the coffee through the cream. (If St. Patrick's Day is warm and sunny, use the recipe for Iced Irish Coffee on page 22.)

Sauces and Accompaniments

Lemon Butter Sauce

Yields Approximately ½ Cup

4 tablespoons lemon juice
¼ teaspoon salt

¼ pound butter
⅛ teaspoon white pepper

Heat lemon juice and salt just to boiling. Beat in butter, 1 tablespoon at a time until mixture is creamy. Beat in pepper.

Can be served with asparagus, spinach, artichokes or broccoli.

Barbecue Sauce

Yields 1 Quart

6 tablespoons prepared
  mustard
1 (14 ounce) bottle catsup
1 (5 ounce) bottle
  Worcestershire sauce
4 tablespoons lemon juice
8 tablespoons sugar

1 tablespoon salt
1 tablespoon pepper
2 tablespoons white vinegar
1 tablespoon chili powder
⅛ teaspoon Tabasco
½ cup butter

Combine mustard and catsup first, then add other ingredients. Simmer over low heat for 30 minutes.

Barbecue Sauce

Yields 2 Quarts

3½ cups catsup
7 ounces prepared mustard
1¾ cups white vinegar
7 ounces Worcestershire
  sauce

1 tablespoon salt
1 tablespoon pepper, or less
1 whole lemon
¼ cup butter

Stir catsup, mustard and pepper in large saucepan until smooth. Add other ingredients and cook slowly, stirring occasionally for 1 hour, or until lemon gets soft. Remove lemon and add butter, blending well.

Tigner Barbecue Sauce   Yields 1 Cup

1 teaspoon salt
½ teaspoon dry mustard
1 teaspoon black pepper
1 tablespoon brown sugar
Dash cayenne

2 egg yolks
⅓ cup white vinegar
½ cup water
1 tablespoon butter

Mix dry ingredients then add liquid. Cook over boiling water, stirring to keep smooth.

For basting meat while cooking, omit egg yolks.

Homemade Mustard   Yields 1½ Cups

4 tablespoons dry mustard
3 tablespoons sugar
2 eggs, whipped

¾ cup cider vinegar
2 tablespoons olive oil

Mix thoroughly mustard and sugar. Add eggs slowly. Bring vinegar almost to a boil. Put vinegar into mustard mixture; return to heat until thickened. Add olive oil when cool.

Hot Sweet Mustard   Yields 2½ Cups

3 (1⅛ ounce) cans dry
   mustard
1 cup red wine vinegar

3 eggs
1 cup sugar

Mix mustard with wine vinegar and put in refrigerator overnight.

Beat eggs; add sugar. Mix with mustard in saucepan and stir over medium heat until thick, stirring constantly. Refrigerate.

Keeps indefinitely.

Béarnaise Sauce

Serves 8

3 tablespoons red wine
  vinegar
1 tablespoon green onion,
  chopped
1 tablespoon tarragon leaves
¼ teaspoon black pepper,
  cracked

⅛ teaspoon cayenne pepper
9 egg yolks
1½ cups butter or margarine,
  softened
1 tablespoon parsley

In top of double boiler, combine wine vinegar, green onion, tarragon and peppers. Heat to boiling directly over high heat. Boil about 7 minutes or until vinegar is reduced to about 1 tablespoon. Place double boiler top over double boiler bottom with hot (not boiling) water. Add egg yolks and cook, beating constantly with wire whisk until slightly thickened. Add butter or margarine about 3 tablespoons at a time, beating constantly with wire whisk until butter is melted and mixture thickened. Stir in parsley. Add an egg yolk if mixture separates.

Albert's Béarnaise Sauce

Yields Approximately 2½ Cups

½ teaspoon *Kerbel* (German
  Herb), optional
½ cup tarragon vinegar
½ cup dry white wine
½ teaspoon tarragon leaves
1 tablespoon shallots,
  chopped
Salt, to taste
6 egg yolks

2 cups butter, melted
Juice of 1 lemon
1 teaspoon Worcestershire
  sauce
Dash of Tabasco
1 tablespoon parsley, chopped
1 teaspoon tarragon leaves,
  freshly chopped

Mix together first 6 ingredients and boil until reduced to about one-third. Remove from heat and strain. Combine eggs in saucepan and place over low heat. Beat eggs constantly as you slowly add strained liquid. Beat until thick and fluffy. Slowly beat in melted butter, lemon juice and Worcestershire sauce. Add a touch of Tabasco, salt to taste, chopped parsley and tarragon leaves. Keep warm, but not hot.

Lillie Mae's Hollandaise

Yields 1½ Cups

1 cup butter
2 tablespoons boiling water
Yolks of 2 eggs, beaten

1½ tablespoons lemon juice
Pinch salt

Prepare in double boiler and stir with a silver spoon.

Melt ½ cup butter in top of double boiler. Add 2 tablespoons boiling water, beaten egg yolks, lemon juice and salt. Cut remaining butter into 3 equal parts and stir one lump at a time into egg mixture making sure each lump is melted before adding another. If mixture curdles, stir in one teaspoon cream or hot water.

Sauce Robert

Yields Sauce for 4 to 6 Chops

¼ cup dry white wine
   (sauterne)
1 bay leaf
2 tablespoons scallions,
   finely chopped
1½ teaspoons onion,
   chopped
1 small clove garlic, minced
½ teaspoon thyme

½ cup tomato sauce
½ cup chicken stock
½ cup beef gravy (brown gravy
   mix can be used)
½ cup sour gherkins or dills,
   minced
2 tablespoons parsley, chopped
1 tablespoon Dijon mustard
2 tablespoons butter

Combine first 6 ingredients in skillet. Simmer until wine is reduced to 2 tablespoons. Add next 3 ingredients and cook slowly, stirring occasionally. Remove bay leaf. Bring to a boil and remove from heat. Add pickles, stir in mustard and swirl in the butter. Serve hot. Do not cook further.

Serve over grilled pork chops.

Can be frozen or doubled.

Mustard Cream Sauce With Capers

Yields Approximately ½ Cup

2 tablespoons butter
2 tablespoons flour
1 cup half-and-half
Salt, to taste
White pepper, freshly
  ground

1 tablespoon Dijon mustard
1 teaspoon dry mustard
2 tablespoons capers, well
  drained

Melt butter in top of double boiler, then mix in flour with a wooden spatula until a smooth paste. Cook over moderate heat, stirring constantly for 2 to 3 minutes. Stir in half-and-half until smooth. Cook over simmering water, whipping constantly with a wire whisk, until the sauce has thickened. Remove from heat and whip in the pepper and two mustards until smooth. Stir in capers. Place over simmering water to keep warm.

Horseradish Sauce

Yields Approximately 1 Cup

½ cup heavy cream
4 tablespoons horseradish,
  freshly grated

Few drops onion juice
Dash cayenne
1½ tablespoons cider vinegar

Whip cream and fold remaining ingredients into it. Chill and serve with beef.

Tartar Sauce

Yields 1⅔ Cups

1 cup mayonnaise
⅓ cup dill pickle, chopped
⅓ cup onion, chopped

1½ teaspoons capers, chopped
½ teaspoon mustard
½ teaspoon lemon juice

Mix all ingredients and refrigerate an hour before serving with seafood.

Marinade For Beef

Yields Marinade for
5 to 6 Pounds of Beef

½ cup oil
¼ cup red wine vinegar
½ cup tomato puree
½ cup prepared marinara
  sauce
¼ cup Burgundy

½ cup dry sherry
½ teaspoon salt
¼ teaspoon onion salt
¼ teaspoon garlic salt
⅛ teaspoon pepper

Mix all ingredients in large casserole. Slice cooked, cooled beef (not too thick) and place in marinade. Refrigerate, covered, overnight or at least 12 hours.

Can be served warm with marinade, heated and poured over meat or used cold for picnics, served as open-faced sandwich on pumpernickel.

Pork Marinade

Yields Approximately 2 Cups

1 bay leaf
2 tablespoons brown sugar
½ teaspoon salt
4 drops Tabasco
1 cup water
Garlic, optional
½ cup oil or butter

4 tablespoons Worcestershire
  sauce
2 tablespoons lemon juice or
  cider vinegar·
3 tablespoons catsup
1 tablespoon cornstarch, soaked
  in ¼ cup water

Combine all ingredients except cornstarch in a saucepan; bring to a boil and cook for about 10 minutes. Thicken with cornstarch. Remove from heat, let cool, then emulsify the marinade in a blender. Marinate pork for at least 1 hour before cooking.

Marinade For Chicken

Yields ¾ Cup

4 tablespoons wine vinegar
4 tablespoons olive oil
2 cloves garlic, sliced
2 tablespoons parsley, chopped

1 tablespoon rosemary leaves, crushed
Salt and freshly ground pepper, to taste

Combine all ingredients. Mix well. Use to baste chicken while cooking in the oven or on the grill.

Sauce For Lamb

Yields Approximately ½ Cup

2 tablespoons prepared mustard
½ teaspoon salt
1 teaspoon Worcestershire sauce
½ teaspoon black pepper, freshly ground

4 tablespoons brown sugar
2 tablespoons apricot puree or apricot preserves
2 teaspoons soy sauce
2 tablespoons olive oil
½ clove garlic, crushed
⅓ cup lemon juice, strained

Mix all ingredients together well in an air tight container and store in refrigerator 3 days before using. Brush mixture on lamb before grilling and frequently during cooking.

Baked Curried Bananas

Serves 8

4 large, firm bananas
¼ cup butter

1 teaspoon curry powder
2 tablespoons light brown sugar

Cut bananas lengthwise, then in half crosswise. Melt butter in baking dish in preheated 350°F oven. Stir in curry, dip bananas in butter, turning to cover well. Sprinkle with brown sugar and bake 12 to 15 minutes.

Good with lamb or pork.

Hot Curried Georgia Peaches   Serves 8 to 10
(allowing 2 peaches per person)

2 (28 ounce) jars spiced or   ¾ cup light brown sugar
  pickled peaches   2 tablespoons cornstarch
¼ cup butter, melted   1½ teaspoons curry powder

Drain peaches and place in a greased, 2-quart casserole. Blend melted butter with sugar, cornstarch and curry powder. Pour the butter-sugar mixture over peaches. Bake at 350°F for 40 minutes.

Hot Curried Fruit   Serves 10

½ cup butter   20 ounces pineapple chunks in
2 tablespoons curry powder   natural juice
1 cup dark brown sugar   16 ounces canned fruit cocktail,
20 ounces canned pear   optional
  halves   4 ounces maraschino cherries,
20 ounces canned peach   optional
  halves

Melt butter in saucepan. Sprinkle curry powder into butter and let bubble for a minute. Dissolve sugar in butter and add a little water, if needed. Arrange fruit in baking dish, cut side up, and pour sauce over and around fruit. Bake at 350°F for 1 hour.

Cranberry Relish   Serves 6

1 (3 ounce) package   1 medium orange, unpeeled
  strawberry gelatin   and ground
1 cup sugar   1 tart apple, unpeeled and
1 cup boiling water   finely chopped
½ cup lemon juice   1 cup celery, finely diced
¼ cup cold water   1 cup pecans, chopped
1 pound fresh cranberries,   8¼ ounces canned crushed
  ground   pineapple, drained

Dissolve gelatin and sugar in one cup of boiling water. Add lemon juice and ¼ cup cold water. Grind cranberries and orange in meat grinder. Add to gelatin along with chopped apple, celery, nuts and pineapple. Chill and serve.

Orange Sauce For Game

Yields 2 Cups

3 tablespoons butter
¼ cup flour
1½ cups chicken stock
Pinch salt

⅓ cup orange juice
½ teaspoon orange rind, grated
1 tablespoon sherry
Dash Tabasco

Melt butter and stir in flour. Add chicken stock slowly, then add salt. Keep in double boiler over hot water. Before serving, stir in orange juice, orange rind, sherry and Tabasco.

Excellent with wild duck or goose.

Tomato Sauce For Venison Loaf

Yields Approximately 2 Cups

12 to 16 ounces tomatoes
1 tablespoon sugar
2 tablespoons flour
2 tablespoons brown sugar
1 tablespoon cider vinegar

½ teaspoon salt
⅛ teaspoon black pepper
1 teaspoon Worcestershire
  sauce

Puree tomatoes in blender or food processor. Pour into a small saucepan; add remaining ingredients. Bring to a boil and cook a few minutes until sauce thickens.

Mustard Ring For Ham

Serves 8

6 eggs
1 cup sugar
1 package unflavored
  gelatin
2 tablespoons dry mustard

½ teaspoon turmeric
¼ teaspoon salt
1 cup water
½ cup cider vinegar
1 cup heavy cream

Beat eggs in top of double boiler.. Mix together sugar and gelatin; stir in mustard, turmeric and salt. Add water and vinegar to eggs; stir in sugar mixture and cook over boiling water until slightly thickened. Cool until thick. Whip cream; fold into egg mixture. Chill in 1 quart mold.

Garnish with lettuce, onions, celery, etc.

Bibliography

Books:

Bell, Malcolm, Jr. *Savannah, Ahoy!* 1959. Reprint edition. Savannah: The Pigeonhole Press, 1962.

Birmingham, Stephen. *Life at the Dakota.* New York: Random House, 1979.

Burke, Emily. *Pleasure and Pain: Reminiscences of Georgia in the 1840's.* 1850. New edition with introduction by Felicity Calhoun. Savannah: The Beehive Press, 1978.

Cay, John Eugene, Jr. *Ducks, Dogs and Friends.* Savannah: Published for the author, 1979.

Davis, Harold E. *The Fledgling Province: Social and Cultural Life in Colonial Georgia 1733-1776.* Chapel Hill: University of North Carolina Press, 1976.

Harden, William. *A History of Savannah and South Georgia.* Volume 1. 1913. Reprint edition. Atlanta: Cherokee Publishing Company, 1969.

King, Spencer Bidwell. *Ebb Tide.* Athens: University of Georgia Press, 1958.

McAllister, Ward, *Society As I Have Found It.* New York: Cassell Publishing Company, 1890.

Waring, Joseph Frederick. *Cerveau's Savannah.* Savannah: The Georgia Historical Society, 1973.

Warwick, The Earl of. *Memories of Sixty Years.* London: Cassell and Company, Ltd., 1917.

Lane, Mills. *Savannah Revisited.* Savannah: The Beehive Press, 1977.

Other Sources:

Bell, Malcom, Jr. "Notes on the Good Life." A series of short articles written for the Chatham Club, Savannah, Georgia.

——————. "The Romantic Wines of Madeira." *The Georgia Historical Quarterly.* Volume 38, Number 4.

Carpenter, Annie Schley Haines. "Chronicle of a Happy Childhood in Savannah, Georgia." Unpublished manuscript in Meldrim Family Files at Georgia Historical Society.

Gordon, Arthur, "Low Country Chritmas." *Woman's Day,* December, 1963.

Johnston, Edith D. "Christmas Festivities in Savannah at the End of the Nineteenth Century." Paper read at meeting of the Savannah Historical Research Association, December 28, 1934, at Georgia Historical Society.

Johnston, Eugenia M. "Social Life and Interesting Events in Savannah Between 1880 and 1890." Paper read at meeting of the Savannah Historical Research Association, March 27, 1935, at Georgia Historical Society.

Jones, George Noble. "The Vernon River in the Gay Nineties." Paper read at meeting of Savannah Historical Research Association, November 31, 1949, at Georgia Historical Society.

Lawrence, Daisy Gordon. "Christmas at the Old House." Unpublished manuscript on deposit at the Juliette Gordon Low Girl Scout National Center.

Morrison, Mary Lane. Research Notes on Jasper Ward on deposit at the Georgia Historical Society.

Savannah. The Georgia Historical Society. Jeremiah Evarts Diary, 1822.

Savannah. The Georgia Historical Society. Mrs. E. H. Allen Paper, 1831.

Waring, Martha Gallaudet. "The Gay Nineties in Savannah: Notes on the Fin De Siècle and Its Ways." Paper read at meeting of Savannah Historical Research Association, November 27, 1934, at Georgia Historical Society.

——————. "The Striving Seventies in Savannah." Paper read at meeting of Savannah Historical Research Association, December 30, 1934, at Georgia Historical Society.

Index

Index

Savannah Style Cookbook
P. O. Box 1864, 41 W. Broad St.
Savannah, Georgia 31402

Please send me _____ copies of *Savannah Style* at $16.95 per book. I am enclosing $2.50 to cover postage and handling. Georgia residents please add $1.01 per book for sales tax.

Name _____

Address _____

City _____ State _____ Zip _____

Savannah Style Cookbook
P. O. Box 1864, 41 W. Broad St.
Savannah, Georgia 31402

Please send me _____ copies of *Savannah Style* at $16.95 per book. I am enclosing $2.50 to cover postage and handling. Georgia residents please add $1.01 per book for sales tax.

Name _____

Address _____

City _____ State _____ Zip _____

Savannah Style Cookbook
P. O. Box 1864, 41 W. Broad St.
Savannah, Georgia 31402

Please send me _____ copies of *Savannah Style* at $16.95 per book. I am enclosing $2.50 to cover postage and handling. Georgia residents please add $1.01 per book for sales tax.

Name _____

Address _____

City _____ State _____ Zip _____

Reorder Additional Copies

SAVE $1.00 on your reorder! Just send us the name and addresses of two gift, gourmet, or book stores in your area that sell cookbooks - and deduct $1.00 from your order on the reverse side.

Name of Store _____

Address _____

City _____ State _____ Zip _____

Name of Store _____

Address _____

City _____ State _____ Zip _____

SAVE $1.00 on your reorder! Just send us the name and addresses of two gift, gourmet, or book stores in your area that sell cookbooks - and deduct $1.00 from your order on the reverse side.

Name of Store _____

Address _____

City _____ State _____ Zip _____

Name of Store _____

Address _____

City _____ State _____ Zip _____

SAVE $1.00 on your reorder! Just send us the name and addresses of two gift, gourmet, or book stores in your area that sell cookbooks - and deduct $1.00 from your order on the reverse side.

Name of Store _____

Address _____

City _____ State _____ Zip _____

Name of Store _____

Address _____

City _____ State _____ Zip _____